Arabs and Muslims in the Me

CRITICAL CULTURAL COMMUNICATION

General Editors: Sarah Banet-Weiser and Kent A. Ono

Dangerous Curves: Latina Bodies in the Media
Isabel Molina-Guzmán

The Net Effect: Technology, Romanticism, Capitalism
Thomas Streeter

Our Biometric Future: The Pursuit of Automated Facial Perception
Kelly A. Gates

Critical Rhetorics of Race
Edited by Michael G. Lacy and Kent A. Ono

Circuits of Visibility: Gender and Transnational Media Cultures
Edited by Radha S. Hegde

Commodity Activism: Cultural Resistance in Neoliberal Times
Edited by Roopali Mukherjee and Sarah Banet-Weiser

Arabs and Muslims in the Media: Race and Representation after 9/11
Evelyn Alsultany

Visualizing Atrocity: Arendt, Evil, and the Optics of Thoughtlessness
Valerie Hartouni

Arabs and Muslims in the Media

Race and Representation after 9/11

Evelyn Alsultany

NEW YORK UNIVERSITY PRESS
New York and London

NEW YORK UNIVERSITY PRESS
New York and London
www.nyupress.org

References to Internet Websites (URLs) were accurate at the time of writing. Neither the author nor New York University Press is responsible for URLs that may have expired or changed since the manuscript was prepared.

Library of Congress Cataloging-in-Publication Data
Alsultany, Evelyn.
Arabs and Muslims in the media : race and representation after 9/11 /
Evelyn Alsultany.
p. cm. — (Critical cultural communication)
Includes bibliographical references and index.
ISBN 978-0-8147-0731-9 (cl : alk. paper)
ISBN 978-0-8147-0732-6 (pb : alk. paper)
ISBN 978-0-8147-2917-5 (ebook)
ISBN 978-0-8147-3814-6 (ebook)
1. Arabs on television.   2. Muslims on television.   3. Stereotypes (Social psychology) on television.   4. Television programs—United States—History—21st century.   I. Title.
PN1992.8.A7A58   2012
305.6′970973—dc23   2011051502

New York University Press books are printed on acid-free paper, and their binding materials are chosen for strength and durability. We strive to use environmentally responsible suppliers and materials to the greatest extent possible in publishing our books.

Manufactured in the United States of America

c 10 9 8 7 6 5 4 3 2 1
p 10 9 8 7 6 5 4 3 2 1

For my father, Kamal Ali Alsultany
1941–2011

In the idealized desire for national unity served up nightly on evening cable and network newscasts, new actors—this time Arabs, Palestinians, Islamic fundamentalists—have quickly become the bodies and cultures that the logic of race marks as different and therefore potentially threatening to the national order. Television's role in this process is absolutely central, for it is television that makes these images and representations of difference meaningful, legible, and familiar.
—Herman Gray, *Watching Race*

Contents

Acknowledgments   ix

Introduction   1

1   Challenging the Terrorist Stereotype   18

2   Mourning the Suspension of Arab American Civil Rights   47

3   Evoking Sympathy for the Muslim Woman   71

4   Regulating Sympathy for the Muslim Man   100

5   Selling Muslim American Identity   132

Epilogue   163

Notes   179

Bibliography   205

Index   221

About the Author   227

Acknowledgments

This book began at Stanford University where I was fortunate to work with and learn from exceptional scholars. David Palumbo-Liu, Akhil Gupta, and Cherríe Moraga advised and challenged me, believing in my project on Arab Americans even before the current renaissance in the field. Jackie Armijo-Hussein, Ahmad Dallal, Purnima Mankekar, Paula Moya, and Renato Rosaldo encouraged me to pursue my interests. Monica Moore and Jan Hafner at Modern Thought and Literature provided invaluable administrative and moral support. My colleagues were both supportive and inspirational. I thank Lisa Arellano, Yael Ben-zvi, Julia Carpenter, Raul Coronado Jr., Manishita Dass, Eman Desouky, Maya Dodd, Nicole Fleetwood, Vida Mia Garcia, Mishuana Goeman, Shona Jackson, Jackie Jenkins, Steven Lee, Bakirathi Mani, Allegra McLeod, Hilton Obenzinger, Marcia Ochoa, Flavio Paniagua, Beth Piatote, Sarah Ramirez, Rola Razek, Helle Rytkonen, Richard Simpson, Nirvana Tanoukhi, Lisa B. Thompson, Kyla Wazana Tompkins, Tim'm T. West, and Michelle Zamora. I am especially grateful to *mis compañeras* Madgalena Barrera and Marisol Negrón. It is difficult to find the words to acknowledge Ebony Coletu, who accompanied me throughout my years at Stanford. Ebony gave me meticulous feedback, pushing me to think in new ways, dazzling me with her brilliance and her friendship.

This project has been directly and indirectly shaped by several key mentors. Dorothy Duff Brown has counseled me through my years as an assistant professor. I would not have completed this book with my sanity intact had it not been for our many conversations over the past few years and her encouragement, guidance, and wisdom. The mentorship of M. Jacqui Alexander, Drucilla Cornell, Penny Eckert, and Cherríe Moraga has had a lasting impact. Penny Von Eschen's mentorship and support have been a source of sustenance. Jack G. Shaheen's work has been foundational and inspirational. I am moved by his support and faith in me. As for Melani McAlister, it is an embarrassment of riches that she has read three versions of this manuscript and offered her close engagement, feedback, and support. Her belief in the project and targeted feedback were instrumental to its fruition.

Ella Shohat has read the full manuscript in its various forms, providing extensive feedback. She has also given me emotional support, guidance, and friendship for over a decade and is an inspiration and tremendous influence on my work.

I have been fortunate to be surrounded by many wonderful colleagues at the University of Michigan: Paul Anderson, Catherine Benamou, Stephen Berry, Bruce Conforth, Maria Cotera, Matthew Countryman, Julie Ellison, Amal Fadlallah, Jonathan Freedman, Mary Freiman, Colin Gunckel, Sandra Gunning, Jesse Hoffnung-Garskof, Judy Gray, June Howard, Mary C. Kelley, Scott Kurashige, Larry LaFountain-Stokes, Jayati Lal, Emily Lawsin, Lora Lempert, Richard Meisler, Victor Mendoza, Tiya Miles, Marlene Moore, Susan Najita, Silvia Pedraza, Brooklyn Posler, Daniel Ramirez, Tabitha Rohn, Damon Salesa, Sarita See, Amy Stillman, Gustavo Verdesio, Alan Wald, Michael Witgen, and Magdalena Zaborowska. In particular, I thank Matthew Briones, Philip Deloria, Vince Diaz, Greg Dowd, Kristin Hass, Nadine Naber, Yeidy Rivero, Andrea Smith, Amy Stillman, and Penny Von Eschen for either participating in my manuscript workshop or providing comments on my manuscript. They challenged me to make this the best book possible. I especially thank Kristin and Penny for their close and constructive engagement with multiple iterations of the manuscript. I am also grateful for support and comments from my writing group: Lori Brooks, Anthony Mora, and Amy Carroll. Amy's insightful feedback and camaraderie have shaped some of the key ideas in this book.

I am fortunate to have a community of Arab and Muslim American Studies colleagues and friends: Rabab Abdulhadi, Sawsan Abdulrahim, Wadad Abed, Nasrine Shah-Aboushakra, Devon Akmon, Barbara Aswad, Moulouk Berry, Leila Buck, Louise Cainkar, Christina Dennaoui, Carol Fadda-Conrey, Jonathan Friedlander, Reem Gibriel, Randa Jarrar, John Karam, Sylvia Chan-Malek, Joan Mandell, Khaled Mattawa, Joe Namy, Rola Nashef, Junaid Rana, Huda and Jeff Rosen, Therese Saliba, May Seikaly, Matthew Stiffler, William Youmans, and Kathy Zarur. I am honored to be in such good company, and would especially like to thank Thomas Abowd, Deborah Al-Najjar, Anan Ameri, Salah Hassan, Amira Jarmakani, Sunaina Maira, and Steven Salaita for their support and friendship. Amira and Steven also gave vital feedback on parts of the manuscript.

It has been a pleasure to work with bright and wonderful research assistants, many of whom are the next generation of cutting edge scholars: Ryah Aqel, Rabia Belt, Monika Raj, Mejdulene Shomali, Emily Rosengren, Lani Teves, and Eliot Truesdell. The passionate work of graduate students Yamil Avivi, Sarah Gothie, Andrew McBride, Hannah Noel, Wendy Sung, and Rachel Afi Quinn is infectious. Rachel has also been a kind source of encouragement.

Eric Zinner has been a fantastic editor who has believed and advocated for this project from the beginning. I thank series editors Sarah Banet-Weiser and

Kent A. Ono for their interest and support. I am also grateful to Ciara McLaughlin for her assistance along the way. This project also benefited from feedback from anonymous readers. I am grateful to freelance editor David Lobenstine for his painstakingly detailed work. It was a challenging and enriching experience to develop my writing and ideas with David's feedback, and it undoubtedly made this a better work. I also thank copy editor Sheila Berg and production editor Tim Roberts. For financial support, I thank the Program in American Culture, Office for Vice President for Research, LSA Dean's Office, and the Center for International and Comparative Studies at the University of Michigan.

I am indebted to many friends for emotional support. Nadine Naber has been my dear friend, colleague, and co-conspirator. She read different versions of the manuscript and helped me develop as a scholar and writer. We have spent countless hours together writing our respective books and collaborating on other projects. The impact of her solidarity is immeasurable both professionally and personally. Kathryn Babayan and Rima Hassouneh nourished me with food and friendship. I could always count on them for emotional support and to remind me of life beyond writing. I am grateful to other friends in Ann Arbor, Deirdre de la Cruz, Shazia Iftkhar, Osman Khan, and Atef Said, who make Ann Arbor feel like home. Dahlia Petrus conducted extensive and meticulous research for me from which I could probably write multiple books. She has offered me her invaluable support and friendship. It has been such good fortune to commiserate with someone about media representations of Arabs and Muslims who is equally passionate about it.

I am appreciative of my dear friends and family who believed in me before I believed in myself and who are still an important part of my life: Joseph Battle, Michael Bobbitt, Christianne and Helen Cejas, Erskine Childers, Vivia and Stratos Costalas, Amber Donell, Elena Fiallo, Litsa Flores, Catherine Groves, Sandra Hanna, Anya Hurwitz, Florencia Masri, Nichole Diaz Mendoza, Douglas Pineda, Lavinia Pinto, Solade Rowe, Shahid Siddiqui, Brad Verebay, and Juan Carlos Sobrino. I thank Fernando Rodriguez, Anita, Lourdes, and Leonor Garcia, and Gilda Rodriguez for their support. I am grateful to my ladies who anchor me in life: Mireille Abelin, Elif Bali, Nacisse Demeksa, Mona El-Ghobashy, Vanessa Primiani, and Lauren Rosenthal. Mireille and Mona have shared this journey with me while on their own parallel paths. Mireille reminds me every day of how far I've come. Mona breathes each minute detail with me, and there is nothing like having her accompany me for each play-by-play. Her friendship has enhanced this book and my life. Christine Burmeister-Guivernau is my biggest cheerleader. She celebrates my accomplishments no matter how small and has encouraged me each step of the way while also lending her scrupulous editorial services.

People often laugh at me when I acknowledge my pets, but those of you who live with animals understand how they contribute to one's emotional well-being on a day-to-day level. I offer my thanks to Nubian, Zeeza, and Monaluna for enriching my life and for keeping me sane. My husband, Benefo Ofosu-Benefo, has seen me through this project from its inception to this finished book. His faith in me has been unyielding and has carried me through. He has provided the calm and comfort needed to write this book and has also shared in the outrage and enthusiasm that fill its pages.

I am blessed with a supportive family. I thank Sara, Kwadwo (aka Papa, 1935–2011), Nana, and Osei Ofosu-Benefo for their belief in me. For always being there, thanks to Martha Jaramillo, Maria Jimenez, Steven Cuevas, and Jimmy and Fatima Chavez. Thanks to my brother, Fabian, for dreaming big with me. I could always count on my parents for love and support. They encouraged me throughout this process even when they didn't understand why I chose this difficult path. From my mother, Maggie, I have learned the commitment required to complete a project like this.

This book is dedicated to my father who is the ultimate inspiration for this project. As a child, witnessing all the assumptions and stereotypes he was confronted with as an Arab Muslim in the United States made me painfully aware of the politics of culture. My father passed away as this book went into production. This is for you, Dad.

Introduction

JACK BAUER (COUNTER TERRORISM UNIT AGENT): How long have you been planning this operation? Two years? Five years? Ten? All this planning for one day. You do realize that if all the reactors melt down, hundreds of thousands of people will die?

DINA ARAZ (TERRORIST): Every war has casualties.

JACK BAUER: These people do not know about your war. These people are innocent.

DINA ARAZ: No one is innocent.

JACK BAUER: You really believe that?

DINA ARAZ: As strongly as you believe in what you believe. So I won't waste your time or mine trying to explain something you can never understand.

—24, "Day 4: 3–4 p.m."

REVEREND CAMDEN (TO NEIGHBORS): I know everyone is boycotting that party tonight because they think the Duprees are French, but they're not. The Duprees are from Glen Oak.

NEIGHBOR 1: Well, that's good to know.

REV. CAMDEN: And they're Muslim. [Long pause by neighbors.] I had to see it with my own eyes.

NEIGHBOR 2: See what?

REV. CAMDEN: Prejudice, narrow mindedness . . . racism.

—7th Heaven, "Getting to Know You"

On September 11, 2001, nineteen Arab Muslim men hijacked four airplanes and flew them into two of the greatest icons of power in the United States—the World Trade Center and the Pentagon. Nearly three thousand people were killed. In response, the U.S. government, under President George W. Bush, initiated the self-proclaimed War on Terror—a military, political, and legal campaign targeting Arabs and Muslims both in the United States and around the world.

After this tragic event, and amid growing U.S. American[1] rancor toward the Arab world and violence against individuals with brown skin, I was surprised to find an abundance of sympathetic portrayals of Arabs and Muslims on U.S.

television. My surprise was twofold. First, at such an opportune moment for further stereotyping—a moment of mourning, fear, trauma, anger, and presumably justifiable racism against the entire Arab and Muslim population—this wave of sympathetic representations seemed both unprecedented and unlikely. Demonizing the enemy is so common during times of war—a brief list, just over the last century, would include the Japanese during World War II and the Russians during the Cold War—I assumed that 9/11/01[2] and the War on Terror would ignite the blanket demonization of all Arabs and Muslims. Second, given that the U.S. media has stereotyped and misrepresented Arabs and Muslims for over a century, with very few exceptions, I couldn't believe that sympathetic portrayals would appear during such a fraught moment.[3]

Like many others in the days and weeks (and then months and years) after September 11, I remained glued to my television. I watched the endless clips of the planes crashing, of the towers falling, of people pressing photos of the missing toward the news cameras, of the photos of the nineteen Arab Muslim men responsible for the attack. I grieved for all those who lost loved ones and simultaneously grieved in anticipation for the backlash that was to come against us as Arabs and Muslims. In the midst of the flurry of news reports, my amazement grew. I watched President Bush reassure Americans, taking pains to distinguish between Arabs and Muslim "friends" and "enemies." He stated, "The enemy of America is not our many Muslim friends; it is not our many Arab friends. Our enemy is a radical network of terrorists, and every government that supports them."[4] I watched news reporters interview Arab and Muslim Americans, seemingly eager to include their perspectives on the terrorist attacks, careful to point out their experiences with hate crimes.[5] I watched dozens of TV dramas in which Arab and Muslim Americans were portrayed as the unjust target of hate crimes.

Certainly, xenophobia and outright racism flourished on the airwaves; the pundits of FOX News were always a reliable source of antagonism. At the same time, a slew of TV dramas cashed in on the salacious possibilities of Arab or Muslim terrorist threats and assured viewers with depictions of the U.S. government's heroic efforts to combat this new, pulse-quickening terrorism. These shows, from network and cable channels alike, include—but are not limited to—24, *Sleeper Cell*, *NCIS*, *JAG*, *The Grid*, *The Agency*, *LAX*, *Threat Matrix*. The series 24, from which the first of this chapter's epigraphs is drawn, is a culture-shaping action drama centered on Jack Bauer, the ubiquitous counterterrorism agent who, season after season, races against the clock to disrupt terrorist plots in the United States. Amid his debate with Dina Araz, Bauer subverts a nuclear attack by apparent "Middle Easterners" partially orchestrated by the Araz family, which has lived in the United States for years, secretly conspiring with others to attack this country and murder hundreds of thousands of innocent Americans. The reasons for these attempts are never fully explained, leaving open two opposed possibilities: we don't need a reason—isn't terrorism what Arabs and/or Muslims do, after all?—or any such rationale would be incomprehensible to Americans.

Often, however, these very same TV dramas narrated stories about innocent Arab and Muslim Americans facing unjust post–September 11 hatred. In the years after the attacks, shows as diverse as *The Practice, Boston Public, Law and Order, Law and Order SVU, NYPD Blue, 7th Heaven, The Education of Max Bickford, The Guardian*, and *The West Wing* all featured Arab and Muslim Americans as hardworking, often patriotic, victims. The second epigraph, for example, is from an episode of *7th Heaven*, a family drama about Reverend Camden and his wife and their seven children. In this episode, a Muslim American family moves to the neighborhood and the Camden family plans a party to welcome them. The other neighbors decide to boycott the party because they erroneously assume the new residents are French, and since France did not support the U.S. government's decision to invade Iraq as part of the War on Terror, they, like many Americans, are boycotting anything and everything French.[6] When the neighbors realize that the new residents are not French but Muslim American, their impulse to boycott the party is reaffirmed. After Reverend Camden articulates his deep disappointment at the nationalist strand of racism he has witnessed from his neighbors, they reflect on their assumptions about and attitudes toward Muslims, see the error in their ways, and decide to join in welcoming their new Muslim American neighbors.

On another episode of *7th Heaven*, twelve-year-old Ruthie takes a principled stance and quits her private school because the school board refuses to admit her Muslim friend.[7] On *Boston Public*, two innocent Arab American students are investigated by the FBI for connections to terrorism and harassed by their classmates.[8] The principal assembles the student body and gives a speech stating that when we terrorize Arab and Muslim Americans out of fear and prejudice, "we" are the terrorists. On *The Education of Max Bickford*, after a Muslim student receives a note under her dorm room door stating, "Muslim bitch, keep your family off our campus or die," Professor Haskel devotes a week of class time to discussing the impact of September 11 on everyday life, including a debate on the racial profiling of Arab Americans.[9] Typical of the broad gamut of quality in American television, some of these episodes were incredibly moving, others near nausea-inducing in their sentimentality. Nevertheless, the message was clear: we should not resort to stereotyping and racism; we should not blame our innocent Arab and Muslim neighbors for something they had nothing to do with.[10]

Something else besides the increase in sympathetic representations of Arab and Muslim Americans in the U.S. media after 9/11 puzzled me: certain friends and colleagues expressed pride and relief. They claimed that Americans were at the dawn of a new era. They stated that racism against Arabs and Muslims after 9/11 was "not so bad" because we were not rounded up and placed in internment camps, as was done with Japanese Americans during World War II. Often at on-campus teach-ins and other public forums, they expressed nationalist pride that the U.S. government was not repeating past racism by indiscriminately demonizing an entire ethnic group. Sympathetic representations—whether Bush's speeches, TV dramas, news reports, or public service announcements—were cited as examples of a new era of multicultural sensitivity. The case of Arabs and Muslims post-9/11 was discussed as a symbol of racial progress. I, too, felt comforted by these TV dramas that evoked sympathy for Arab and Muslim Americans, yet wondered to what extent we had really "progressed" as a nation. I wondered, how were these sympathetic representations being consumed amid the dominant meanings that were circulating about Islam as a threat to U.S. national security? How were sympathetic representations of Arabs and Muslims in government discourses and media representations during the War on Terror projecting this presumed new era of multicultural sensitivity?

Such optimism was quickly tempered by a more complex reality. At the same time that sympathetic portrayals of Arab and Muslim Americans proliferated on U.S. commercial television in the weeks and months after 9/11, hate crimes, workplace discrimination, bias incidents, and airline discrimination targeting Arab and Muslim Americans increased exponentially. According to the FBI, hate crimes against Arabs and Muslims multiplied by 1,600 percent from 2000 to 2001.[11] In just the first weeks and months after 9/11, Amnesty International, the Council on American-Islamic Relations, the American-Arab Anti-Discrimination Committee, and other organizations documented hundreds of violent incidents experienced by Arab and Muslim Americans and people mistaken for Arabs or Muslim Americans, including several murders. Dozens of airline passengers perceived to be Arab or Muslim were removed from flights. Hundreds of Arab and Muslim Americans reported discrimination at work, receiving hate mail, physical assaults, and their property, mosques, and community centers vandalized or set on fire.[12] Some communities organized escorts to accompany Arab and Muslim Americans in public in the hope of protecting them from hate crimes. And some non-Muslim women even began wearing the hijab (head scarf) as an act of solidarity.[13] Across the decade after 9/11, such racist acts have persisted.

As individual citizens were taking the law into their own hands, the U.S. government passed legislation that targeted Arabs and Muslims (both inside and outside the United States) and legalized the suspension of constitutional rights.[14] The USA PATRIOT Act, passed by Congress in October 2001 and renewed in 2005, 2006, 2010, and 2011 legalized the following (previously illegal) acts and thus enabled anti-Arab and Muslim racism:[15] monitoring Arab and Muslim groups; granting the U.S. Attorney General the right to indefinitely detain noncitizens whom he suspects might have ties to terrorism; searching and wiretapping secretly, without probable cause; arresting and holding a person as a "material witness" whose testimony might assist in a case; using secret evidence, without granting the accused access to that evidence; trying those designated as "enemy combatants" in military tribunals (as opposed to civilian courts);[16] and deportation based on guilt by association (not on what someone has done).[17] Other measures included the Absconder Apprehension Initiative that tracked down and deported 6,000 men from unnamed Middle Eastern countries, in most cases for overstaying a visa. In the weeks after 9/11 at least 1,200 Muslim men were rounded up and detained without criminal charges.[18] The National Security Entry-Exit Registration System (NSEERS), required males from twenty-four Muslim countries to be photographed and fingerprinted and to register their addresses with the Immigration and Naturalization Service every few months; anyone who refused would face deportation. Under this "Special Registration" approximately 80,000 men complied, 2,870 of whom were detained and 13,799 placed in deportation proceedings within two years after 9/11.[19] The government submitted young Arab and Muslim men to a "voluntary interview" program, based on the assumption that they would have information about terrorism because of their religion, gender, and national origin.[20] Nearly 200,000 Arab and Muslim men were interviewed. Many Muslim charities were either closed by the government or "voluntarily" shut down because Muslims feared that they would be investigated if they continued to engage in charitable giving.[21]

Post-9/11 government measures had a psychological impact on Arab and Muslim Americans, causing depression, sadness, and shock. Arab and Muslim Americans reported being fearful and censoring their behavior in public to avoid ethnic or religious markers.[22] The trauma of the terrorist attacks coupled with the increased suspicion and hostility from the public led many Arab and Muslim Americans to feel excluded from the process of grieving in the United States because they were associated with the enemy.[23] As a result, many Arab and Muslim Americans isolated themselves; they stayed home, they stopped attending their mosques, all to protect themselves from potential harm.[24] Thousands of Pakistani Muslims were so fearful of being targeted by these government policies that they "voluntarily" returned to Pakistan.[25] Nadine Naber writes that some Arab Americans experienced "internment of the psyche," psychological distress due to the fear that one might be considered guilty by association or secretly monitored.[26]

Ironically, though often seen as the enemy, Arab and Muslim Americans were not alone. Fear was evident across the United States, often stoked by the rhetoric and policies of the Bush administration, news reports, and other cultural productions that reminded the public of an ever-present, unresolved, and often-mysterious threat. The Homeland Security Advisory System—the much-derided, color-coded terrorist alert system—still in place ten years later, has for many epitomized this state of endless fear. President Bush justified these policies, contending that securing the nation was imperative. The U.S. government therefore "secured the nation" domestically by legalizing heightened surveillance measures and reenforcing anti-immigration laws. Abroad, "securing the nation" was achieved through all-out war in Iraq and Afghanistan. To put it mildly, the explicit targeting of Arabs and Muslims by government policies, based on their identity as opposed to their criminality, contradicts claims to racial progress.

These racial policies have been heatedly debated. The political right has often argued that government measures, such as the USA PATRIOT Act, are needed for national security and accuse the left of being willing to risk national security in order to be racially or culturally sensitive. Michelle Malkin, advocating for racial profiling, writes, "When our national security is on the line, 'racial profiling'—or more precisely, threat profiling based on race, religion or nationality—is justified. Targeted intelligence-gathering at mosques and in local Muslim communities, for example, makes perfect sense when we are at war with Islamic extremists."[27] The political right tends to diminish concerns about advancing racist policies through accusations of political correctness. One Republican congressman put it most succinctly when he stated that "political correctness kills," arguing that political correctness intimidates Americans from speaking out against a potential threat because they do not want to be perceived as racist. He claims that political correctness is destroying the nation.[28] In contrast, the political left has often argued that these measures not only amount to racial profiling, but compromise civil liberties for Arab and Muslim Americans, are ineffective in fighting terrorism, and afford the government excessive power by promoting a culture of fear. Anti-Arab racism continues to be acceptable and legitimized in conservative circles and beyond, often by people who claim that the United States is multicultural and beyond racism.

The question of whether or not, or the extent to which, the U.S. government was institutionalizing racism was far less important to some after the terrorist attacks. More visceral questions, and knee-jerk reactions, ruled the day. Many Americans asked, "Why do they hate us?" The U.S. government offered a decisive answer that had the power to frame and hijack the system of meaning during the War on Terror: "They hate us for our freedom." This question and answer—which was in turn widely circulated in television and print journalism, and before too long in television dramas as well—effectively foreclosed the many other possible conversations. Public discourse rarely focused on debating the impact of U.S. foreign policies on human life around the globe or the U.S. government's involvement in proxy wars, including their own role, during the Cold War, in the creation of Al Qaeda.[29]

While the focus of my exploration is on the War on Terror portrayed by television shows and news reporting, and not specifically about the ways that the U.S. government has portrayed recent history, the two are inextricably linked. As a result, I refer to interrelated "government and media discourses"; I see them together forming a hegemonic field of meaning. As a crucial aspect of the War on Terror—particularly in our information-soaked age—the Bush administration needed to frame the ways that people across the country thought about and talked about the events of 9/11, and the ways that we should respond to such events. The "they hate us for our freedom" discourse provided the logic and justification needed to pass racist foreign and domestic policies and provided the suspicion needed for many citizens to tolerate the targeting of Arabs and Muslims, often without any evidence that they were involved in terrorist activities. As I consider the government's ongoing effort to shape the national conversation, the media can be seen as a similarly ongoing attempt to process or negotiate a new political reality. In the days and weeks following 9/11, the government's overt propaganda of war was palatable to many citizens on edge and regarded with suspicion by others. As such propaganda has become less effective and more controversial, the production and circulation of "positive" representations of the "enemy" has become essential to projecting the United States as benevolent, especially in its declaration of war and passage of racist policies. TV dramas have become essential, though often unwitting, collaborators in the forming of a new postrace racism.

Arabs and Muslims in the U.S. Media before 9/11

The significance of increased sympathetic representations of Arab and Muslim identities must be understood in relation to the lengthy history of Orientalist tropes of Arabs. Across the twentieth century, Arabs have most often been seen as rich oil sheiks, sultry belly dancers, harem girls, veiled oppressed women, and, most notably, terrorists. The trajectory of Arab representations in television mirrors that in film. Early silent films that represented the Middle East, such as *Fatima* (1897), *The Sheik* (1921), and *The Thief of Baghdad* (1924), portrayed the region as faraway, exotic, and magical; a place reminiscent of biblical stories and fairy tales; a desert populated by genies, flying carpets, mummies, belly dancers, harem girls, and rich Arab men living in opulent palaces (or equally opulent tents). This trend continued into the era of Technicolor and sound, as can be seen in films such as *Arabian Nights* (1942), *Road to Morocco* (1942), and *Harum Scarum* (1965), to name but a few. These films, made at a time when parts of the Middle East were colonized by European powers, reflect the fantasies of the colonizer and a logic that legitimizes colonialism.[30] It was not unusual for both "good" and "bad" Arabs to be represented and for a white man to save the day—saving the good Arabs from the bad Arabs, freeing the female Arab slaves from their captors, and rescuing white women from Arab rapists.[31]

The year 1945 figures as an important historical moment, marking the decline of European colonialism at the end of World War II, the beginning of the Cold War, the creation of Israel in the shadow of the Holocaust, and the emergence of the United States as a global power.[32] As the United States began its geopolitical ascendancy, representations of the "foreign" contributed to the making of American national identity; the projection of erotic and exotic fantasies onto the Middle East began to shift to more ominous representations of violence and terrorism.[33] Representations of Arabs as terrorists emerged with the inauguration of the state of Israel in 1948, the Arab-Israeli war and subsequent Israeli occupation of Palestinian territories in 1967, and the formation of Palestinian resistance movements. As Jack G. Shaheen writes:

> The image began to intensify in the late 1940s when the state of Israel was founded on Palestinian land. From that preemptive point on—through the Arab-Israeli wars of 1948, 1967, and 1973, the hijacking of planes, the disruptive 1973 Arab oil embargo, along with the rise of Libya's Muammar Qaddafi and Iran's Ayatollah Khomeini—shot after shot delivered the relentless drum beat that all Arabs were and are Public Enemy No. 1.[34]

From the late 1940s into the 1970s and 1980s, images of Arab men shifted from lazy sheikhs reclining on thrones to new images of rich, flashy oil sheikhs who threaten the U.S. economy and dangerous terrorists who threaten national security.[35] As for representations of Arab women, before World War II they were represented as alluring harem girls and belly dancers.[36] In the first decades after World War II images of Arab women became largely absent from the representational field, but in the 1970s they reemerged as sexy but deadly terrorists and in the 1980s as veiled and oppressed.[37]

Significant shifts toward portraying Arab and/or Muslims as terrorists in the 1970s are evident not only in Hollywood filmmaking but also in U.S. corporate news media. Melani McAlister argues that Americans' association of the Middle East with the Christian Holy Land or Arab oil wealth shifted to a place of Muslim terror through news reporting on the Munich Olympics (1972), the Arab oil embargo (1973), the Iran hostage crisis (1979–80), and airplane hijackings in the 1970s and 1980s.[38] The news media came to play a crucial role in making the Middle East, and Islam in particular, meaningful to Americans as a place that breeds terrorism. This genealogy of the emergence of the Arab terrorist threat in the U.S. commercial media reveals that while 9/11 is a new historical moment, it is also part of a longer history in which viewers have been primed by the media to equate Arabs and Muslims first with dissoluteness and patriarchy/misogyny and then with terrorism.[39]

The Iran hostage crisis was an important moment in conflating Arab, Muslim, and Middle Eastern identities. Though Iran is not an Arab country, during the hostage crisis Iran came to stand in for Arabs, the Middle East, Islam, and terrorism, all of which terms came to be used interchangeably. It is commonly assumed that Iranians and Pakistanis are Arab and that all Arabs are Muslim and all Muslims Arab, despite the fact that there are 1.2 billion Muslims worldwide and that approximately 15 to 20 percent of them are Arab. The majority of the world's Muslim population is concentrated in Indonesia, Pakistan, Bangladesh, and India, with sizable populations in Senegal, Uzbekistan, China, and Malaysia.[40] Why are these categories interchangeable when most Muslims are not Arab and when none of the most populous countries are Arab? This conflation enables a particular racial Othering that would not operate in the same way through another conflation, such as, for example, Arab/Christian, Arab/Jew, or Indonesian/Muslim. The result is particularly damaging, since it reduces the inherent—and enormous—variety of the world's Muslim population, projecting all Muslims as one very particular type: fanatical, misogynistic, anti-American. This recurring conflation, advanced by U.S. government and media discourses at this historical juncture, serves a larger narrative about an evil Other that can be powerfully and easily mobilized during times of war. The Arab/Muslim conflation is strategically useful to the U.S government during the War on Terror because it comes with baggage. It draws on centuries-old Orientalist narratives of patriarchal societies and oppressed women, of Muslim fundamentalism and anti-Semitism, of irrational violence and suicide bombings. With this conflation established, it is easy to conceptualize the United States as the inverse of everything that is "Arab/Muslim": the United States is thus a land of equality and democracy, culturally diverse and civilized, a land of progressive men and liberated women.

Casting for TV dramas and films has historically contributed to this conflation. TV dramas participate in the construction of a phenotype and the fiction of an Arab or Muslim "race" and hence the notion that Arabs and Muslims can be racially profiled. In Sleeper Cell, the lead terrorist is Arab/Muslim but portrayed by an Israeli Jewish actor, Oded Fehr, who has played Arab roles before, most notably in The Mummy films (1999, 2001). In season 2 of 24, the

Arab terrorist is played by Francesco Quinn, who is Mexican American (his father, Anthony Quinn, has often played Arab characters). During the fourth season of 24, Marwan Habib, the Arab/Muslim terrorist, is played by Arnold Vosloo, a South African actor who also featured (as an ancient Egyptian) in *The Mummy* (1999, 2001). Nestor Serrano who is Latino, Shoreh Aghdashloo who is Iranian, and Jonathan Adhout who is Iranian American play the terrorist sleeper cell family—mother, father, and teenage son. The other terrorists include Tony Plana who is Cuban American and Anil Kumar who is South Asian. In the sixth season of 24, Alexander Siddig, who is Sudanese British, plays Hamri Al-Assad, the reformed terrorist who helps CTU in its investigation. The "good Arab American" CTU agent, Nadia Yassir, is played by Marisol Nichols, who is Mexican-Hungarian-Romanian. The villains are played by Kal Penn and Shaun Majumder and Adonis Maropis, South Asian Americans and Greek American respectively.

Most of the actors who play Arab/Muslim terrorists, at least in the past decade, are Latinos, South Asians, and Greeks.[41] The point here is not that only Arabs should portray Arab characters but rather that casting lends itself to the visual construction of an Arab/Muslim race that supports the conflation of Arab and Muslim identities. This construction of a conflated Arab/Muslim "look" in turn supports policies like racial profiling; even if unintentional, it does the ideological work of making racial profiling seem like an effective tool when it is in fact an unrealistic endeavor.

Such representations make it difficult to disentangle the Arab/Muslim conflation and to speak with more precision. Thus, when referring to representations in which the identity could be either Arab or Muslim and to refer to the conflated identity, I use "Arab/Muslim." When there is a distinct identity to designate, whether Arab, Muslim, Arab American, or Muslim American, I use that particular term. More often, I use the term "Arab and Muslim identities" to capture that the identity in question could be either American or not. This is especially significant given that immediately after 9/11, it seemed that Arab and Muslim Americans would be represented sympathetically and Arabs and Muslims would not. However, as the "sleeper cell" threat permeated, all Arab and Muslim identities came to be suspect, and the "good" Arabs and Muslims became those who would help the United States fight Arab/Muslim terrorism—whether or not they were American.

Many of the representational modes examined in this book began in the late 1990s and then became common after 9/11. The shift around 9/11 is not one in which Arabs are represented solely as terrorists to one in which Arabs are represented sympathetically. It is from a few exceptional, sympathetic representations of Arabs and Muslim identities to a new representational strategy whereby sympathetic representations are standardized as a stock feature of media narratives. A few films in the late 1990s—*The Siege* (1998) and *Three Kings* (1999) in particular—challenged the trend of representing Arabs and Muslims as one-dimensional stereotypes; these films offered a multidimensional terrorist character and included a "good" Arab or victimized Arab American when representing an evil Arab.[42] During the era of the multicultural movement, when these films were produced, these strategies were considered "new" and "exceptional." After 9/11 these strategies, especially that of including a "good" Arab American to counteract the "bad" or terrorist Arab, came to define the new standard when representing Arabs.

Post-9/11 as Post-Race?

While many associate the declaration of a postracial society with the 2008 election of Barack Obama, the first black president of the United States, the first pronouncement of a postracial society can be traced to shortly after the Civil War.[43] Eighteen years after slavery was abolished in 1865, the Supreme Court, having made great strides to remedy racial inequality, was ready to declare the United States a postracial society and therefore requiring no further legal measures to combat racial discrimination.[44] Postracial discourses have reappeared at landmark moments of racial contest, for example, at the end of the civil rights movement in the 1960s, after the multicultural movement in the 1990s, and after Obama's election. Each time it has gained more and more momentum and cultural credibility. Such discourses consist of a set of beliefs that converge to posit that the United States has made such notable racial progress that racial discrimination has become rare and therefore governments should no longer consider race in their decision making.[45] It perceives progress since the times of slavery, Jim Crow laws, and Japanese American internment as complete and has cross-ideological appeal, holding resonance for those who identify with the political right and left. This way of thinking was carried into the post-9/11 moment in which some citizens perceived the TV dramas and government speeches that portrayed Arabs and Muslims favorably as signaling, or even confirming, a postracial era. Some (i.e., the political right) even went as far as to say that racial profiling had nothing to do with racism and everything to do with national security. Racist policies and practices are advanced often through the very stance that purports to disavow it.

This move toward advancing a post-race ideology is linked to a co-optation of movements for racial equality. The civil rights movement led to a shift in U.S. government approaches to race and racism, from institutionalized white supremacy to recognition of racial inequality as a problem and to institutionalizing antiracist policies.[46] Howard Winant argues that while on the surface institutions implemented policies that advocated racial equality, in practice a repackaged version of white supremacy in the guise of color blindness was produced.[47] In this notion of color blindness, racial inequality persists by "still resorting to exclusionism and scapegoating when politically necessary, still invoking the supposed superiority of 'mainstream' (aka white) values, and cheerfully maintaining that equality has been largely achieved."[48] Within this new racial formation that Jodi Melamed calls "neoliberal multiculturalism" and that Eduardo Bonilla-Silva calls "color-blind racism," "racism constantly appears as disappearing according to conventional race categories, even as it takes on new forms that can signify as nonracial or even antiracist."[49] These new antiracist forms are aptly apparent when Guantanamo Bay prisoners are provided with copies of the Qur'an and time to pray as evidence of the cultural sensitivity of their captors; or when the USA PATRIOT Act contains a section that condemns discrimination against Arab and Muslim Americans. Such gestures attempt to subvert the focus from the violation of civil and human rights in favor of highlighting multiculturalism and racial sensitivity.[50] The emergence of sympathetic representations of Arabs, Muslims, Arab Americans, and Muslim Americans similarly deflects attention from the persistence of racist policies and practices post-9/11.

While the civil rights movement focused on rectifying centuries of institutionalized racism, the multicultural movement, which began in the 1960s and culminated in the 1990s, sought to highlight and challenge the patriarchal, Eurocentric ideologies endemic to U.S. culture. These perspectives had become utterly normalized, and were evident in everything from educational curricula to media representations to everyday speech that, for example, referred to humans as "man" and figured white men as the standard identity. The multicultural movement of the 1990s shed light on how language and representations appeared to be neutral while in fact powerfully naturalizing inequalities. It influenced education by multiculturalizing curricula and influenced the media by multiculturalizing representations. It succeeded in shifting what was considered publicly acceptable language by introducing neutral language and practices regarding women, minorities, and differently abled people.

The efforts of multicultural activists, not surprisingly, were fiercely challenged and resisted by conservatives who dubbed the multicultural movement the "politically correct" (PC) movement. They claimed that multicultural activists were jeopardizing free speech by insisting on "politically correct" language and objected to being called racist or sexist if they expressed themselves freely. They also objected to curricular changes, claiming that multiculturalism posed a threat to a unified national identity that emerged from studying the history of achievements of white men. Most important, they insisted that the goals of equality had been reached and that antiracist policies were no longer needed. They used a post-race argument against affirmative action policies in the 1990s, resulting in a series of legal cases that ended affirmative action in some states.[51] Despite the racial progress that has undoubtedly been made, post-race declarations tend to deny the ongoing persistence of racism and "allows opponents of race-based remedies and programs to seem noble rather than racist."[52]

Just as the objectives of the civil rights movement were co-opted and diffused through government policies, the objectives of the multicultural movement were co-opted by the media, corporations, education, and government in the guise of "progressive gestures in the name of 'diversity.'"[53] The U.S. government, during the 1991 Gulf War, redefined its global image in representations of the military as racially diverse, ideologically united, and winning the war in Iraq. McAlister demonstrates how the U.S. government and media strategically portrayed the U.S. military as a force for multiculturalism and democracy while unresolved and heated debates over multiculturalism continued at home, providing the United States with a mandate to intervene globally. Similarly, television, news reporting, and film adopted the discourse of multiculturalism and diffused it, for example, by projecting a multicultural society (e.g., a black and white duo of cops fighting crime together) without addressing the persistence of structures of inequality (e.g., criminals are bad people, as opposed to being shaped by structures of inequality). As a result of the media's co-optation of multiculturalism, explicit war propaganda, demonizing the enemy, and stereotyping are no longer the order of the day. Yet demonizing the enemy during times of war is not a thing of the past. Rather, it has assumed new forms.

Beyond Positive Representations

The notion that the United States has overcome racism, while tantalizing, is deceptive. If we take these positive portrayals at face value, if we believe that complex characterizations of terrorists and valiant portrayals of patriotic Muslims do solve the problem of stereotyping, then racist policies and practices will persist under the guise of antiracism. A diversity of representations, even an abundance of sympathetic characters, does not in itself demonstrate the end of racism, nor does it solve the problem of racial stereotyping. As Ella Shohat, Robert Stam, Herman Gray, and other cultural studies scholars have shown, focusing on whether or not a particular image is either good or bad does not necessarily address the complexity of representation.[54] Rather, it is important to examine the ideological work performed by images and story lines. Shohat and Stam write:

The focus on "good" and "bad" characters in image analysis confronts racist discourse on that discourse's favored ground. It easily elides into *moralism*, and thus into fruitless debates about the relative virtues of fictive characters (seen not as constructs but as if they were real flesh-and-blood people) and the correctness of their fictional actions. This kind of anthropocentric moralism, deeply rooted in Manichean schemas of good and evil, leads to the treatment of complex political issues as if they were matters of individual ethics, in a manner reminiscent of the morality plays staged by the right, in which virtuous American heroes do battle against demonized Third World villains.[55]

The critical cultural studies approach that I employ strategically privileges the analysis of ideological work performed by images and story lines, as opposed to reading an image as negative or positive, and therefore gets us beyond reading a positive image as if it will eliminate stereotyping. If we interpret an image as either positive or negative, then we can conclude that the problem of racial stereotyping is over because of the appearance of sympathetic images of Arabs and Muslims during the War on Terror. However, an examination of the image in relation to its narrative context reveals how it participates in a larger field of meaning about Arabs and Muslims. The notion of a field of meaning, or an ideological field, is a means to encompass the range of acceptable ideas about the War on Terror, including highlighting the ideas that are on the margins and are therefore deemed unacceptable.

A critical cultural studies approach moves beyond linear race rehabilitation theories that suggest both that representations of Arabs in U.S. popular culture are following a trajectory from negative to positive images and that other racialized groups have followed this trajectory as a rite of passage toward assimilation.[56] There is indeed a process of rehabilitation taking place, but it is one in which images of *acceptable* Arab and Muslim Americans are produced through the figure of the Arab American patriot or victim of post-9/11 hate crimes. This process of rehabilitation is certainly not unique to Arab and Muslim Americans. Native American images in Hollywood, for example, shifted from savages to noble savages in the 1930s, best typified by the Lone Ranger's Native American sidekick, Tonto.[57]

The representational mode that has become standard since 9/11 seeks to balance a negative representation with a positive one, what I refer to throughout this book as "simplified complex representations."[58] This has meant that if an Arab/Muslim terrorist is represented in the story line of a TV drama or film, then a "positive" representation of an Arab, Muslim, Arab American, or Muslim American is typically included, seemingly to offset the stereotype of the Arab/Muslim terrorist. This feature of post-9/11 representations is consistent with Mahmood Mamdani's claim that the public debate since the terrorist attacks has involved a discourse about "good" and "bad" Muslims in which all Muslims are assumed to be bad until they perform and prove their allegiance to the U.S. nation.[59] What makes a Muslim "good" or "bad" in this paradigm is not his or her relationship to Islam but rather to the United States. Though rare in U.S. history, after 9/11 this mode of representing "the enemy" became standard.

The result of the good/bad coupling is startling: at its most effective, the strategy creates a post-race illusion that absolves viewers from confronting the persistence of institutionalized racism.[60] This reflects Gray's argument that representations of the black middle-class family in television sitcoms of the 1980s and 1990s contributed to an illusion of racial equality.[61] Gray acknowledges *The Cosby Show* for successfully recoding blackness away from images of the welfare queen and the drug dealer while simultaneously noting that it participated in rearticulating a new and more enlightened form of racism and contributed to an illusion of "feel-good multiculturalism and racial cooperation."[62] Sympathetic images of Arabs and Muslims after 9/11 give the impression that racism is not tolerated in the United States, despite the slew of policies that have targeted and disproportionately affected Arabs and Muslims.

Television dramas are critical sites for understanding the cultural politics of the War on Terror. The TV dramas I examine are a sampling of the broad genre of prime-time TV dramas. Nielsen ratings indicate that during these prime-time hours on any night of the week somewhere between 18 million and 30 million viewers will likely tune in to any given program on a major television network (ABC, CBS, NBC, FOX). The majority of these programs are sitcoms, "reality" shows, and dramas. Of these three prime-time genres, dramatic series are considered more likely to be "quality" television—a disputed category, needless to say, in itself—because they address controversial, realistic issues that either reflect current news stories or fundamental cultural, historical, or emotional conflicts. By analyzing prime-time TV dramas, their intersections with news reporting, and also nonprofit advertising, the parameters of the War on Terror's ideological field is revealed. Nonprofit advertising, moveover, provides an important contrast to the commercial media's representations of Arabs and Islam during the War on Terror.

A range of media, from the news and talk shows to TV dramas and even nonprofit advertising, have since September 11 engaged in debates on which measures were appropriate or justifiable in securing the nation—from racial profiling at airports to wiretapping telephones to indefinitely detaining or deporting Arab or Muslim men. Amid the increase in hate crimes and government policies that targeted and criminalized Arab and Muslim identities, and amid public support for such policies, how can we understand the proliferation of sympathetic representations of Arabs and Muslims in the U.S. commercial media after 9/11? The discrepancy between the proliferation of sympathetic images about Arabs and Muslims and the simultaneous enactment of racist policies and practices that criminalized Arab and Muslim identities is the central problematic of this book. I am particularly concerned with the standardization of "positive," sympathetic representations of Arab and Muslim identities during—and the myriad significance of these representations for—the Bush administration's War on Terror, from September 11, 2001, to the end of his term in January 2009.

These seemingly positive representations of Arabs and Muslims have helped to form a new kind of racism, one that projects antiracism and multiculturalism on the surface but simultaneously produces the logics and affects necessary to legitimize racist policies and practices. It is no longer the case that the Other is explicitly demonized to justify war or injustice. Now, the Other is portrayed sympathetically in order to project the United States as an enlightened country that has entered a postracial era. This is accomplished through the following mechanisms: deploying seemingly complex story lines and characters that are in fact predictable and formulaic (chapter 1); evoking sympathy for the Arab/Muslim American plight while narrating the logic of exception (chapter 2); eliciting an excess of affect for oppressed Muslim women (chapter 3) while regulating sympathy for Muslim men (chapter 4); and producing narratives of multicultural inclusion that reproduce restrictive notions of Americanness and acceptable forms of Muslim American identity (chapter 5).

The book is organized in three parts: logics, affects, and challenges. Chapters 1 and 2 focus on the dual process of producing multicultural representations while advancing exclusionary logics. Chapter 1 explores how writers and producers of TV dramas deployed numerous representational strategies to circumvent reinscribing the stereotype of Arab/Muslim terrorists. I also examine how the debate about torture during the War on Terror often took place through debates about representations in TV dramas, demonstrating that TV dramas have been important sites that mediate the War on Terror. Chapter 2 examines representations of the Arab American plight in post-9/11 TV dramas, stories in which Arab Americans are victims of hate crimes and viewers are positioned to sympathize with their plight. I show how these sympathetic representations can reproduce logics of exception that are central to the War on Terror and justify the denial of rights to Arabs and Muslims.

Chapters 3 and 4 argue that the logics central to the War on Terror are not possible without their accompanying affects, showing how certain Muslim identities are designated as worthy of feeling while others are not. Chapters 3 and 4 are mirror images of each other, exploring the ways in which the boundaries of feeling are policed differently in the case of Muslim women and Muslim men. Chapter 3 examines how Muslim women have for the most part become sites of public sympathy and moral outrage, and chapter 4 examines how Muslim men have become sites of moral disengagement. In the case of women, I pay special attention to the ways in which discourses of multiculturalism and feminism are co-opted by the government and media during the War on Terror. In the case of men, I trace how some journalists have located the causes of 9/11 in the dispositions of Muslim men, showing how sympathy toward Muslim men is strictly regulated through coding race, gender, religion, and sexuality.

Chapter 5 and the epilogue turn to the efforts of nonprofit organizations, civil rights groups, and sitcom writers and producers to challenge ideas that Arab culture and Islam are incompatible with and oppositional to the United States. Chapter 5 demonstrates how the government, a nonprofit organization, and a civil rights group used nonprofit advertising campaigns after 9/11 to mobilize a version of multiculturalism that I term "diversity patriotism." I examine the ways in which public service announcements narrated Islam and the United States as compatible in an effort to inspire national unity during a time of crisis. The epilogue assesses the representational terrain almost a decade after 9/11 under the Obama administration. It considers whether there have been any changes since the Bush administration's War on Terror and reviews recent sitcoms that present alternative representations of Arab and Muslim identities. In the book as a whole, I examine the role of the government and media in producing ideas about race, gender, sexuality, religion, civilization, and violence in the making, unmaking, and remaking of the War on Terror.

1　Challenging the Terrorist Stereotype

Am I crazy or is attacking torture by lobbying the producers of 24
almost as ridiculous as trying to make nuclear power plants safer by urging the producers of *The Simpsons* to stop letting Homer play with
plutonium in the lunchroom of the Springfield nuke plant?
—Peter Carlson, *Washington Post*

Intentionally or not—and for better and for worse—fiction can play a real role in the
construction of political reality. Amid the global war on terror, those in Hollywood
and those in Washington would do well to take heed of this fact about fiction.
—Kelly M. Greenhill, *Los Angeles Times*

In 2004 the Council on American-Islamic Relations (CAIR) accused the TV
drama 24 of perpetuating stereotypes of Arabs and Muslims.[1] CAIR objected
to the persistent portrayal of Arabs and Muslims in the context of terrorism,
stating that "repeated association of acts of terrorism with Islam will only serve
to increase anti-Muslim prejudice."[2] CAIR's critics have retorted that programs
like 24 are cutting edge, reflecting one of the most pressing social and political
issues of the moment, the War on Terror. Some critics further contend that
CAIR is trying to deflect the reality of Muslim terrorism by confining television writers to politically correct themes.[3]

The writers and producers of 24 have responded to CAIR's concerns in a
number of ways. For one, the show often includes sympathetic portrayals of
Arabs and Muslims, in which they are the "good guys" or in some way on the
side of the United States. Representatives of 24 state that the show has "made a
concerted effort to show ethnic, religious and political groups as multi-dimen-
sional, and political issues are debated from multiple viewpoints."[4] The villains on the eight seasons of 24 are Russian, German, Latino, Arab/Muslim,
Euro-American, and African, even the fictional president of the United States.
Rotating the identity of the "bad guy" is one of the many strategies used by
TV dramas to avoid reproducing the Arab/Muslim terrorist stereotype (or any
other stereotypes, for that matter).[5] 24's responsiveness to such criticism even
extended to creating a public service announcement (PSA) that was broadcast
in February 2005, during one of the program's commercial breaks. The PSA
featured the lead actor, Kiefer Sutherland, staring deadpan into the camera,
reminding viewers that "the American Muslim community stands firmly beside

their fellow Americans in denouncing and resisting all forms of terrorism" and urging us to "please bear that in mind" while watching the program.[6]

CAIR is not the only organization that has lobbied 24 to change its representations. Whereas CAIR objected to stereotyping Arabs and Muslims as terrorists, the Parents Television Council, Human Rights First, and faculty from West Point Military Academy objected to 24's portrayal of torture as an effective method of interrogation. The Parents Television Council was concerned that children would become desensitized to torture; Human Rights First was concerned that viewers might come to perceive certain human beings as deserving of torture, not worthy of human rights; and the West Point faculty were concerned that some of their cadets believed torture was an effective method of interrogation because of 24's portrayal of it. Tony Lagouranis, former army interrogator, stated, "Among the things that I saw people doing [in Iraq] that they got from television was water-boarding, mock execution, using mock torture."[7]

Howard Gordon, one of the writers, responded by stating, "I think people can differentiate between a television show and reality."[8] The writers and producers of 24 explained that the show was fictional, that it was not intended as a documentary or military manual. They went on to say that the torture scenes are for dramatic, entertainment purposes only. Furthermore, the writers and producers of 24 stated that although the character Bauer uses torture and is a U.S. hero, torture is not glamorized because Bauer is traumatized by his use of torture. However, Joel Surnow, executive producer, defended the use of torture in the show, claiming, "We've had all of these torture experts come by recently, and they say, 'You don't realize how many people are affected by this. Be careful.' They say torture doesn't work. But I don't believe that. I don't think it's honest to say that if someone you love was being held, and you had five minutes to save them, you wouldn't do it." In contrast, Sutherland expressed concern about the "unintended consequences of the show." Fox Television network executive David Nevins admits that the show conveys a clear message on the War on Terror: "There's definitely a political attitude of the show, which is that extreme measures are sometimes necessary for the greater good. . . . The show doesn't have much patience for the niceties of civil liberties or due process."[9]

In November 2006 members of Human Rights First and West Point met with the writers and producers of 24 to address the potential impact of their representations of torture.[10] David Danzig, manager at Human Rights First, explained that the meeting was difficult for 24's writers and producers because "they have a hugely popular show, and we were suggesting to them that they do something actually a little bit risky, which is change their format. And there's obviously a lot of money at stake." Though the 24 crew insisted their depiction of torture should not have an influence on its viewers, it is interesting to note that the story line of the next season (which debuted on January 13, 2008, fourteen months after the meeting) involved Jack Bauer being tried by the U.S. government for his illegal use of torture.

This chapter explores this slippery realm between representations and their potential impacts. Through each facet of this discussion, what arises is a fact that is utterly taken for granted: television mediates the War on Terror. Between 2001 and 2009 the fictional creations of a tiny number of artists and executives shaped the ways that viewer-citizens engaged with the very real war going on around us. As indicated in the opening epigraph, the journalist Peter Carlson thinks that it is ridiculous that a TV drama, rather than the U.S. government, was criticized for its role in torture (and for its *representation* at that). Whether ridiculous or not, the journalist Kelly Greenhill asserts that it is important to take seriously the power of TV dramas to shape public perceptions of the War on Terror. Throughout the Bush years, TV shows became a crucial way that Americans saw, thought about, and talked about the United States in a state of emergency after 9/11. Public debate, it sometimes seemed, was displaced onto TV dramas. The slippage between debating a television show and debating a government's policies and practices demonstrates the significance of TV dramas during the War on Terror.

After September 11, 2001, a number of TV dramas were created using the War on Terror as their central theme. Dramas such as *24* (2001–11), *Threat Matrix* (2003–4), *The Grid* (2004), *Sleeper Cell* (2005–6), and *The Wanted* (2009) depict U.S. government agencies and officials heroically working to make the nation safe by battling terrorism.[11] A prominent feature of these television shows is Arab and Muslim characters, most of which are portrayed as grave threats to U.S. national security. But in response to increased popular awareness of ethnic stereotyping and the active monitoring of Arab and Muslim watchdog groups, television writers have had to adjust their story lines to avoid blatant, crude stereotyping.

24 and *Sleeper Cell* were among the most popular of the fast-emerging post-9/11 genre of terrorism dramas. *24* centered on Jack Bauer, a brooding and embattled agent of the government's Counter-Terrorism Unit (CTU) who raced a ticking clock to subvert impending terrorist attacks on the United States. The title refers to a twenty-four-hour state of emergency, and each of a given season's twenty-four episodes represented one hour of "real" time. *Sleeper Cell* was not as popular as *24*, partly because it was broadcast on the cable network Showtime and therefore had a much smaller audience. While *24* lasted eight seasons, *Sleeper Cell* lasted two. *Sleeper Cell*'s story line revolved around an undercover African American Muslim FBI agent who infiltrates a group of homegrown terrorists (the "cell" of the show's title) in order to subvert their planned attack on the United States.

This chapter draws from the many TV dramas but especially 24 and *Sleeper Cell* that either revolved around themes of terrorism or the War on Terror or included a few episodes on these themes. I begin by mapping the representational strategies that have become standard since the multicultural movement of the 1990s and discussing the ideological work performed by them through simplified complex representations. I then ask, If writers and producers of TV dramas are making efforts at more complex representations, how are viewers responding to them? Finally, I address the concerns expressed by various organizations regarding representations of torture on TV dramas.

Simplified Complex Representations

Simplified complex representations are strategies used by television producers, writers, and directors to give the impression that the representations they are producing are complex. While I focus on television, film uses these strategies as well. Below I lay out what I have found to be the most common ways that writers and producers of television dramas have depicted Arab and Muslim characters after 9/11. While some of these were used more frequently (and to greater narrative success) than others, they all help to shape the many layers of simplified complexity. I argue that simplified complex representations are the representational mode of the so-called post-race era, signifying a new era of racial representation. These representations appear to challenge or complicate former stereotypes and contribute to a multicultural or post-race illusion. Yet at the same time, most of the programs that employ simplified complex representational strategies promote logics that legitimize racist policies and practices, such as torturing Arabs and Muslims. I create a list of some of these strategies in order to outline the parameters of simplified complex representations and to facilitate ways to identify such strategies.

Strategy #1: Inserting Patriotic Arab or Muslim Americans

Between 2001 and 2009 television writers increasingly created "positive" Arab and Muslim characters to show that they are sensitive to negative stereotyping. Such characters usually take the form of a patriotic Arab or Muslim American who assists the U.S. government in its fight against Arab/Muslim terrorism, either as a government agent or as a civilian. Some examples of this strategy include Mohammad "Mo" Hassain, an Arab American Muslim character who is part of the USA Homeland Security Force on the show *Threat Matrix*;

Figure 1.1. Strategies 1 and 6, the cast of 24, Season 4. Marisol Nichols, who plays Counter Terrorism Unit agent Nadia Yasir, is pictured on the far right (strategy 1). The multicultural cast (strategy 6) includes an African American president, Wayne Palmer, played by D. B. Woodside, pictured fourth from the left.

Nadia Yassir, in season 6 of 24, a dedicated member of the CTU;[12] and in *Sleeper Cell* the lead African American character, Darwyn Al-Sayeed, a "good" Muslim who is an undercover FBI agent who proclaims to his colleagues that terrorists have nothing to do with his faith and cautions them not to confuse the two.[13] In a fourth-season episode of 24, two Arab American brothers say they are tired of being unjustly blamed for terrorist attacks and insist on helping to fight terrorism alongside Jack Bauer.[14] Islam is sometimes portrayed as inspiring U.S. patriotism rather than terrorism.[15] This bevy of characters makes up the most common group of post-9/11 Arab/Muslim depictions. This strategy challenges the notion that Arabs and Muslims are not American and/or un-American. Judging from the numbers of these patriots, it appears that writers have embraced this strategy as the most direct method to counteract charges of stereotyping.

Strategy #2: Sympathizing with the Plight of Arab and Muslim Americans after 9/11

Multiple stories appeared on TV dramas with Arab/Muslim Americans as the unjust victims of violence and harassment (see chapter 2). The viewer is nearly always positioned to sympathize with their plight. In an episode of *The Practice* the government detains an innocent Arab American without due process or explanation, and an attorney steps in to defend his rights.[16] On *7th Heaven* Ruthie's Muslim friend, Yasmine, is harassed on her way to school, prompting the Camden family and their larger neighborhood to stand together to fight discrimination.[17] This emphasis on victimization and sympathy challenges long-standing representations that have inspired a lack of sympathy and even a sense of celebration when the Arab/Muslim character is killed.

Strategy #3: Challenging the Arab/Muslim Conflation with Diverse Muslim Identities

Sleeper Cell prides itself on being unique among TV dramas that deal with the topic of terrorism because of its diverse cast of Muslim terrorists. It challenges the common conflation of Arab and Muslim identities. While the ringleader of the cell, Faris al-Farik, is an Arab, the other members are not: they are Bosnian, French, Euro-American, Western European, and Latino; one character is a gay Iraqi Brit. Portraying diverse sleeper cell members strategically challenges how Arab and Muslim identities are often conflated by government discourses and media representations by demonstrating that all Arabs are not Muslim and all Muslims are not Arab and, further, that not all Arabs and Muslims are heterosexual. In addition, the program highlights a struggle within Islam over who will define the religion, thus demonstrating that not all Muslims advocate terrorism. For example, in one episode a Yemeni imam comes to Los Angeles to deprogram Muslim extremists and plans to issue a fatwa against terrorism.[18] These diverse characters, and their heated debates for and against terrorism, indeed distinguish *Sleeper Cell* from the rest of the genre. But this strategy of challenging the Arab/Muslim conflation is remarkable in part because of its infrequency.

Strategy #4: Flipping the Enemy

"Flipping the enemy" involves leading the viewer to believe that Muslim terrorists are plotting to destroy the United States and then revealing that those Muslims are merely pawns for Euro-American or European terrorists. The identity of the enemy is thus flipped: viewers discover that the terrorist is not Arab, or they find that the Arab or Muslim terrorist is part of a larger network of international terrorists. On *24*, Bauer spends the first half of season 2 tracking down a Middle Eastern terrorist cell, ultimately subverting a nuclear attack. In the second half of the season, we discover that European and Euro-American businessmen are behind the attack, goading the United States into declaring a war on the Middle East in order to benefit from the increase in oil prices. Related to this subversion of expectations, *24* does not glorify the United States; in numerous ways the show dismantles the notion that the United States is perfect and the rest of the world flawed. FBI and CIA agents

Figure 1.2. Strategy 3, Challenging the Arab/Muslim conflation and representing diverse Muslim identities. DVD cover of *Sleeper Cell*.

are incompetent; other government agents conspire with the terrorists; the terrorists (Arab and Muslim alike) are portrayed as very intelligent. Flipping the enemy demonstrates that terrorism is not an Arab or Muslim monopoly.

Strategy #5: Humanizing the Terrorist

Most Arab and Muslim terrorists in film or on television before 9/11 were stock villains, one-dimensional bad guys who were presumably bad because of their ethnic background or religious beliefs.[19] In contrast, post-9/11 terrorist characters are humanized in a variety of ways. We see them in a family context, as loving fathers and husbands; we come to learn their back stories and glimpse moments that have brought them to the precipice of terror. In 2005 *24* introduced viewers to a Middle Eastern family for the first time on U.S. network

Figure 1.3. Strategy 4, Flipping the Enemy. During Season 5 of *24*, Gregory Itzen plays U.S. President Charles Logan, who conspires with the terrorists.

television (in a recurring role for most of the season, as opposed to a one-time appearance). In their first scene they seem like an "ordinary" family—mother, father, and teenage son—preparing breakfast. It is soon revealed, however, that they are a sleeper cell; in the episodes that follow, each family member's relationship to terrorism is explored. The father is willing to kill his wife and son in order to complete his mission; the mother reconsiders her involvement with terrorism only to protect her son; and the teenage son, raised in the United States, is portrayed with an evolving sense of humanity that ultimately prevents him from being a terrorist. This strategy—humanizing the terrorists by focusing on their interpersonal relationships, motives, and back stories—is also central to *Sleeper Cell*. Each member has his or her personal motivation for joining the cell: to rebel against a leftist liberal parent (a professor at the University of California, Berkeley); to seek revenge against the United States for the death of family members (one character's husband was killed by U.S. forces in Iraq). Adding multiple dimensions to the formerly one-dimensional bad guy has become increasingly common since 9/11.

Strategy #6: Projecting a Multicultural U.S. Society

Projecting a multicultural U.S. society is another strategy to circumvent accusations of racism while representing Arabs and Muslims as terrorists. In *Sleeper Cell*, the terrorists are of diverse ethnic backgrounds, and Darwyn, the African American FBI agent, is in an interracial relationship with a white woman. For several seasons of *24*, the U.S. president was African American, his press secretary Asian American; the Counter Terrorist Unit is equally diverse, peppered with Latinos and African Americans throughout the show's eight seasons. The sum total of the casting decisions creates the impression of a United States in which multiculturalism abounds. The projected society is one in which people of different racial backgrounds work together and racism is socially unacceptable.

Strategy #7: Fictionalizing the Middle Eastern or Muslim Country

It has become increasingly common for the country of the terrorist characters in television dramas to go unnamed. This strategy rests on the assumption that leaving the nationality of the villain open eliminates the potential for offensiveness; if no specific country or ethnicity is named, then there is less reason for any particular group to be offended by the portrayal. In season 4 of *24*, the terrorist family is from an unnamed Middle Eastern country, possibly Turkey; it is, we assume, intentionally left ambiguous. In *The West Wing*, the fictional country "Qumar" is a source of terrorist plots; in season 8 of *24*, it is "Kamistan." But the name of country doesn't always connote the Middle East. For example, in season 7 of *24*, the African country "Sangala" is an important source of terrorism. Fictionalizing the country of the terrorist can give a show more latitude in creating salacious story lines that might be criticized if identified with an actual country.

The seven representational strategies I have found are not exhaustive, nor are they all new to our post-9/11 world. Rather, these strategies collectively outline some of the ways in which writers and producers of television (and film) have sought to improve representations of Arabs (and other racial and ethnic groups). These strategies are an astounding shift in the mass entertainment landscape. They present an important departure from stereotypes into more challenging stories and characters. This new breed of terrorism programs reflects a growing sensitivity to the negative impact of stereotyping. These new representational strategies seek to make the point—indeed, often with strenuous effort—that

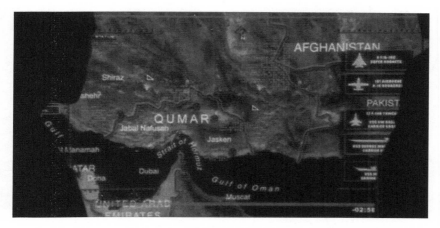

Figure 1.4. Strategy 7: Fictionalizing the Middle Eastern or Muslim country. A map of Qumar, *The West Wing.*

not all Arabs are terrorists and not all terrorists are Arabs. However, for all their innovations, these programs remain wedded to a script that represents Arabs and Muslims only in the context of terrorism and therefore do not effectively challenge the stereotypical representations of Arabs and Muslims.

Stuart Hall has claimed that even those with the best intentions, liberal writers and producers who seek to subvert racial hierarchies, may inadvertently participate in inferential racism, that is, "apparently naturalized representations of events and situations relating to race, whether 'factual' or 'fictional,' which have racist premises and propositions inscribed in them as a set of unquestioned assumptions."[20] The persistent unquestioned assumption in these TV dramas is that Arabs and Muslims are terrorists, despite writers' efforts to create a wider range of Arab and Muslim characters. The primary objective of commercial television networks is not education, social justice, or social change. Rather, the goal is financial, to keep as many viewers watching for as long as possible. Television must therefore strike a balance between keeping its products as engaging as possible and not offending potential viewers. Writers thus seem to be constrained and influenced by two factors: viewers have been primed to assume that Arabs/Muslims are terrorists, and therefore writers create what viewers expect and what will sell; at the same time, some viewers are particularly sensitive and fed up with stereotypes, and therefore writers must create a more diverse world of characters. The results are some modifications to avoid being offensive while perpetuating core stereotypes that continue to have cultural capital.[21] Post-9/11 television is testimony to the fact that the stereotypes that held sway for much of the twentieth century are no longer socially acceptable—at least in their most blatant forms. But this does not mean that such stereotypes (and viewers' taste for them) have actually gone away; they have only become covert. Simplified complex representational strategies reflect the commodification of the civil rights and multiculturalist movements. The commodification of multiculturalism, while reflecting the sensibilities of some viewers, is submerged under the more prominent consumable message that Arabs and Muslims pose a terrorist threat to American life and freedom.

These strategies attempt to make representations complex, yet do so in a simplified way; they are predictable strategies that can be relied on if the plot involves an Arab or Muslim terrorist but are a new standard alternative to (and seem a great improvement on) the stock ethnic villains of the past. Under the guise of complexity, these representational strategies construct "good" and "bad" Arabs and Muslims, reinforcing a narrow conception of what constitutes a "good" Arab or Muslim.[22] "Bad" Arabs or Muslims are the terrorists, and their "good" counterparts are those who help the U.S. government fight terrorism. Despite the shift away from the more blatant stereotypes of previous decades, Arab and Muslim identities are still understood and evaluated primarily in relation to terrorism. This binary focus, in turn, overpowers the strategies described above. Though some television writers might certainly have humane motives and though some producers might honestly desire to create innovative shows, devoid of stereotypes, any such efforts are overwhelmed by the sheer momentum of our current representational scheme. Thus representations of Arab and Muslim identities in contexts that have nothing to do with terrorism remain strikingly unusual in the U.S. commercial media.[23]

Inserting a patriotic Arab or Muslim American or fictionalizing Middle Eastern countries are ineffectual devices if Arabs, Muslims, Arab Americans, and Muslim Americans continue to be portrayed through the narrow lens of "good" or "bad" in the fight against terrorism. Casting actors of color to give the impression of a postracial society propagates the comforting notion of an enlightened society that has resolved all its racial problems. The various strategies used in the first decade of the War on Terror are akin to a Band-Aid over a still-festering wound. They give the impression of comfort, perhaps even of cure, but the fundamental problem remains.

While these representational strategies that challenge the stereotyping of Arabs and Muslims were being broadcast, circulated, and consumed, real Arabs and Muslims were being detained, deported, held without due process, and tortured. Certainly not all Arabs and Muslims were subject to post-9/11 harassment. Nonetheless, what I am arguing is that simplified complex racial representations—a new representational mode collectively constructed by these multiple representational strategies—performs the ideological work of producing a post-race moment in which denying the severity of the persistence of institutionalized racism becomes possible. These TV dramas produce reassurance that racial sensitivity is the norm in U.S. society while simultaneously perpetuating the dominant perception of Arabs and Muslims as threats to U.S. national security.

These complex characters and story lines fall short of subverting stereotypes. Fictionalizing Arab and Muslim countries, for example, tends to add to the conflation and generalization of Arab and Muslim identities by implying that terrorism originates from a fictional country that could be any of a number of Arab/Muslim countries. The specificity of the context becomes irrelevant. Furthermore, viewers are well aware that the fictionalized country is supposed to be Arab or Muslim. These fictionalized countries operate as allegories—standing in as doubles for the "real"—and in turn illustrate how the real sites where the United States is waging its War on Terror (Iraq and Afghanistan) often feel like abstract or even fictional locations to viewers.

This fictionalizing strategy has many precedents. Fictional Latin America, with locations such as San Pasquale in *Commander in Chief* (2005), Tecala in *Proof of Life* (2000), and Curaguay in *The A-Team* (1983–86), has been a staple of mainstream film and television for decades. Similarly, fictional "Arabia" is not a new representational strategy; rather it is a strategy that is making a comeback. The Hollywood film *Harum Scarum* (1965), starring Elvis Presley, for example, takes place in "Abulstan" and "Lunacan." Disney's *Aladdin* (1992) takes place in "Agrabah." Originally set in Baghdad, the location was changed to avoid associating this fairy tale with the Gulf War.[24] These films seek to trade on the West's long-standing, and carefully cultivated, notions of an imaginary, fantastical, and exoticized East. Recent films and television shows emphasize their portrayal of actual locations, to heighten the sense of place and create presumably realistic depictions of current and historical events. Post-9/11 TV dramas have merely conflated their methods, emphasizing their "realistic" story lines—"ripped from the headlines," as *Law and Order* and others advertise—in the ideological safety of fictionalized locations.

Simplified complex representations are also deceptive: they offer a limited field of explanation of the War on Terror under the guise of an expanded field of explanation. Audiences are given the impression that multiple positions and perspectives have been considered, for example, by exploring the motives of terrorists. Terrorism, according to *Sleeper Cell*, is caused by disaffected non-Arabs who turn to fundamentalist Islam and Arabs who embrace fundamentalist ideologies. Consistent with what Mamdani calls "culture talk"—the notion that terrorism can be explained merely by examining Arab or Muslim "culture"— the series perpetuates the idea, circulating in popular culture since at least the

1970s, that Arabs and Muslims have a monopoly on terrorism.[25] The motives for terrorism that are presented often lack real depth or exploration. These plot lines are, however, gripping, making it is easy to ignore all that remains unchanged and the way in which the dominant discourse of the United States as an innocent victim of terrorism is maintained.

Simplified complex representational strategies attempt to challenge the Arab/Muslim terrorist stereotype by making concessions to how violence, sympathy, and context are framed. The Arab terrorist stereotype has emerged not only through repeating this one-dimensional character in films, news reports, and government speeches but also through its particular framing. The Arab terrorist stereotype was born from a fundamental distinction: violence perpetrated by Arabs and Muslims is framed as illegitimate; violence committed by the United States is legitimate, indeed necessary to democracy, freedom, and peace. What makes a terrorist a "terrorist"—a pejorative term, in comparison to "freedom fighter"—is that the violence is illegitimate because it is targeting innocents and because it is senseless or without a moral outcome. "Arab/Muslim terrorists" in the U.S. media have historically been portrayed as seeking power or chaos; the United States, in contrast, is consistently portrayed as fighting to preserve equality. Recent television dramas seem to challenge this basic distinction. Behind the grim certainty of Jack Bauer's fatalism, 24 seems to relish its portrayals of the U.S. government as flawed and at moments even morally bankrupt. Similarly, Sleeper Cell provides its terrorist characters with ample opportunity to state their grievances; their backstories appear to lend a degree of legitimacy to their violence. However, in the broader arc of these shows—with their eventual, if tortured, triumph against evil—such grievances are ultimately framed as illegitimate. The complexities of history and religion are eventually boiled down to Arab/Muslim individuals spewing nonsensical, hateful rhetoric at the United States or Israel. Furthermore, the portrayal of Arab/Muslim terrorists as well organized and intelligent, while a departure from previous representations of incompetent Arab/Muslim terrorists, conveys the idea that the threat is "real" and that the United States is still smarter since the terrorists are outsmarted in TV dramas.

As with all instances of framing, what is not shown is as important as what is.[26] While it has become increasingly common to show the verbal tirades of Arab terrorists, promising to free their country from U.S. foreign policies, it is uncommon for the context of such references to be adequately addressed. The concept of freeing an Arab country from the negative impacts of U.S. foreign policies remains abstract, since viewers don't see the daily realities of those countries. Both the suffering of Palestinians living under Israeli military occupation that is supported by U.S. policies and the suffering of the Iraqi people as a result of a decade of U.S. sanctions are absent from the story line. This absence operates to ensure that any consideration of their violence as legitimate remains taboo. Thus while simplified complex representational strategies make concessions to complexity—giving voice to the grievances of terrorist characters, allowing us to see them in the context of their families—"their" violence remains incomprehensible, beyond reason, and in the service of hatred.

How violence is framed, including what parts of the story are intentionally left absent, is intimately connected to how sympathy is framed and who is represented as deserving or undeserving of the audience's sympathies. Because terrorists commit senseless acts of violence, because they are the "bad" guys, they are not deserving of sympathy. By contrast, the "good" Arab/Muslim characters—patriotic Americans and innocent victims of post-9/11 hate crimes—are positioned as worthy of sympathy. These dramas are remarkable in that they encourage a post-9/11 audience to root for certain Arab and Muslim characters and to feel sadness—even outrage—when those characters are unfairly attacked. But such sympathy, it becomes clear, is possible only because of the basic good/bad binary. We root for these unlikely good guys because they challenge (though they don't overturn) our cultural assumption that the Arab/Muslim character is the bad guy. These concessions are reflective of the "post-race" moment. Gray states that representations of blackness in the 1980s and 1990s rewrote "a strife-ridden past into a harmonized vision of possibility" and in so doing made it difficult to differentiate between "progressive political possibilities" and "neoliberal and conservative rewrites of the same old racial narratives."[27] Similarly, post-9/11 TV dramas, through multidimensional characters and story lines, construct an internal logic of racial sensitivity and diversity that makes it increasingly difficult to differentiate between new Arab and Muslim representations and the reinscription of long-standing stereotypes.

Responding to Simplified Complex Representations

Television executives are complicating their story lines in an effort to avoid reproducing stereotypes and to project racial sensitivity. Their choices reflect an era in which blatant racism is for the most part no longer tolerated by mainstream U.S. culture. So if TV shows are responding to broader cultural trends, what about the flipside: how is the broader culture responding to them? To what extent do simplified complex representations influence viewer responses? What do TV critics and viewers say about portrayals of Arabs and Muslims?

The range of critiques offered by film and television critics tends to fall along ideological lines. Yet, surprisingly, the differentiation is not that drastic. Taking *Sleeper Cell* as a case study of viewer responses, we find that political

conservatives, or those on the right, tend toward harsh criticism of these representational strategies, claiming that they prioritize political correctness over
an accurate portrayal of the very real Arab/Muslim threat to U.S. national
security. Political liberals, or those on the left, tend to acknowledge *Sleeper
Cell's* attempt to offer alternative representations of Muslims but nevertheless
criticize it for being pedantic. Both sets of responses demonstrate the limited
impact of these representational strategies and how—despite their efforts at
complexity—they devolve toward a problematic simplicity.

The conservative writer Dorothy Rabinowitz, in her review for the *Wall
Street Journal*, states:

> SHOWTIME'S *Sleeper Cell* won't make viewers particularly happy, its intention
> being, evidently, to teach rather than to delight—a worthy enterprise in this case,
> and one, it turns out that's also highly compelling most of the time. The 10-part
> series . . . is clearly meant to represent varying aspects of Muslim society—in particu-
> lar attitudes towards terrorism. . . . with a didactic streak more than a little evident.
>
> Its strains and balancing efforts aside, it is soon obvious that there's much in
> this story about the day-to-day planning and training for a terror strike that should
> enthrall—and chill—audiences.[28]

Rabinowitz describes *Sleeper Cell's* teaching mission and its intention to give
voice to "Muslims opposed to Islamic extremists" as efforts that will not please
viewers. What will please audiences, she goes on to say, are the parts of the
show that portray views that "are common in numerous quarters of the radical Islamic world"—in other words, its portrayal of the Muslim threat to U.S.
national security.

The criticism of liberal writers tends to focus on how the educational thrust
of *Sleeper Cell* compromises its entertainment quality. A reviewer for the *Village
Voice*, Joy Press, writes:

> *Sleeper Cell* moves way too slowly to get anyone's pulse racing—except maybe the
> Arab American community, which will almost certainly protest, despite the writ-
> ers' awkward attempts to give equal screen time to "good" and "bad" Muslims. . . .
> Not only does *Sleeper Cell* fan free-form paranoia about Arabs, foreigners, and
> loners (hey, maybe that next-door neighbor with the funny accent is a terrorist after
> all!), but it plants the idea that the people meant to be protecting us from amor-
> phous terror might be as inept as Inspector Clouseau—or even former FEMA chief
> Michael Brown. What could be scarier than that?[29]

This reviewer conflates Arabs and Muslims, despite *Sleeper Cell's* efforts to challenge that conflation, and criticizes the TV drama for fueling the public's fears
about sleeper cells and inept government officials. While conservative perspectives tend to praise TV dramas such as *Sleeper Cell* for instilling fear in the

American public (though they are critical of portrayals of the US government as inept), liberal perspectives tend to be critical of fear-mongering.

The show's attempt to challenge the Arab/Muslim/Sikh conflation does not go unnoticed by Gillian Flynn, though she finds plenty of other faults with the show. She writes for *Entertainment Weekly*:

> Strange that only four years after we were forced to add phrases like sleeper cell to our vocabulary so much of a series about terrorists on American soil can feel cliché. Showtime's nine-part *Sleeper Cell*, about a small group of Muslim extremists and the undercover agent who's infiltrated their band, has every feature that every movie involving post-9/11 terrorism seems to deem essential. The optimistically named agent Darwyn al-Sayeed (Michael Ealy) is himself a Muslim, leading to the obligatory declaration that the extremists are distorting the word of the Koran. "These guys have nothing to do with my faith," he proclaims. At various points, the terrorists decry football and American arrogance, a trait highlighted in one scene in which some frat types harass a Sikh, mistaking him for an Arab, and allowing Mr. Survival of the Fittest to explain to them and us the differences between the cultures. These are all certainly important points, but Sleeper makes them artlessly—yet with a confounding confidence that it's teaching us something new. . . . We know it, we've heard it, find a slicker approach.[30]

Some liberal television critics, in other words, claim that the pedantic quality of these representational strategies compromise their entertainment value. John Leonard writes for *New York* magazine, "*Sleeper Cell* tries laudably to entertain us and to complicate us simultaneously. But we also experience the Stockholm syndrome in reverse. The more time we spend with these people, the less we care about them."[31] And Joan Juliet Buck writes for *Vogue*, "The earnest realism of *Sleeper Cell* adds up to an exploitative and inept piece of garbage."[32]

In contrast to television critics who acknowledge and criticize these representational strategies, many viewer posts on the Internet tend to praise *Sleeper Cell* for educating the public—not on the diversity of Muslims, but on the ongoing Arab/Muslim terrorist threat to national security. Not surprisingly, there are a wide array of viewer responses on Internet forums devoted to television shows. Some (e.g., tampafilmfan.com) are run by individuals, others (e.g., tvsquad.com) by corporations such as AOL and News Corporation. These websites allow everyone and anyone to be a critic and to anonymously "talk back"— consistent with the new culture of viewer feedback initiated by major networks such as CNN, which has shifted its news format to invite and include viewer perspectives. Some viewer posts focus on whether 24 or *Sleeper Cell* is more entertaining; others discuss the "hotness" of the actors; still others say what they would like to see happen in the story line—who will fall in love, who will be avenged, and so on. My focus here is on a particular strain of responses—those that focus on the realism of the show and reflect a collapsed distinction between television and politics.

A recurring theme in viewer comments is *Sleeper Cell's* realism, its presumed "realistic" portrayal of the War on Terror and the Muslim threat to U.S. national security. One viewer, Mike Rankin, writes:

> I loved it for being fearlessly honest when it comes to the true face of our real
> enemies—not turning them into generic, PC comicbook versions of themselves....
> Unlike most political thrillers from Hollywood, the bad guys didn't turn out to be
> the American military or the military-industrial complex or the oil companies or our
> own corrupt politicians. The enemy was the enemy, from start to finish—Islamic
> extremists who would be happy to see our entire civilization turned to dust.[33]

Rankin is discussing the "flipping the enemy" strategy and indirectly critiquing 24 (and a smattering of Hollywood films) for portraying Americans as complicit in terrorism. He articulates a preference for *Sleeper Cell* over other TV dramas because Muslims are the sole enemy; no others are implicated along the way; no one else diffuses the potency of an Arab/Muslim threat. This post reflects how TV dramas can be used to make claims to "truth" and "realness"—and how viewers can use them to confirm their own suspicions about what is real. The emphasis here is not on an appreciation for representing diverse Muslims but rather on educating the public on the War on Terror and the Arab/Muslim terrorist threat. This viewer seeks programming that affirms an "us" and a "them" and appreciates a drama that reinscribes conceptions of the domestic and foreign wherein the foreign is signified as a threat.

Similar commentary is made by a poster who identifies himself as a military officer:

> I am an NCO in the United States Army. After four over seas tours in the last four
> and a half years I was beginning to get a little tired of my job. Then *Sleeper Cell* fell
> into my lap. It truly reminded me why I do what I do every day. I Sit and watch the
> tv and hear all the negative stuff the media puts out and I get very discouraged. I
> am out here everyday watching along with my brothers and sisters in arms as we
> rebuild a torn country. I see us out there working with the MUSLIM society giving
> entire cities electricity for the first time ever, giving school supplies and clothing to
> kids, watching as grown Iraqi men break down and cry because we put a new roof
> on his adobe house and many other things that never make the news. I know this
> is a fictional story but it is so real to life that it made me get right back in the fight
> and remember why I am over here doing what I do. I beg Showtime to continue
> this show if for nothing else but to make America aware of the real terror that faces
> our blessed nation. Plus it make for one hell of a pass time. BRING THE SHOW
> BACK SHOWTIME!!!!SGT SIEBRASSEBALAD IRAQ.[34]

The military officer acknowledges that *Sleeper Cell* is fictional, yet insists that it is realistic to the extent that it inspires him to continue participating in the War on Terror. Drawing on dominant discourses from the Bush administration, Sergeant Siebrasse articulates the benevolent role of the United States during the War on the Terror. According to him, "the Muslim" is either a terrorist or a victim in need of rescue by the United States.

Other viewers have also emphasized the realism of this "educational" drama on the War on Terror and expressed disappointment that the show was not renewed for a third season:

> I am so upset that they have totally taken off *Sleeper Cell*. . . . We should fight for this show to be put back on, it is the world we live in today with these *Sleeper Cells* living among us they would just soon chop our heads off. These are doctors, teachers, nanny's so this show is so important to know the knowledge of these TERRORIST living among us and our children. So for them to take off a show full of info. is down right stupid. Instead they want to put on filth, yea don't educate us any on the TERRORIST who want us all dead.[35]

This Internet poster, Isebella, discusses *Sleeper Cell* as if there is no distinction between the show and the War on Terror itself. The people she refers to as terrorists living among us, nannies and teachers, are the covers of two of the show's characters.

Such elisions between televised fiction and historical reality are common across fan forums. Statements like these are perhaps the greatest possible compliment for a show like *Sleeper Cell*, whose claim to artistic significance draws primarily on its urgent declarations of its authenticity. Writers and producers of *Sleeper Cell* pride themselves on their realism, in particular, their use of current events in the plotlines, filming at actual locations (e.g., Los Angeles International Airport), and consulting with members of the FBI and experts on Islam. These elisions are also a backhanded compliment to the mainstream news media, which has made television reporting into a similarly urgent, fast-paced action narrative that aspires to hold viewers in the grip of its dramatic authenticity. When these two cultural strands are both successful, their borders blur; TV dramas about the War on Terror often come to stand in for non-fictional accounts of the War on Terror.

Surprisingly, many post-9/11 TV dramas whose central theme is the War on Terror did not succeed past a season or two; some did not last longer than a few episodes. Why did they fail to capture audiences given the ripped-from-the-headlines relevance of their plots and ability to capitalize on post-9/11 fear? *The Wanted*, meant to be a documentary version of 24 with CIA agents investigating and combating terrorism, lasted a mere two episodes. It was attacked by critics for promoting questionable journalistic standards and by viewers for being contrived, empty propaganda. In contrast, *Sleeper Cell* was often criticized for being preachy and for trying to teach rather than entertain.[36] 24 was the only show that succeeded for multiple seasons; it was applauded for the ticking time bomb scenario that defines the show and keeps viewers on the edge of their seats. One of the keys to its success, at least as evidenced from the fan forums, is an apparent absence of pedagogy. It seems that viewers and critics alike criticize shows with an educational thrust. However, the "education" that is the focus of criticism is the diverse portrayals of Arab and Muslim identities, as opposed to the presumed "education" on the "reality" of the Arab/Muslim threat.

Some viewers reject the paranoid message of *Sleeper Cell*. One viewer, "TrentB," fed up with fear-mongering, posted the following to metacritic.com (a division of CBS Interactive):

> More mindless neocon propaganda vomited onto our screens. This country is going to collapse into a police state if people are actually believing this garbage. Fellow citizens, start questioning your government for God's sake! They're taking away our liberties and expanding federal police control over states and cities. Terrorists don't have any power over us—in fact they have less power to threaten us than street criminals. It's all a facade, and the Feds are using it to grab more control over our lives.[37]

Not all Internet posters accept *Sleeper Cell*'s message about an impending terrorist attack; not all accept its claims to realism. Some explicitly reject the message about the perpetual threat of terrorism and criticize TV dramas for capitalizing on post-9/11 fear, needed to support the U.S. government's War on Terror. Trent B. asserts that terrorism is a screen for the government to amass more power and that what should be feared is not terrorism but government control. Nonetheless, the vast majority of posts engage in the TV drama as a stand-in for the actual War on Terror.

One poster's comments elide the War on Terror and the 1995 Oklahoma City bombing, perpetrated by Timothy McVeigh and Terry Nichols.

> Having lived in OKC at the time of the Murrah bombing and being a federal government employee, I have an intense interest in terrorism issues. I believe the time will come when the world will finally understand that the OKC bombing was conducted by middle-eastern terrorists using *Sleeper Cell*s to accomplish the mission while employing "lily white" accomplices, Tim McVeigh and Terry Nichols. There was so much covered up by the FBI, and ordered by higher government officials. Records have been destroyed and evidence has been withheld.[38]

For this viewer, Sue Barnham, *Sleeper Cell* is not only a lens through which to understand the War on Terror but also a lens through which to reevaluate earlier instances of terrorism. Though two white men were convicted for the Oklahoma City bombing, she claims it must have been perpetuated by Muslims.

Barnham joins a large number of fellow posters, as well as TV critics on the right, in the idea that there is an incessant need to protect the domestic from the foreign (and to project any potential domestic threats onto foreign enemies). She "flips the enemy" in reverse: rather than say that there are white accomplices to Arab/Muslim terrorism, she asserts that there are Middle Eastern terrorists behind the Oklahoma City bombing. This poster insists on the unique connection between terrorism and Arab and Muslim identities.

Unlike responses from film and television critics, viewer posts to the Internet represent an unstable archive; they are often anonymous, and the source cannot be verified. They are fragments of larger sentiments, operating like eavesdropping into conversations for which the larger context is absent. Juana Maria Rodriguez refers to online exchanges as "textual performances: fleeting, transient, ephemeral, already post. Like the text of a play, they leave a trace to which meaning can be assigned, but these traces are haunted by the absence that was the performance itself, its reception, and its emotive power."[39] After being immersed in the often rabid and frequently misspelled rantings on Internet fan message boards, it is tempting to conclude that these posters are a very small subsection of the United States and that they certainly do not represent a mainstream perspective. Such a temptation, however, must be resisted, because these same voices are found among mainstream cultural critics. They also comment on the realism of the show and participate in blurring the boundaries between the War on Terror waged by the U.S. government and its fictional representations on television. Dan Iverson, for example, who writes for IGN Entertainment (a division of News Corporation), stated:

> [Sleeper Cell] never sides with the radical Muslims, and it never makes you feel like what they are doing is justified, but what it does is gives you a window into their culture and the terrorists' perversion of their religion in order to see what would drive people to do what they are doing. For this reason alone, Sleeper Cell should have a larger American audience - as we are waging war with this same enemy, and yet we know nothing about them or the religion that fuels their hatred for us. If more television programs were to responsibly give this type of attention to their radical fundamentalist enemies we might not be so ignorant of current events.[40]

Like many posters, Iverson laments the perceived "ignorance" of his fellow Americans. The pessimistic vision of his country, however, is less startling than the faith he has in fictional television: equivalent to news education, bettering our understanding of an entire religion and group of people.

Michael Medved, film critic and conservative political commentator, also has faith in the power of television. Regarding the film *Syriana*, he writes: "The problem, it seems to me, in a lot of these new films, is not that they humanized terrorists, that's good dramatically, the problem is that they're sympathetic to terrorists, that they erase the distinction between terrorists and those who are fighting terrorism and that's a terrible thing."[41] Medved contends that there is a moral difference between those who kill innocent people and those who kill the killers of innocent people and states that this should be accurately reflected in films, highlighting his investment in narratives of U.S. exceptionalism. He is committed to a particular configuration of blame that maintains the United States as innocent and heroic and Arabs and Muslims as committing senseless violence, upholding the dominant "they hate us for our freedom" discourse. However, Medved need not be concerned that humanizing the terrorists will make viewers sympathize with them. Despite the range of representational strategies identified above, viewer responses suggest that for most the dominant message remains the same: the United States is at war against terrorism because Arabs and Muslims are a threat. There is a tension between writers and producers' intentions on the one hand and critic and viewer responses on the other hand. Writers and producers create multiple representational strategies to circumvent accusations of racism and to maintain the largest viewership possible. Yet most critics dismiss such strategies for being too politically correct, preachy, or artless, and many viewers take away the message that Arabs/Muslims are a threat to U.S. national security despite the multiple representational strategies that would seem to counter that hypothesis. Despite efforts to convey that all Arab and Muslims are not terrorists, viewer and critic responses demonstrate that the impact of these representational strategies is limited. Viewers do not comment on how they have come to understand the diversity of Arab and Muslim identities. Ultimately, these representational strategies pay lip service to racism. Simplified complex representations do not necessarily result in viewers expressing sensitivity regarding Arab and Muslim identities. Rather, stereotyping persists because the message of these TV dramas is that Arabs and Muslims are a threat to U.S. national security, despite a few Arab and Muslim characters that are against terrorism. Ultimately, fear-mongering trumps multicultural sensitivity.

Although the impact of their particular representational strategies is limited, the impact of the TV dramas themselves is far-reaching. Operating as sites to discuss and debate the War on Terror, TV dramas have participated in mediating the war itself. They do this by producing a public around it, by lifting "people from the realm of their idiosyncratic interests, their 'particularity,' towards the realm of common interests, the 'universal' values that join them together and define a collectivity of spectators as precisely a 'public.'"[42] TV dramas turn the War on Terror into a common interest on at least two levels. First, TV dramas base their story lines on current events, thereby establishing a relationship to pressing political concerns. Despite being fictional,

TV dramas are intimately involved with the particulars of the War on Terror, creating a product that can feel more real to viewers than the news media. In other words, through TV dramas viewers can imagine the War on Terror in a nonabstract way: they can watch U.S. government agencies at work to combat terrorism; they get to know the terrorists and get to virtually visit Afghanistan and other sites where the War on Terror is waged. Second, in addition to or as an extension of political forums, viewers discuss the War on Terror on Internet forums, which in turn become places where government policies are discussed and debated, which in turn further blurs the boundaries between the War on Terror and its representation. The fact that various groups have lobbied particular TV dramas to change their representation of Arabs/Muslims or of torture in order to manage the potential adverse impact on public perceptions demonstrates how powerfully television mediates the War on Terror. Writers and producers of TV dramas are pressured to be accountable to the possibility of viewers consuming their representations as a clone of the War on Terror.

TV dramas that represent the War on Terror have an intimate relationship with what comes to be imagined and understood as "the real," by which I mean the "truth" produced by the U.S. government about the War on Terror. Because TV dramas have a semblance of "the real"—indeed, they take great pains to create a sense of authenticity—they can become an extension of it.[43] According to Jean Baudrillard, at this historical moment it is not that the representation threatens to replace the original but rather that the distinction between the original and its representation has broken down. Representations of reality—images, symbols, signs, media—have come to stand in for "the real" to the extent that the representation becomes indistinguishable from the original, or what he terms "clones of the real."[44] Some viewers experience and make sense of the War on Terror through its simulation. As Susan Willis writes:

> America lives its history as a cultural production. The post-9/11 era, as one defined by individual uncertainty in the face of an over-certain but often mistaken and repressive state, has seen a tremendous burgeoning of cultural forms meant to explain and manage the crisis. Daily life in America is articulated across an array of competing popular fictions.[45]

The fictional dramas and news dramas examined in this book are cultural forms that participate in explaining and managing the War on Terror. Viewers' experiences of the War on Terror, in turn, are intimately linked to these cultural forms.

Prime-Time Torture

The controversy surrounding 24's depiction of torture arose shortly after the revelation that U.S. military personnel had tortured inmates at Iraq's Abu Ghraib prison.[46] Leaked photos showed Iraqi prisoners being physically, psychologically, and sexually abused. The horrific photos intensified the debate about whether or not the U.S. government was sanctioning torture. In the view of the right-wing commentator Rush Limbaugh, the photos did not reveal torture but rather the U.S. military "blowing off steam"; he questioned what the public was so worried about since the torture victims "are trying to kill us."[47]

Here I explore the extent to which TV dramas mediate the War on Terror by normalizing logics that legitimize torture. The apparent contradiction here is a key example of how simplified complex representations operate: in the case of 24, multiple strategies are employed to avoid a simple conflation of Arabs and Muslims with terrorism, yet at the same time for many Americans 24 has helped make the real torture of Arabs and Muslims seem like a necessary evil—regrettable, perhaps, but essential for the safety of our nation.

In 24 this process works in various ways, all of which ultimately create a sense of urgent realism, a sense that disaster could strike at any moment, and thus that quick decisions must be made (even if they are difficult ones). One such device is the use of a split screen in order to present the show's multiple plotlines and a version of "real time." The most important of these techniques, however, is the "ticking time bomb scenario,"[48] one of the show's foundational plot devices. Agent Jack Bauer knows that a deadly bomb will be detonated within the next few hours; he therefore must make the difficult decision to torture a suspect in order to obtain the necessary information to disarm the bomb. The "real time" and ticking time bomb scenarios create an environment of immediate urgency. However, creating a sense of realism and a realistic portrayal are very distinct objectives; the ticking time bomb scenario as a symbol of the War on Terror might effectively create dramatic realism but is not necessarily realistic. The ticking time bomb scenario has powerfully influenced the public discourse on the War on Terror, particularly the debate on torture. Right-wing politicians and advocates reason that torture is necessary precisely because of this specter of an impending attack. President Bush in a nationally televised speech told citizens that the CIA, in successfully capturing and questioning terrorist Khalid Sheik Mohammed, extracted timely information using procedures that stopped further terrorist attacks.[49] In other words, the ticking time bomb scenario represented in 24 was used as a justification for torture in the War on Terror.

As I mentioned at the beginning of this chapter, the writers and producers of 24 repeatedly claimed that their show is entertainment as opposed to a realistic or educational program on the War on Terror. And as I mentioned, the show has been criticized by a range of groups for its depiction of terror. These groups fear that the show will sway its viewers into perceiving torture as a necessary and effective technique. The frequency, and intensity, of these attacks are perhaps the most compelling evidence of just how gripping the show's depiction of torture is. Again and again in 24, Jack Bauer employs any means necessary to capture terrorists and thwart terrorist attacks. Across the show's eight seasons, viewers have witnessed Bauer choking, suffocating, electrocuting, stabbing, and shooting suspects in the hope of extracting information. As an outlaw hero, Bauer's heroism relies on his breaking the rules to save the day. Thus viewers are frequently reminded that Bauer's actions are illegal to heighten the dramatic quality of his actions. Furthermore, he doesn't *want* to be doing this, but he *has* to do it—for the sake of all of us. Jack Bauer breaks the law in order to (often single-handedly) stop terrorism and save lives. He is a stunningly successful manifestation of situational morality: he is the good guy who does bad things because they are justifiable. The show thus positions viewers to admire his bravery, even if repelled by his actions; Bauer's choices are portrayed as difficult and sad, perhaps even terrible, but nonetheless necessary.[50] According to the logic of 24, we would all be dead if it weren't for Jack Bauer.

As mentioned, the Parents Television Council has expressed concern that children who watch 24's torture scenes may become desensitized to violence and may perceive torture favorably. Human Rights First has expressed concern that viewers might conclude that not all human beings are deserving of basic human rights. Military faculty from West Point have expressed concern that 24 will have an undue influence on U.S. interrogators in the field and on cadets in training. Because torture has been found to be an ineffective method of interrogation, they wanted the show to make torture scenes realistic: subjects do not necessarily "break" in a few minutes or hours—as they so often do under Bauer's coercion—and then provide truthful information.[51] West Point faculty stated that it is not uncommon for a tortured suspect to provide false information in order to stop whatever is being done to him; it can take weeks or even months for a suspect to break, and some die in the process. They stated that a more realistic scenario would be to spend months with a prisoner establishing trust (which is how *Sleeper Cell* portrayed torture). West Point faculty have witnessed military cadets disregard their training in order to mimic Jack Bauer. Tony Lagouranis, a former U.S. Army interrogator at Abu Ghraib, stated that such programs can trump the military training that soldiers receive. Brigadier-General Patrick Finnegan, dean of West Point, stated that Bauer's illegal behavior, persistent violation of protocols, and use of torture was influencing young soldiers in the field: "the disturbing thing is that although torture may cause

Jack Bauer some angst, it is always the patriotic thing to do."[52] In other words, 24, whether intended or not, has successfully linked torture to patriotism.

Following the Abu Ghraib scandal, debates ensued in newspapers on whether the torture scenes in 24 were influencing the public to support torture by representing it as an effective, and therefore legitimate, tactic in the War on Terror. It became part of the public discourse. Kelly M. Greenhill, in an editorial in the *Los Angeles Times*, reported that during the May 15, 2007, Republican presidential debate, candidate Tom Tancredo said about the War on Terror, "I am looking for Jack Bauer at this point"; and Rudolph Giuliani argued that interrogators should use "any method they can think of." Giuliani's statement was met with applause.[53] Supreme Court Justice Antonin Scalia, in a speech defending the use of torture, stated, "Jack Bauer saved Los Angeles. . . . He saved hundreds of thousands of lives. . . . Are you going to convict Jack Bauer?"[54] According to Dahlia Lithwick of *Newsweek*, the Bush administration lawyers who designed interrogation methods in the War on Terror and redefined torture cited Jack Bauer more often than the U.S. Constitution.[55] Secretary of Homeland Security Michael Chertoff gave a speech at a Heritage Foundation dinner, "Fact vs. Fiction in the War on Terror," on the ways in which 24 does and does not mirror real life.[56] Even an Arab American defended 24 in an editorial in the *Wall Street Journal*, stating, "Well, here's the hard cold truth: When Islamic terrorists stop being a threat to America's survival, viewers will lose interest in 24, because it will have lost its relevancy. Until such time, I will continue to watch 24—because, believe it or not, the idea that there are Jack Bauers out there in real life risking their lives to save ours does mean something to me. . . . Because terrorists and their supporters continue to hide amongst us in plain sight, we need Jack Bauer, now more than ever."[57] 24 became a vehicle for the government to discuss the War on Terror and particularly to recognize the counterterrorism efforts of government agents, thus revealing how TV dramas have mediated the War on Terror, not only by representing current events, but, more important, by normalizing the need for torture given the impending threat Arab/Muslim terrorists pose to U.S. national security.

Furthermore, Jack Bauer stands in for the U.S. government: he confronts multiple dilemmas inherent in war and demonstrates the difficult necessity of his actions. He also brings comfort to Americans that everything possible is being done to protect them. It is not only his determination that brings comfort but also portrayals of the U.S. government's technological capabilities. Caren Kaplan writes that since the Gulf War the media has focused on technological advances during war, in particular, precision targeting. She writes, "'Space power' and the vast resources of the military-industrial-media-entertainment network generated discourses of precision that obscured information about civilian deaths or rendered them inconsequential. The representations of the war were less embodied than previous representations of wars, with U.S. military casualties going undercover or under the radar, as it were, as well."[58] This concept of "precision war" has seeped into television shows. Despite the intense violence in many TV dramas, and even moments where government agencies are portrayed as making grave errors, technology is central to the ultimate heroism of the United States. 24 has high-tech means to defeat the terrorists—from tracking their locations to eavesdropping on important conversations to recovering crucial information from damaged hard drives and precision bombing of targets. This emphasis on precision extends from technology to torture techniques; Bauer precision torture extracts needed information.

Human Rights First and the Parents Television Council have documented that representations of torture on U.S. television have increased exponentially since 2000. They report that from 1996 to 2001 there were 102 scenes of torture. From 2002 to 2005 torture scenes increased to 624. The 67 torture scenes in 24's first five seasons placed it at the forefront of prime-time depictions.[59] In addition to an increase in representations of torture on prime-time television, there also has been a shift in the identity of the torturer. In the history of U.S. television, the torturer had usually been the bad guy, not the good guy. Historically, torture was used as a technique by writers and producers to villainize a character; it was considered immoral and therefore a stock tool of the bad guys—who included the Russians during the Cold War, the Viet Cong during the Vietnam War, and Latin American and Middle Eastern dictators in the 1980s and 1990s. Since 9/11, and especially through the character of Jack Bauer, the hero has become the torturer. Torture is now used for the greater good, as opposed to being used in the service of evil or power.

Polls indicate that representing the good American hero as the torturer changed public opinion on torture.[60] A poll conducted by ABC News and the Washington Post in 2004 revealed that the majority of Americans—65 percent—are against torture, while 35 percent believe that torture is acceptable in some cases.[61] However, it also indicated that the public made a distinction between torture and physical abuse. While the majority of respondents indicated that torture was unacceptable, 46 percent indicated that physical abuse is acceptable. Among the actions deemed acceptable were sleep deprivation (approved by 66 percent of respondents), hooding (57 percent), noise bombing (54 percent), threatening to shoot a suspect or expose him or her to extreme heat or cold (40 percent), punching and kicking (29 percent), and sexual humiliation (16 percent). The same poll revealed that 60 percent of the public perceived the Abu Ghraib prison scandal to constitute "abuse," not "torture." What emerges here is a wide gray area in which morality becomes a slippery slope, in which there are always exceptions to the rules. It turns out the news media itself may have aided this growing acceptance of torture, or at least of some of its manifestations. Brigitte L. Nacos and Oscar Torres-Reyna write, "An ironic consequence of the Abu Ghraib revelations was the drastic decline of the use of the T-word in pertinent news accounts. Instead, anchors, correspondents, and reporters themselves preferred terms like 'abuse,' 'alleged abuse,' 'mistreatment,' and 'wrongdoing.'"[62] Government officials and journalists came to distinguish between "hard-core torture," "torture lite," and "coercion."[63] Nacos and Torres-Reyna note that after the Abu Ghraib prison scandal, "Americans were less inclined to agree with the statement that torture is "never justified" as a means to force suspected terrorists to reveal important information. By December 2004, more than seven months after the Abu Ghraib story broke, only 27 percent of the public rejected the torture of terrorist suspects categorically, while 69 percent found it justified to varying degrees."[64] The operating cultural logic shifted from one in which torture was considered illegal and morally wrong to an exceptionalist logic in which torture was considered wrong but necessary and effective in moments of national crisis. But public opinion polls also demonstrate an ideologically fractured populace, in which approximately half of the public agree and other half disagree that there is a difference between "torture" and "abuse," or that either is acceptable.

Certainly 24 alone is not responsible for shifting perspectives in favor of justifying torture or "abuse." Representations of torture on 24 are part of a larger field of meaning and exist alongside the Bush administration's enormous public relations efforts to make torture palatable to the American mainstream and make torture legally acceptable, often despite its clear violation of the Geneva Conventions. The news media and government officials succeeded in making torture acceptable and necessary, and TV dramas participated in doing the ideological work (even as they offered post-9/11 representational strategies that resisted stereotyping) to justify the U.S. government's actions during the War on Terror.

After the meeting in 2006 with Human Rights First, West Point faculty, and members of the FBI and CIA, the writers and producers of 24 introduced a new plot to the show. In season 7, which aired in 2008, the U.S. government puts Bauer on trial for his use of torture. Bauer is depicted as a broken human being, seemingly haunted by all the people he has tortured. His actions are questioned throughout the season by other characters who maintain that torture is not only illegal but also morally wrong. The antitorture message, it seems, is clear. And yet this plotline becomes, in effect, another simplified complex representational strategy: this explicit portrayal of the terrible consequences of inflicting violence on others is continually called into question by the season's other, far more urgent events. As Bauer is confronted with one ticking time bomb scenario after another, the rest of the plot seems to be an advertisement for the unfortunate necessity of torture to divert terrorist attacks, consistent with simplified complex representational modes.

These terrorist dramas are built on a basic paradox, between representational strategies that project a postracial, multicultural United States and the logics that legitimize racism and torture. These processes are simultaneous and interlinked. Simplified complex representations enable logics that justify torture; or more specifically, they make a successful case for torture, because the suspension of Arab and Muslim American civil rights relies on them as evidence that racism is no longer a factor in the decisions most Americans make. Therefore, if the actions of the government, or the military, are not racist, then the people the United States fights must be the bad guys. TV dramas, by co-opting multiculturalism and standardizing these seemingly humanistic representations of the Other, produce a post-race illusion of good if problematic intentions. This illusion makes logics that legitimize racism appear as though they are not racist.

The television landscape shifted on 9/11 as the vague, ominous threat to U.S. national security took center stage. The story lines in TV dramas such as 24 and *Sleeper Cell* reinforce the government's need for a War on Terror; these shows have, in numerous guises, replayed the tragedy of 9/11 weekly to U.S. audiences, keeping the trauma fresh in the collective memory. These cultural productions, despite employing a range of strategies to avoid reproducing stereotypes, offer a very specific story that keeps viewer-citizens living and reliving the War on Terror. There is a fundamental contradiction between representational strategies that project an enlightened, postracial culture yet maintain the relevance of the threat. So long as Arabs and Muslims are represented primarily in the context of terrorism, our current crop of representational strategies—for all their apparent innovations—will have a minimal impact on viewers' perceptions of Arabs and Muslims and, far worse, will perpetuate a simplistic vision of good and evil under the guise of complexity and sensitivity.

What is most strongly conveyed by these post-9/11 TV dramas is that Arabs and Muslims pose a threat to U.S. peace and security. The articulated fear, similar to that during the Cold War, is that the enemy is among "us," so that we must live in a state of constant fear and vigilance. According to Douglas L. Howard, "For all we know, our neighborhoods, our businesses, and our highways have been or are being targeted even as we speak, but we are (and we must feel) powerless to protect ourselves from what we cannot see and what we do not know. . . . 24, in all its violent glory, makes us believe that, if the terrorists are out here, something, everything, in fact, is being done to stop them and to keep us safe."[65] 24 and *Sleeper Cell*, despite their representational strategies, do the ideological work of perpetually reenacting the Arab/Muslim threat.

Above all, what is depicted in these TV dramas is a nation in perpetual danger. As McAlister has written, "The continuing sense of threat provides support for the power of the state, but it also provides the groundwork for securing 'the nation' as a cultural and social entity. The 'imagined community' of the nation finds continuing rearticulation in the rhetoric of danger."[66] Writers and producers create an "imagined community" of virtual viewer-citizens,[67] many of whom are interpellated into a sense of impending threat that supports the state.[68] Television is the fundamental way such a threat can be conveyed to a nation. In addition to being the disseminator of this threat, television capitalizes on it, keeping viewers both fearful and captivated.

Mourning the Suspension of Arab American Civil Rights

Racial profiling is a terrible thing, but the reality is—it has become necessary.
—Attorney Lindsey Dole, *The Practice*

Having experienced all kinds of racism, I can say that racism is never as malicious as when it becomes insidious and in turn is presented as open-minded or enlightened.
—Steven Salaita, *Anti-Arab Racism in the U.S.A.*

After 9/11 the news media and the public alike seemed eager to debate, and to disagree about, the manifold issues and anxieties unleashed by the terrorist attacks: whether the USA PATRIOT Act should be passed; whether Arabs and Muslims should be racially profiled, detained, and/or deported; and whether or not, or the extent to which, it was justifiable to suspend or violate the U.S. Constitution during a time of crisis. Political conservatives often argued—both in the harrowing days after September 11 and in the months and years following—that it was not possible to be both safe and free, that freedoms must inevitably be sacrificed in the interest of safety and security. These same critics typically argued that racial profiling was a reasonable and necessary method of law enforcement. Richard Cohen, for example, in the *Washington Post*, argued, "We have become driveling idiots on matters of race and ethnicity. One hundred percent of the terrorists involved in the Sept. 11 mass murder were Arabs. Their accomplices, if any, were probably Arabs too, or at least Muslims. Ethnicity and religion are the very basis of their movement. It hardly makes sense, therefore, to ignore that fact and, say, give Swedish au pair girls heading to the United States the same scrutiny as Arab men coming from the Middle East."[1] Mona Charen, writing for *Jewish World Review*, chimed in, "Let's not pretend that 'ethnic profiling' is out of the question. It is absolutely necessary. If a young unmarried man from Iraq, Egypt, Syria, Lebanon or a half dozen other nations buys a ticket on a plane, boat or train in the next ten years and does not receive a thorough background check and pat down at the gate, we are not defending ourselves."[2] The Louisiana congressman John Cooksey summarized such logic with startling candor: "If I see someone come in that's got a diaper on his head, and a fan belt wrapped around that diaper on his head, that guy needs to be pulled over."[3]

In contrast, the American Civil Liberties Union (ACLU) insisted that "we can, and must be, both safe and free" by relying on the collection of facts and evidence in all law enforcement investigations and by upholding civil rights without exception.[4] The ACLU and other opponents of the PATRIOT Act claimed that racial profiling could be counterproductive and undermine national security "by distracting security officials from less clumsy and more reliable forms of individual suspicion."[5] These critics argued that violating the Constitution during crisis threatens "the institutions of our democracy instead of . . . the terrorists that threaten it."[6]

Always quick to seize on the pulse of the public, TV dramas soon after 9/11 began to incorporate these debates into their story lines. In turn, they became forums for articulating and working through the events and aftermath of 9/11, including policies such as racial profiling and the detention of Arabs/Muslims and Arab/Muslim Americans, as well as considering the parameters of patriotism. TV dramas typically featured post-9/11 government policies by representing positions on both the left and the right. During the War on Terror, as always, television studios and networks sought to maintain the widest possible viewership. As a result, programs that are usually considered "liberal" in their viewpoint nevertheless contain "conservative" elements, and "conservative" programs also contain "liberal" ideological elements.[7] In other words, "liberal" TV dramas that convey an antiracism message, sympathize with the Arab and Muslim American plight, or seem to critique racial profiling, will often take the opposing perspective into consideration so as not to alienate viewers. And likewise with "conservative" TV programs that focus on capturing Arab/Muslim terrorists. George Lipsitz writes:

> To make their dramas compelling and their narrative resolutions dynamic, the media also reflect the plurality of consumer experiences. A system that seeks to enlist everyone in the role of consumer must appear to be addressing all possible circumstances; a system that proclaims consensus and unanimity must acknowledge and explain obvious differences within the polity, if for no other reason than to co-opt or trivialize potential opposition. Television, and other forms of electronic mass media, so effectively recapitulate the ideology of the historical bloc in which they operate that they touch on all aspects of social life—even its antagonistic contradictions.[8]

Lipsitz stresses the role of the "consumer" over that of the "citizen" because TV dramas are driven by viewer ratings and corporate sponsors eager to sell their products in prime-time slots. Maintaining the largest number of viewers depends on addressing a range of perspectives when dealing with a political or controversial issue.

John Fiske and John Hartley offer a useful lens through which to view these terrorism dramas, as they point out that the active contradictions articulated in a given episode reveal how the available ways of seeing are not fixed and subject to change. At the same time, despite this mass appeal strategy, any given TV drama contains a "preferred meaning," usually located in the final notes, or the resolution of the plot of each episode.

> Hence the television discourse presents us daily with a constantly up-dated version of social relations and cultural perceptions. Its own messages respond to changes in these relations and perceptions, so that its audience is made aware of the multiple and contradictory choices available from day to day which have the potential to be selected for future ways of seeing. Of course, the picture does not appear to be so fluid as we watch: there are "preferred" meanings inherent in every message.[9]

Here I delineate the range of perspectives in specific episodes of several TV dramas, and how the fluidity of potential messages eventually dissolves into one preferred meaning. I will examine one representational strategy in depth: the plight of Arab and Muslim Americans after September 11. Plots using this strategy typically focus on characters who are subject to hate crimes and unfairly blamed for the terrorist attacks based solely on their ethnicity or religion. The plots highlight their innocence, evoke sympathy for Arabs and Muslims from the viewer, and seek to delink individual Arab and Muslim characters from monolithic portrayals of terrorism. The particular episodes in question appear to contest the dominant positioning of Arabs/Muslims as terrorists, Islam as a violent extremist ideology, and Arabs and Islam as antithetical to U.S. citizenship and the U.S. nation.

TV dramas that focus on the Arab/Muslim American plight post-9/11 tend to evoke a particular cluster of emotions: sympathy, remorse, and mourning. Stories about Arab/Muslim Americans as the unjust victims of hate crimes or as victims of post-9/11 government policies evoke feelings of sorrow for their misfortune (sympathy), feelings of regret that a better decision could not be made under the circumstances that would not adversely affect their civil rights or well-being (remorse), and feelings of grief that their plight reveals certain compromises in American ideals (mourning). This set of emotions, what I refer to as benevolent emotions, contribute to a sense of benevolence in the ideal viewer, a sense that viewers, and Americans more broadly, are well meaning in even the most difficult circumstances.

I will examine two episodes of the prime-time dramatic series *The Practice*, one episode of *NYPD Blue*, and one episode of *Law and Order* in order to investigate the articulated logic and preferred meaning embedded in these programs. As I began to explore in chapter 1, I contend that there is a revealing discrepancy at the heart of these shows, between the projection of racially sensitive images and the ultimate exclusion of Arab and Muslim Americans from civil rights. Despite taking multiple viewpoints into consideration and staging a debate, these TV dramas usually advance a logic that legitimizes racism in the present moment through the preferred meaning in the final scene of the episode, for example, that racism is wrong but necessary or that the plight of Arab and Muslim Americans will soon pass and racial equality will prevail as the norm in U.S. society.

The TV dramas examined in this chapter are based in institutions of authority: a government agency, the police, or the legal system.[10] *The Practice*, broadcast on ABC from 1997 to 2004, focuses on the lawyers and cases of Robert, Donnell and Associates in Boston; each episode ends with a courtroom verdict. *Law and Order*, broadcast on NBC from 1990 to 2010, seeks to demonstrate how the police and courts work in conjunction to maintain "law and order"; each episode tracks a criminal case from the police investigations through the trial and similarly culminates in a courtroom verdict. *NYPD Blue*, broadcast on ABC from 1993 to 2005, is about the ongoing personal and professional struggles of the officers in one New York City police precinct. Collectively, these prime-time TV dramas, all winners of numerous Emmy awards and each with an average audience of over 20 million, epitomize the institutions of authority at the heart of American culture and offer the stories of a variety of individuals struggling to pursue justice in the face of ethical and moral dilemmas.

Through a close reading of these four episodes, this chapter unpacks sympathetic representations of Arab/Muslim Americans in post-9/11 TV dramas on three levels. First, it scrutinizes the preferred meanings articulated in TV dramas that foreground the Arab/Muslim American plight to show a fundamental tension between positive or antiracist portrayals and logic that justifies racism. Second, it examines how benevolent emotions are a key ingredient in producing "post-race racism," that is, racism that is enacted but then denied or minimized because of assertions by the commercial media and the government that the United States has entered a "post-race" era. Third, it sketches how a particular narrative of racism in U.S. history, as told in TV dramas, participates in advancing an exceptional logic. As I will demonstrate, sympathetic representations of Arabs and Muslims after 9/11 can participate in justifying the suspension of Arab and Muslim civil rights through a logic of exception. An exceptional or emergency situation lends credibility to arguments that would otherwise be discredited as unfair or illegal. The logic that 9/11 is an exceptional moment of crisis—and therefore demands exceptional measures—becomes crucial in producing a new kind of racism, one that purports to be antiracist while perpetrating and justifying racism. I argue that sympathetic representations of Arab and Muslim Americans in TV dramas participate in normalizing a logic of exception that is central to producing post-race racism. Racism is presented as an aberration, as opposed to the norm, and the United States is portrayed as having resolved its history of racism. Crucial to the success of these ideas is a show's ability to cultivate benevolent emotions in the viewer.

Ambivalent Racism, Exceptional Racism

Every episode of *The Practice* takes viewers into the courtroom. After 9/11 a common theme was debates about the rights of Arab and Muslim Americans. On "Bad to Worse,"[11] an episode initially aired on December 1, 2002, and rebroadcast several times since, an airline in the months after 9/11 seeks to bar Arabs/Muslims from flying on their airplanes in the name of safety and security. An Arab American man is suing the airline for discrimination, and the preliminary case goes to court. It is clear that the Arab American man, a university professor, is innocent and the unfair target of discrimination, but the case is heard to determine whether or not the racial profiling of Arabs and Muslims after 9/11 can be justified. Ms. Dole, a young white female lawyer, is hired to defend the airline, whose slogan is "We Don't Fly Arabs" and that strives to be known as "the most security conscious airline in the new world." Ms. Dole is conflicted about defending the airline, aware of the racism and injustice inherent in the case, but takes it on to further her career. Multiple debates ensue in the courtroom: Is racial profiling justified? Can certain biases be considered reasonable? Are there legitimate forms of racism?

This episode and others correlate with actual events. Within three months after 9/11, for example, over one hundred Muslims reported to the Council on American-Islamic Relations that non-Muslim passengers complained about (and in some cases refused to fly with) them; some of these people, deemed untrustworthy because of their skin color or their headdress, were removed from flights. A Muslim man was escorted off his America West flight at Newark Airport two days after 9/11 because other passengers were uncomfortable with his presence; the pilot later defended his decision, saying that the discomfort of his passengers gave him the right to exclude the Muslim passenger.[12] An Arab American Secret Service agent on his way from Washington, D.C., to President Bush's ranch in Texas was barred from an American Airlines flight because the pilot thought he looked suspicious.[13] In Lincoln, Nebraska, a Muslim woman was asked to remove her hijab in public before boarding an American Airlines flight.[14] Dozens of Arab, Muslim, and South Asian Americans filed suits after being barred from flying; many others submitted complaints about being subjected to extra searches and racial profiling. Meanwhile, news programs featured debates on whether or not it was fair to racially profile Arab and Muslim Americans in order to ensure safety. The Republican writer Ann Coulter, infamous, among other things, for her post-9/11 comment that the United States should invade Muslim countries, "kill their leaders and convert them to Christianity,"[5] furthered the national debate on racial profiling when she publicly expressed the opinion that airlines ought to advertise the number of civil rights lawsuits filed against them by Arabs in order to boost business. When asked how Arabs should fly if discriminated against, she replied, "They could use flying carpets."[16]

In this episode of *The Practice*, like so many dramas concerning the War on Terror, the viewing audience is implicitly invited to participate in the debates. Here, viewers literally sit alongside the jurors, hearing both sides of the case. Toby Miller's description of watching television is apt here: "The audience participates in the most uniformly global (but national), collective (yet private), and individually time consuming practice of meaning making in the history of the world. . . . So viewing television involves solitary interpretation as well as collective behavior."[17] In other words, it involves imagining the self as part of a collective, in this case as citizen of the U.S. nation and a virtual participant in national debates.

The debate in the virtual courtroom of *The Practice* is limited to the extreme positions of the left and the right. Citizens have one of two options: political correctness or safety, or being PC or being alive. The better choice becomes clear. If you choose political correctness to avoid being racist, then your safety is forfeited. And if you elect safety over discrimination, rest assured that not all racisms are alike: some are reasonable, others are not. Within the frame of safety, racism is reduced to political correctness and political correctness reduced to useless etiquette.

The articulated logic is as follows: racism is wrong, except during *exceptional* times of crisis. The CEO of Seaboard Airlines, the episode's fictional airline, claims it would not be reasonable to discriminate against African Americans, but it is reasonable to discriminate against Arabs and Arab Americans and against Muslims and Muslim Americans. As is often the case, "Arab," "Arab American," "Muslim," and "Muslim American" are conflated and used interchangeably as if they denote the same identity. As the episode heads toward a climax, the attorney for the Arab American client, Mr. First, and the airline CEO debate the issue of political correctness versus safety in court:

> **MR. FIRST:** What if research showed that blacks were more likely to commit mayhem on a plane?
>
> **AIRLINE CEO:** I would never exclude against blacks because I would consider that bias to be unreasonable. This prejudice isn't.
>
> **MR. FIRST:** There are 1.6 billion Muslims in the world. So you're discriminating against all of them because of the actions of 19? That's reasonable?
>
> **AIRLINE CEO:** Start your own company and run it the way you'd like. I should get the same courtesy.

MR. FIRST: We don't give people the right to be a bigot in this country.

AIRLINE CEO: How about the right to be safe?

The CEO's language is revealing: airlines should have "the right," he says, to bar Arabs from their flights. Moreover, as a CEO, he wants "the right" to run his company as he desires. A discourse on constitutional rights is thus invoked. What "rights" will be protected? Do people have the "right" to be racist? The "right" to run their business as they wish? The "right" to be safe? Do Arab and Muslim Americans have citizenship "rights"? According to the terms of this debate, safety trumps all other rights during times of crisis. Safety requires racism, and eliminating racism compromises safety. Ultimately, according to the CEO, it is more important to be safe than it is to not discriminate; times are too urgent to be concerned with being politically correct.

According to the political philosopher Giorgio Agamben, ambivalence—the ability to regard the same act as both unjustifiable and necessary—is central to the sovereign power of modern democracies. Such a breech in logic comes to be reasoned through "exceptional" moments of crisis, which the state uses to suspend established codes and procedures and to legitimize government abuses of power. Agamben claims that what characterizes modern democratic Western politics is that the exceptions have become the rule. The state of exception, he writes, becomes "the hidden foundation on which the entire political system rest[s]."[18] Thus the United States was not necessarily in an exceptional state of crisis during George Bush's War on Terror but rather operated through a perpetual "state of exception"—from the Cold War through the continued War on Terror. In the past decade, the triumph of ambivalence has justified the exercise of unilateral power, such as denying due process to Arabs and Muslims and initiating wars in Afghanistan and Iraq. These current justifications, Agamben reminds us, are the latest in a decades-long American tradition.

This ambivalence is central to post-9/11 racial logic, especially since explicit racism has for the past few decades become a social taboo. In order for this illogical ambivalence to acquire weight, race and racism had to be reconfigured after 9/11. This was accomplished through media projections of a diverse and united U.S. citizenry and simultaneous racialization and criminalization of Arabs and Islam by the Bush administration. Rachad Antonius refers to this process of justifying racism directed specifically against Arabs and Muslims as "respectable racism."[19] By defining racism against Arabs and Muslims as legitimate or respectable, even necessary, not only are individual acts such as hate crimes or employment discrimination condoned, but government practices of detaining and deporting Arabs and Muslims without due process are enabled. By racializing Arabs and Islam, touting diversity as the paradigm of U.S. citizenry, and articulating ambivalent racism, the Constitution and principles of democracy could be "logically" suspended by the Bush administration based on exceptionalism and thus simultaneously further U.S. imperial power. In this episode of *The Practice*, African Americans are invoked to establish that racism is wrong and passé. The airline CEO explicitly states that discriminating against African Americans would be unreasonable or illogical; thus the logic of ambivalence allows him to reason that racism is both wrong and necessary against Arabs and Muslims.

The safety/political correctness debate is elaborated in the closing arguments of *The Practice*. Mr. First and Ms. Dole present their opposing arguments, delineating common arguments made by the right and left. Mr. First concedes that Americans are understandably suspicious of Muslims because of the terrorist attacks of September 11. He says that while "we" felt violated by the events of September 11, this case violates the very freedom that defines the United States. He recounts that he routinely has a conversation with his nine-year-old daughter over breakfast in which they exchange stories about work and school. His daughter told him that week that she was learning about Rosa Parks and was surprised to learn that African Americans used to be required by law to sit at the back of the bus. He points to how the court is in the process of justifying and legalizing injustice. Mr. First states that it is the people who define the nation and asks in an emotional plea:

> Well who are we? Do we really stand for liberty? Are we truly the champions of equal rights? Are Martin Luther King's words about judging a person by the content of their character and not by the color of their skin? Do we live by these words? Or are they just credos that we trumpet when we're not running scared?

In Ms. Dole's closing remarks, she states that Americans, "We the people," want justice and revenge but above all security. She says that the desire for security is sound and credible rather than paranoia, especially given that the government warns Americans every day about the possibility of another terrorist attack. In order to prevent another plane from becoming a flying bomb, Ms. Dole claims, it is necessary to stop Arabs from boarding planes. She states, "Racial profiling is a terrible thing, but the reality is—it has become necessary," because the terrorist enemy is unusual: educated, trained, willing to sacrifice themselves, and living among us as neighbors. Since it is impossible to identify them by their behavior, she argues, the best way to ensure safety is through racial profiling, a right that airlines ought to be able to practice. Her dream is for her son to grow up in an America that is a land of freedom and opportunity: "I want him to able to get on a plane that won't be used as a bomb. And I don't think you can dismiss that as paranoia, Your Honor, when our own leaders are telling us to be afraid."

The closing arguments center on defining the U.S. nation and its borders. Mr. First concedes that is it in fact reasonable to be suspicious of "Muslims" ("They blew up the World Trade Center for God's sake!") but encourages people to put those feelings aside and to consider larger and more important issues, namely, "our civil rights," "our freedom," and how we define this country. In so doing, he sets up an us/them dichotomy: "they" blew up the World Trade Center, but "we" need to think about who "we" are as a people and whether or not "we" stand for equal rights; and although "they" violated "us," "we" cannot in turn violate "our" freedom. He defends his client's rights but fails to acknowledge that his Arab/ Muslim client is American too and entitled to the same rights as other Americans.

Mr. First draws a parallel between barring Arabs from flying on airplanes and segregating African Americans from the white population, pointing to a history of legitimizing and legalizing injustice and inequality. Through this historical and comparative parallel, viewers are asked if these "presumed reasonable" racisms come to haunt "us" later. Do "we" agree that having African Americans sit at the back of the bus is regrettable and shameful, and do "we" want to repeat this history by barring Arab/Muslim Americans from airplanes? He asks, haven't "we" learned the importance of judging a person by their character and not by the color of their skin? Mr. First makes an important case against repeating a racist past and for defining the nation according to moral principles. His case, however, rests on acknowledging the public's right to be suspicious of Muslims. Though he advocates not acting on feelings of violation, Arab bodies are reinscribed as outside of American citizenship through an appeal to "real" Americans not to be racist because greater moral principles are at stake.

In contrast, Ms. Dole argues that American citizens are entitled to security, and though racial profiling is "a terrible thing . . . it has become necessary." Ms. Dole continues that "we" are faced with an enemy, and that enemy has clear features: they are Arab/Muslim. Contributing to a broader historical mythology of U.S. immigration (and neglecting a history of racist immigration restrictions), Dole says that the United States used to be a land with open borders, a place for any immigrant to fulfill the American dream, but that it is no longer possible so long as planes can be used as weapons. Whereas Mr. First seeks to define the nation according to principles of freedom, civil rights, and equality, Ms. Dole shifts the discourse to defining the nation's borders: the borders should be closed, and Arab Americans should be profiled in order to make U.S. citizens safe. Ms. Dole defines a nation in crisis and uses the very language from the Declaration of Independence ("We the people") to argue for the suspension of its application in specific, racialized configurations—vis-à-vis Arab and Muslim Americans. A new competing discourse on constitutional rights after 9/11 emerges that includes the right to be racist, the right to not be politically correct, and the right to run one's business as one pleases at the expense of equality and civil rights.

Emerging from these different positions, the judge's verdict presents the preferred meaning of this episode. He finds it "almost unimaginable" that whether or not it is legally permissible to discriminate based on ethnicity is even being debated in court. He says such discrimination is a violation of the 1964 Civil Rights Act and that he finds the idea repulsive; he refers to a *New York Times* article written by Thomas Friedman, as if to bolster his liberal credentials. He recalls that Friedman wrote that the events of September 11 were "beyond unimaginable." The judge says to Mr. First that he is being asked to waive legal and moral principles in the face of unimaginable and potentially boundless terrorism. He says to Ms. Dole that he too loves being an American and became a judge to protect the freedoms afforded by the constitution. He concludes his verdict in the following way:

> But the reality is that we make exceptions to our constitutional rights all the time. Be it freedom of speech, religion—none of them is absolute. The legal test for doing something so patently unconstitutional is basically: you better have a damn good reason. There has been one other long-standing reality in this country: If not safe, one can never be free. With great personal disgust, I am denying the plaintiff's motion.

Though this episode seeks to demonstrate sympathy for Arab and Muslim Americans after 9/11 and repeatedly states that discrimination is unjust, the ultimate message veers to the other end of the ideological spectrum. The dramatic shift of the judge's decision makes for good TV. It offers viewers a surprising twist. At the same time, the episode's conclusion is actually in keeping with the popular trope of respectable racism.

This episode of *The Practice* embodies the formation of ambivalence Agamben identifies as necessary to the state of exception and sovereign rule. The judge's words, "If not safe, one can never be free," evoke President Bush's rhetoric of freedom—"they hate us because we are free"—and thus extends the logic to "we must discriminate in order to be free." Ultimately, despite representative sympathy, which comes in the judge's regret, remorse, and even disgust at his own verdict, racism is legitimized: sacrifices to Arab and Muslim American civil rights must be made in the interim. This is not a verdict to celebrate. Ms. Dole is not proud, the judge is filled with disgust, and the Arab American man holds his wife as she cries. Within this apologetic moment, hatred toward Arabs is rendered "understandable," even as the roots of terrorism are "beyond our imaginations."

This plight is indeed represented: it is established that Arab Americans are the unfair targets of discrimination after 9/11. Yet sympathy for the Arab American in the episode is compromised through discourses that hold more weight: namely, the right to be racist and national security threats. Discriminating against Arab/Muslim Americans is reasonable at this time because "they" committed a terrorist act and because the government tells us every day that we are still at risk of another terrorist attack. What the episode ultimately represents is less the "plight" of the Arab/Muslim American since 9/11 and more the national debate on racial profiling and the national anxiety about flying with Arabs and Muslims. Throughout the episode, the Arab American man remains silent and unable to represent himself to the audience while his lawyer, a white man, speaks for him. Thus he remains a foreigner in the minds of American viewers. Furthermore, what America is "supposed to be" is debated in relation to Arab and Muslim Americans. Dole's closing remarks make a larger statement about how America has changed. She suggests that the country should no longer be open to immigrants because "they" ruin it by making "us" unsafe. Through arguing for security, not only is racial profiling justified, but so are closed borders and new INS measures to detain and deport Arabs and Muslims.

The question of how to compromise Arab American civil rights without guilt is thus resolved through three intertwined moves: (1) advancing a logic of exception that establishes that racism is wrong but necessary given the state of crisis; (2) linking the logic of exception to a set of emotions, particularly remorse and disgust that principles of equality are being violated; (3) and invoking a master narrative of U.S. history that advances either the feelings of remorse or the logic of exception. The episode's closing arguments also illustrate the dramatic use of the ideologies from "the right" and "the left." The right, embodied by Ms. Dole, prioritizes safety and argues that protecting Arab/Muslim American civil rights is a demonstration of politeness or political correctness that we can ill afford. The right is unapologetic about denying Arabs and Muslims civil liberties. In contrast, the left, embodied by Mr. First and the judge, affirms that racism is wrong and yet remorsefully concedes that in this exceptional time of crisis, racism might be necessary. The difference between these two positions is that the left *feels* terrible about denying Arab/Muslim American's rights, which operates to absolve liberals of being complicit with racism. Remorse and disgust become central to producing liberal-style racism under the guise of antiracism. The ideal viewer is positioned to feel sympathy for the innocent Arab/Muslim American man who is the victim of discrimination, remorse that the national security crisis is necessitating discrimination, and mourning that such egregious exceptions to the constitution are being made. This set of benevolent emotions signal to the viewer that despite discrimination flourishing and democratic principles eroding, Americans are nonetheless well-intentioned people who stand for democracy and equality.

Apparent here is the important function of racialization and emotion in creating the moment of exception so necessary for the abuse of government power. At the risk of repetition, the specific steps involved are as follows. First, the nation in crisis needs to be established. Given the events of September 11, it is not difficult to make this point: we do not want terrorists, who are likely to be Arab and Muslim and who presumably hate our freedom, to attack and kill again. Second, the necessity of exceptionalism needs to be established. In order to do this, a norm of democracy and freedom for all peoples—regardless of race—needs to be affirmed. Thus it can be stated that it was wrong to discriminate against African Americans and gestures are made to temporarily bring disenfranchised racialized groups into the dominant designation "American." Third, Arabs and Muslims need to undergo a process of racialization in which their ethnic/racial background and religious beliefs make them a potential threat to the nation. And thus it can be stated that racism is wrong but compulsory against this potentially threatening population at this particular exceptional time of crisis. The consequences of this process are vast, and they have enabled the U.S. government to exercise power without necessary constraints and act outside of democratic legal conventions. It is not too much of a stretch to argue that this notion of an exceptional moment coupled with this process of racialization has enabled the U.S. government to implement the USA PATRIOT Act, invade Iraq, initiate a war in Afghanistan, hold and torture prisoners in Guantanamo and Abu Ghraib prisons without legal recourse, and initiate mass deportations of Arabs and Muslims from the United States. This very logic comes to be articulated in TV dramas through the portrayal of a sympathetic Arab American character; while the audience is encouraged to sympathize with the Arab American plight in the wake of 9/11, the TV drama ultimately normalizes the very logic that supports U.S. imperial projects at home and abroad.

The Benevolence of Mourning

Another episode of *The Practice*, "Inter Arma Silent Leges,"[20]—from the Latin, "In war, law is silent"—again represents the plight of Arab and Muslim Americans post-9/11. This episode, first aired on December 9, 2001, also sympathizes with Arab/Muslim American characters while simultaneously narrating a story of the United States as a nation in crisis, invoking a necessary logic of exceptionalism and ambivalence and lamenting the need for security over liberty. However, unlike the episode discussed above, this one articulates a preferred meaning that does not justify the suspension of civil rights in times of crisis but rather objects to it. Here the episode articulates the emotion of mourning to come to terms with perpetuating racism. While the episode "Bad to Worse" focuses on airline discrimination, "Inter Arma Silent

Leges" focuses on the government's practice of interviewing and detaining Arab and Muslim Americans.

In the opening sequence, viewers learn that the U.S. government is unfairly detaining an Arab/Muslim American man. It becomes clear that he refuses to speak to his wife and children and is apologetic to them for "what he has done." What he has done remains a mystery; viewers are left to assume that he was involved with terrorism. Dr. Ford, the white wife of the detainee, hires Ms. Washington, an African American attorney, to find and represent her husband. Dr. Ford admits that her husband's "real name" is Bill Habib, but they both use her maiden name, Ford, signaling that white names are "safer" or more acceptable than Arab ones. Dr. Ford has been unable to get any information on her husband; Ms. Washington quickly learns that the information is classified, requiring security clearance, and that Mr. Habib is being detained without representation, which violates his rights as a U.S. citizen. Ms. Washington appears before a judge to argue, against an FBI representative who is responsible for the detention, that she has a right to see her client. When she asks the FBI representative what Mr. Habib is being charged with, she is informed that he is not being charged with anything but is being held as a material witness to something classified by the Foreign Intelligence Surveillance Act. The judge orders that Mr. Habib be permitted to see his lawyer and wife, stating, "I appreciate your concern for national security, but I'm going to do my part to safeguard what is left of our Constitution." The FBI representative begins to challenge the judge's orders; the judge warns him not to test his authority. Made explicit here is the notion that courts have reduced power during times of war; the judge must fight to resist the complete suspension of the Constitution.

After 9/11 the Justice Department sought to interview thousands of Arab and Muslim immigrant men between the ages of eighteen and thirty-three, those who "fit the criteria of people who might have information regarding terrorism."[21] Many Arab and Muslim Americans feared that any failure to comply would be perceived as unpatriotic and might jeopardize their citizenship and lead to detention or deportation. And in the weeks after 9/11 over a thousand Arabs, Muslims, and South Asians were rounded up and detained across the country. The Justice Department refused to release information on the people detained.[22] As Leti Volpp has written, "While the government refused to release the most basic information about these individuals—their names, where they were held, and the immigration or criminal charges filed against them—the public did know that the vast majority of those detained appeared to be Middle Eastern, Muslim, or South Asian. The majority were identified to the government through suspicions and tips based solely on perceptions of their racial, religious, or ethnic identity."[23] Detaining these particular racialized bodies no doubt comforted some Americans, who felt that the government was being proactive in fighting terror, and simultaneously alarmed proponents of civil rights, who demanded the release of more information and due process.

When Mr. Habib, shackled, is brought to the courtroom, where Ms. Washington seeks to compel the FBI to reveal the charges against Mr. Habib, we learn that he has "voluntarily" turned himself in as an act of patriotism; he objects to Ms. Washington's presence and to the hearing itself. Ms. Washington asks him if he knows why he is being held; he replies, "Help my wife understand: I did what I did because it was right." As Mr. Habib takes the stand, his wife is completely perplexed.

> **MS. WASHINGTON:** Do you know why you're in custody?
>
> **MR. HABIB:** The government believes I may have information about someone, I think, I don't really know. He didn't do anything, but he may have known some people with ties to others who are wanted for questioning.
>
> **MS. WASHINGTON:** What information? What do they think you know?
>
> **FBI REPRESENTATIVE:** Objection.
>
> **JUDGE:** Sustained. You can't know that Ms. Washington.
>
> **MS. WASHINGTON:** You haven't talked to your family in weeks. Why did they keep you from speaking to your family?
>
> **MR. HABIB:** They didn't. I chose not to call my family.
>
> **MS. WASHINGTON:** Why?
>
> **MR. HABIB:** I was told anyone I spoke with would be subject to investigation. I do not want to bring my family into this. My wife and children were born here. They have no connection to any Arab, other than me.
>
> **MS. WASHINGTON:** Have you been interviewed?
>
> **MR. HABIB:** Many times.
>
> **MS. WASHINGTON:** Did you know you had the right to have an attorney present?
>
> **MR. HABIB:** I waived my rights.
>
> **MS. WASHINGTON:** You waived them? Voluntarily?
>
> **MR. HABIB:** I talked to them on my own. They didn't force me. Not in any way.
>
> **MS. WASHINGTON:** Did they make you afraid?
>
> **MR. HABIB:** Am I fearful, I guess I would say yes. But I have made all my decisions voluntarily.

Ms. Washington is baffled by Mr. Habib's "voluntary" decision not to speak to his family. Mr. Habib reiterates that he did not want to risk involving them in any way. The judge asks why Mr. Habib needs to be held in custody when he is clearly cooperating: could he not continue to assist from home? The FBI representative says that Mr. Habib is helping more than he realizes through wiretaps and overseas contacts and that it is necessary to hold him as they are constantly learning new information.

FBI REPRESENTATIVE: We can't risk losing him. Look, we're trying to get the information we need to stop the potential murder of thousands of Americans. That means depriving some Americans of their civil rights. I don't like it, but that's how it is.

MS. WASHINGTON: You're imprisoning an innocent man.

MR. HABIB: Ms. Washington, enough. If my country thinks I should be here, I will stay here.

MS. WASHINGTON: Your country?

MR. HABIB: Yes, I am an American. I am serving my country.

The judge concludes that Mr. Habib will remain in custody, thus proving that "In war, law is silent."

While this Arab American is represented as an über-patriot, willing to give up everything to prove his loyalty and to keep the nation safe, this presumes that Arab and Muslim Americans have information about terrorism by virtue of their race or ethnicity. It is thus not unreasonable to assume that Arabs and Muslims are guilty by association.[24] Bill Habib is helping the government because he might know someone who knows something about someone involved in terrorism. Mr. Habib accepts that he is guilty by association. He proclaims that he is American and that he wants to protect his family from interrogation because they are truly innocent, having no ties to any Arabs (all of whom are presumed terrorist suspects) except for him. Meanwhile, he is of Arab descent, has ties to the Arab world, and therefore accepts a degree of guilt and responsibility. A division is drawn between innocent Americans, Arabs involved with terrorism, and good Arab Americans who go to extreme lengths to assist the U.S. government and prove their loyalty.

"Inter Arma Silent Leges" presents four common positions on the issue of "voluntarily" detaining Arab and Muslim Americans. First, the government violates the Constitution—albeit grudgingly—to ensure U.S. national security; "voluntarism" is an excuse to enable the covert abuse of power. Second, and in contrast, an Arab/Muslim American is represented as complying with the government's suspension of his civil liberties in order to prove his patriotism. Ms. Washington represents a third position; she protests the violation of civil rights and demands that the courts ensure that the Constitution stands even in times of crisis. Fourth, the judge rules that despite his commitment to upholding the Constitution, times of crisis merit different rules and Arab American civil rights cannot be guaranteed.

While the judge's perspective holds the most authority, the preferred meaning of this episode is articulated by Ms. Washington. The episode ends with Ms. Washington in conversation with Ms. Dole (the lawyer in the previous episode who argued for barring Arabs from flying). She is impassioned and outraged that her client's rights are being violated. Comparing Mr. Habib's case to Japanese internment during World War II, Ms. Washington states, "We're back to interning people. Sticking them in prison because of where they were born. It happened during World War II with the Japanese Americans. And it's back. I mean the government will apologize for it later, but it will be too late. Innocent people are having their lives ruined now. Mr. Habib? He thinks being a good American means sacrificing one's rights, instead of fighting for them." Ms. Dole replies that most Americans perceive Arab Americans as Americans and as neighbors but that "we" are justifiably afraid. Ms. Washington ends the conversation and the episode by saying, "Yeah . . . we're back."

Through this conversation, Ms. Washington articulates a narrative of racism in U.S. history, followed by two different assessments of the suspension of civil liberties. Her assessment of the Arab American plight is that the U.S. government is once again engaged in discriminatory practices. Ms. Dole offers a different assessment of the situation: she disagrees that the United States has returned to the era of institutionalized racism and reasons that Americans are simply reacting out of fear after 9/11. Ms. Washington's "Yeah . . . we're back," indicates that there has always been justification for discrimination and that fear is just another one. The last scene is infused with a sense of mourning: for the government's repetition of historical mistakes, for the loss of civil liberties, for the fact that others do not share in Ms. Washington's sense of alarm.

In "Bad to Worse," Ms. Dole wins her case despite her personal feelings of guilt. In this episode the firm's lawyer is arguing for the Arab American character; Ms. Washington is outraged and takes a stand against injustice. However, she is powerless to do anything because the national security crisis trumps all other concerns. Unlike the episode of *The Practice* examined above, this episode does not legitimize racist practices while representing the Arab/Muslim American plight after 9/11. Rather the preferred meaning of the program critiques logic that legitimizes the suspension of Arab and Muslim American civil rights. What viewers are left with at the end of the episode is a sense that mourning is an appropriate emotion when coping with post-9/11 racism, especially because we are powerless to change the situation.

This episode also illuminates the limited ways that Arabs, Muslims, Arab Americans, and Muslim Americans can be represented after 9/11: villains, valorous, or victims. In this case, Mr. Habib is portrayed as both valorous and victimized.[25] As a patriot, he is valorous for voluntarily giving up his rights to help the U.S. government in its fight against terrorism; and he is a victim of the U.S. system that does not protect his rights and requires that he be detained and stop communication with his family. The Arab/Muslim American character and his plight serve as a vehicle to trigger a sense of benevolence in the viewer. The ideal viewer can share in Ms. Washington's indignation and can, alongside her, mourn the loss of civil liberties for Arab and Muslim Americans. Benevolence manifests as caring for the misfortune of others, believing in justice and equality, and experiencing emotions that reflect these good intentions. Mourning the loss of democratic ideals enhances the sense of benevolence.

Patriotic Justice and American Ideals

Some post-9/11 dramas offer a revealing narrative about racism in U.S. history in order to assess anti-Arab racism. This narrative situates the United States as a nation of equality and freedom, a nation whose moments of racism are the exception rather than the norm. This framing tends to minimize the Arab and Muslim American plight even while representing it. I will look at two examples of TV dramas that offer this narrative: one episode of *NYPD Blue* and one episode of *Law and Order*. In both episodes, a white man perpetrates a hate crime in the name of patriotism. As in the above two episodes of *The Practice*, these episodes of *NYPD Blue* and *Law and Order* seek to sympathetically represent the Arab/Muslim American plight after 9/11. In contrast, however, instead of placing Arab and Muslim Americans in the courtroom, white American citizen-patriots are the focus of the legal system, for taking the law in to their own hands.

On *NYPD Blue*'s "Baby Love" (first aired on December 1, 2004) detectives hunt for the arsonist who torched a store owned by Arab/Muslim American brothers.[26] After 9/11 arson was a common hate crime directed at businesses and places of worship of Arab, Muslim, and South Asian Americans. In the two weeks after the terrorist attacks, for instance, a Sikh temple was set on fire in a suburb of Cleveland and a market owned by a Pakistani man was burned down in Long Island.[27] "Baby Love" depicts one such occurrence to reflect on the conflation of racism with patriotism after 9/11. In this episode an Arab American has been hurt in the fire, and family members gather outside the patient's room at the hospital. Detective Andy Sipowicz, a white man in his late fifties, and his partner, Detective Baldwin Jones, an African American man in his thirties, arrive at the hospital.

> **ANDY SIPOWICZ:** Hey, what's this?
>
> **BALDWIN JONES:** That's the family whose case we're workin'.
>
> **ANDY SIPOWICZ:** Pat them down for box cutters?
>
> **BALDWIN JONES:** Hey, c'mon.
>
> **ANDY SIPOWICZ:** You figure they'd give 'em their own hospital until this blows over.
>
> **BALDWIN JONES:** What, and their own drinking fountains too?
>
> **ANDY SIPOWICZ:** Alright. I withdraw the comment.

Detective Sipowicz, who is of Polish descent, is known on the show as a recovering racist; his quips in this scene are typical of his character. His African American partner draws a parallel with African Americans having to drink from separate fountains during the Jim Crow era, and Andy is silenced, although only briefly.

In addition to dealing with racism among police officers and citizens, this episode deals with the mistrust Arab and Muslim Americans have of the police and other government institutions that have treated them as terrorist suspects instead of seeking to protect them from the backlash. One of the Arab/Muslim American store owners insists that he knows who set fire to his store: it's Chris Paget, a white man who has been harassing them. When the detectives doubt his claim and ask for other possible suspects, the store owner wonders whether the police actually investigated the crime.

> **ARAB AMERICAN UNCLE:** Chris Paget did this. I know it.
>
> **WHITE COP:** Sir, we looked into it.
>
> **ARAB AMERICAN UNCLE:** Did you?
>
> **WHITE COP:** Yes, we did.
>
> **ARAB AMERICAN UNCLE:** You're not trying to find who did this. [Relative tries to calm him down.] People don't care because of September 11th.
>
> **WHITE COP:** We lost a lot of people that day. And that fireman who put your fire out today, he lost even more.
>
> **ARAB AMERICAN UNCLE:** You do blame that on us!
>
> **WHITE COP:** I'm telling you that in spite of that we're all doing our job here.

This scene explores Arab/Muslim Americans facing a double plight: first they are victims of a hate crime and then they are treated with suspicion by the police. The Arab/Muslim American store owner is frustrated that he has been treated as a possible terrorist rather than a victimized American; as a result, he has no faith that the police and other government institutions will protect him. He is angry and on edge and tired of being blamed for something he did not do. The police officer's statement that he is doing his job despite what happened suggests that the police are setting "justifiable" racism aside and rising to the greater moral principle of serving and protecting all citizens.

It turns out that it was not Chris Paget who set fire to the store but another white man, Mike Bigalow, who considers himself a patriot and seeks revenge on Arab/Muslim Americans for 9/11. In the final scene, Solomon, the nephew of the Arab/Muslim American store owner, comes to the police department to apologize for his uncle's lack of faith in the police.

> **SOLOMON:** I apologize for what my uncle said at the hospital. It was wrong of him to accuse you of not caring. He was angry and that's not how he really feels because all of us appreciate what this department went through and is going through.

WHITE COP: Well, some things came out of my mouth that I'm not happy about either.

[. . .]

SOLOMON: [In a desperate plea] What can we do? 'Cause my family has lived here for 30 years. I was born here. We're Americans.

SIPOWICZ: There were times in this country when it wasn't a big plus to be Japanese or German.

JONES: Or black.

SIPOWICZ: It'll pass. Hang in there.

After expressing racist views at the beginning of the program, Sipowicz concludes the plotline on a sympathetic note. He shares his gruff, street-hardened wisdom with the young Arab/Muslim American man: this too shall pass.

Two rationales are articulated throughout this episode of *NYPD Blue*. One rationale is that racism is understandable given the trauma and injury inflicted by the Arab Muslim perpetrators of 9/11. The other rationale, and the preferred meaning in the episode, is that racism is wrong and is not to be conflated with patriotism. The backlash against Arab and Muslim Americans is situated as (yet another) exceptional time in U.S. history, but like the others, one whose prejudice will eventually subside. The notion that "this too shall pass" encourages viewers to accept racism against Arabs and Muslims because it is presumably temporary. Mourning is central to this logic as well; the ideal viewer is positioned to mourn the fact that Arab and Muslim Americans are victims and that other Americans react to fear with racism. However, according to *NYPD Blue*, at the other side of mourning is hope for a new day and a return to racial equality as the norm.

This narrative of a history marked by exceptional times of racism presumes that the "normal" times in between are ones of equality. Such normality seems to be supported by an African American and white detective working side by side, the embodiment of racial equality and cooperation, despite their different ideological positions on race. Racism itself is portrayed as exceptional. Hate crimes are depicted as wrong but inevitable given the trauma experienced by Americans as the result of 9/11. The racism evident in hate crimes and the racism evident in U.S. policies that targeted Arabs and Muslims are thus positioned as outside the normal order of affairs; they may define the moment of crisis, but they do not define the nation. This benevolent emotion—regret—enables portraying the United States as a nation founded on justice and equality that will not be defined by another discriminatory moment in its history. From here the episode infers an even more dangerous logical leap: the exceptional racism (including everything from racial profiling to the Patriot Act, from indefinite detention to deportation) during the exceptional post-9/11 moment of crisis, though regrettable, is ultimately what is needed to restore the United States to its presumed "normal" state of affairs. Multiple iterations of the logic of exception are advanced through TV dramas.

"Patriot," an episode of *Law and Order*, deals with the same theme—conflating racism with patriotism after 9/11—while seeming to portray Arab and Muslim characters in a sympathetic light. The episode begins as if it is going to be about the Arab/Muslim American plight and ends up being about the plight of a white American vigilante trying to protect his beloved country. An Arab man, Yusuf Haddad, is found dead in his burning apartment.[28] What appears at first to be a case of arson and an accidental death ends up being murder committed in the name of patriotism. Frank Miller, a former U.S. soldier, suspected that Haddad was involved in terrorist activities and had been secretly monitoring him. The Arab man, we eventually learn, was murdered and then placed in the explosion to make the murder look like arson. The plot twist is as follows: what appears to be a hate crime ends up preventing a terrorist attack. The "patriot" was right to be suspicious. The debate in this episode is over vigilantism: was it justifiable for the patriot to act outside of legal institutions? Unlike the episode of *NYPD Blue*, in which the patriot was wrong and the Arab Americans were innocent victims, in this episode of *Law and Order* the patriot's actions, though illegal, saves lives.

As discussed in chapter 1, a common post-9/11 representational strategy is to flip the viewer's assumptions. Unlike the second episode of *The Practice* examined above, in which the viewer is positioned to assume that the Arab American detainee is guilty but later learns he is innocent, the *Law and Order* episode begins with the viewer assuming that the dead Arab man was unjustly killed. It is later revealed that he was on the verge of killing many innocent Americans.

This episode of *Law and Order*, like so many other post-9/11 TV dramas, makes for gripping television because it reflects the tensions and anxieties and debates of the era. After 9/11 the U.S. government proposed the creation of Operation TIPS—the Terrorist Information and Prevention System program—that encouraged citizens to report suspicious behavior to the government.[29] Operation TIPS was controversial and eventually scrapped; evidence of it has since been deleted from government web pages.[30] Nonetheless, the months after 9/11 made it clear that many individuals did not need the creation of a new government program to take part in a long-standing American tradition; many took it on as their patriotic duty to monitor and report neighbors, coworkers, and strangers who looked like they might be Arab or Muslim or South Asian or Middle Eastern. For example, Eunice Stone, a white woman, saw it as her patriotic duty in September 2002 to call the Georgia police because a group of young Muslim American men were dining at a restaurant; the men were soon arrested, based on this "tip," though after a few hours at the local police station it became clear that they were, in fact, merely dining.[31] Some citizen-patriots alerted local or federal authorities of their suspicions, while others took it on themselves to harass, harm, and kill persons who appeared to be Arab, Muslim, or South Asian. Also in 2002, in Chattanooga, Tennessee, an Arab American man was killed, shot in the back four times, as he was closing his store.[32] In Mesa, Arizona, a Sikh man was killed; on being arrested the white man who killed him shouted, "I am an American!"[33] Police reported that the man claimed he wanted to "kill 'ragheads' responsible for the terrorist attacks."[34] In this episode of *Law and Order*, the former soldier called the FBI, but his information was ignored because there were too many other cases to follow up; he therefore took it upon himself to investigate this Arab man and then assassinated him.

When Frank Miller is arrested, he disputes the charges, claiming that he has devoted his life to defending his country as a soldier. In a precourt meeting, Miller's lawyer continues this argument.

> **DISTRICT ATTORNEY MCCOY:** He murdered a man.
>
> **MILLER'S LAWYER:** He used the skills and training this country gave him and he acted.
>
> **DA MCCOY:** By setting an apartment on fire? To cover his crime? Not exactly the actions of a soldier who thought what he had done was right, Counselor.
>
> **MILLER'S LAWYER:** Do you know what Haddad was doing at that garage he worked at? Learning how to drive 18-wheelers. They had a deal with a trucking company. That's why he wanted that driver's license so badly.
>
> **DA MCCOY:** So we all turn our backs when a cold-blooded murder is committed? We do that and we turn into the very thing we're fighting. The word *terrorism* loses its meaning.
>
> **JUDGE:** I agree with Mr. McCoy. Your client is a civilian, not a soldier.
>
> **MILLER'S LAWYER:** With all due respect, your honor, but we are all soldiers; soldiers in a war against terrorism. I know this because CNN tells me so every day. The Homeland secretary tells us we're all on yellow alert. That has to mean something more than just a color. If Yusef Haddad was indeed a terrorist, then my client was acting in defense of country.

Should Miller be set free because his suspicions about the Arab man were correct? Is he a patriot for diverting a potential terrorist attack? Or did Miller's version of vigilante justice take his self-proclaimed role too far? During the War on Terror, do ordinary rules apply—is murder punished by imprisonment? Or are these times so exceptional that what was previously illegal is now legal? Miller's lawyer argues that we are indeed in a state of exception—a state of national crisis—with CNN as proof. In contrast, the district attorney, Jack McCoy, argues that U.S. citizens who commit murder and acts of violence in the name of patriotism are terrorists themselves. He seeks to resignify "terrorist" from its inscription on Arab bodies to all persons who commit violence against innocent people.

The program ends with a guilty verdict, though the DA and his assistant, Serena, lament the time it took for the jury to reach its decision.

> **SERENA:** Five days of jury deliberations.
>
> **MCCOY:** Which means some of them were ready to acquit.
>
> **JUDGE:** A minority of them may have given in to their fears for a moment. But you were right, Jack. They came to their senses. You think the American dream is still safe?
>
> **MCCOY:** Give us your tired, your poor, your terrorist.

Despite Jack McCoy's weary pessimism, justice is served: patriotism has its limits, and McCoy's trademark morality wins in the end. However, a far more ambiguous message seeps through: though "patriots" should not kill Arabs, this "patriot" was actually right. Arabs and Muslims are invading this country; there are sleeper cells lurking among us; the nation is at risk. Even the district attorney acknowledges this in the episode's last line: "Give us your tired, your poor, your terrorist." McCoy hints that terrorists are jeopardizing the principles of the United States and taking away the liberty and freedom represented by the Statue of Liberty.

While the episode flirts with the idea that exceptional circumstances merit changing the rules, the jury's verdict implies that we must fight to maintain legal standards during times of crisis. The episode's ultimate message, however, is more ambiguous: the logic of exception is indeed critiqued, but the Arab man's identity as a terrorist ultimately confirms that suspicion of all Arabs/Muslims is justified, or at least necessary. According to the preferred meaning of this episode, Arabs are indeed a threat to national security; a seemingly innocent Arab man, after all, who seems to be the victim of a terrible hate crime could actually be a real terrorist. The logic of the episode does not support sympathy for the Arab and Muslim American plight but mourning for the end of the American dream. Ultimately, discourses of the nation in crisis not only trump the Arab and Muslim American plight but also support U.S. government initiatives in the War on Terror. This is achieved through benevolent emotions that connect the viewer's feelings of sympathy, remorse, and mourning to the identity of the nation.

Benevolent Emotions, Benevolent Nation

A logic of exception that has been central to the War on Terror is at times advanced and at other times critiqued by TV dramas. Ironically, it is through this display of multicultural sensitivity that the logic of exception gains legitimacy as "common sense" during the War on Terror. Let me be clear: these representations are indeed sympathetic and are indeed an improvement on the blatantly racist representations typical of both television and film prior to the late 1990s. Some writers and producers of television dramas make an explicit effort to challenge stereotypes. But at the same time, beyond this veneer of sympathy, many of the narratives in which these representations are located simply reinscribe, albeit more subtly, the logic that legitimizes suspending Arab and Muslim civil rights. Several interrelated logics converge in these TV dramas: racism is wrong but regretfully necessary at this exceptional time; the American dream is being threatened by Arab/Muslim terrorists; this moment of intensified racism will pass and the harmonious times that define the United States will soon return. The use of sympathetic representations to create the illusion of a postracial era is how racism operates now, through a denial of itself.

Sympathetic representations of Arab and Muslim characters after 9/11 can in a variety of ways affirm a multicultural, democratic, and benevolent image of the United States. Shohat and Stam have demonstrated that it is not unusual for liberal films to contain positive images of the Other while maintaining a European or Euro-American character as the "center of consciousness":

> Many liberal Hollywood films about the Third World or about minoritarian
> cultures in the First World deploy a European or Euro-American character as a
> mediating "bridge" to other cultures portrayed more or less sympathetically. . . .
> The Third World characters have a subsidiary function in such films and reports,
> even though their plight is the thematic focus. Media liberalism, in sum, does not
> allow subaltern communities to play prominent self-determining roles, a refusal
> homologous to liberal distaste for non-mediated self-assertion in the political
> realm.[35]

In the case of "positive" representations of Arab and Muslim Americans after 9/11, Euro-Americans (as well as African Americans) serve as mediating bridges to sympathy. Arab and Muslim American characters are thus marginalized even when their plight is the central theme of the narrative.[36] Viewers are not positioned to identify directly with the Arab American character but rather to identify with the remorse of the Euro-American or African American character over the plight of this Other. The Arab American character remains in the background; rather than a fully fleshed out individual, he remains an idea, a representation of a salacious topic, and a vehicle for liberal sympathy.

Representing Arab and Muslim Americans sympathetically, and as victims and patriots, in post-9/11 TV dramas has become part of the U.S. narrative of multicultural progress. Conscientious writers, for example, point out the similarities between the detention of Arabs and Muslims and the internment of Japanese Americans during World War II or segregation of blacks during the Jim Crow era; such a critical perspective seems to confirm an enlightened position. Similarly, writers capitalize on the innate desires of our multicultural era—to decry blatant racism, to try to understand others. As a result, these sympathetic portrayals have a touch of self-congratulation. The ability to portray Arabs and Muslims as more than just terrorists is a sign of "progress." These sympathetic representations are the latest rung of an American consciousness that continues to evolve—one that has reckoned with the evils of slavery, that laments past abuses of immigrants, that honors the hard-fought victories of the civil rights movement. These sympathetic representations affirm an image of the United States as democratic, multicultural, and enlightened; an America that many want to live in and an image of Americans that many want to be.

Mourning the plight of Arab and Muslim Americans after 9/11 is central to post-9/11 racial logic. In other words, feelings of remorse operate to relieve viewer-citizens of any blame: viewer-citizens can feel bad, remorseful, and apologetic for the plight of Arab and Muslim Americans while having faith that "this too shall pass." While the United States is detaining and deporting Arabs and Muslims, such benevolent emotions operate as a sign of a benevolent culture and nation; knowing it is wrong makes us "good." Representations of the Arab/Muslim American plight are thus less about coming to understand the Arab or Muslim American experience and are more about enabling benevolent emotions—sympathy, remorse, and mourning, as opposed to revenge and anger—which validate the enlightened, liberal, and "post-race" viewer.

3   Evoking Sympathy for the Muslim Woman

> Without the assault on the senses, it would be impossible for a state to wage war.
> —Judith Butler, *Frames of War*

It is not possible to write about representations of Arabs and Muslims since 9/11 without addressing the quandary of Arab and Muslim women. In innumerable ways, and from both ends of the ideological spectrum, these women have been represented as veiled, oppressed, and in need of rescue. The government and commercial news media have been central to the circulation of stories about the "oppressed Muslim woman" and the imperative to "save brown women from brown men."¹ Yet the figure of the oppressed Muslim woman has not been prominent in post-9/11 TV dramas, which tend to focus on Arab/Muslim American patriots, victims of hate crimes, and Arab/Muslim terrorists. When Arab/Muslim women were represented in TV dramas, like their male counterparts, they tended to fall within these three categories.² For example, *24* portrayed an Arab/Muslim female terrorist (the character Dina Araz) and an Arab/Muslim American patriotic government agent (Nadia Yassir). While these characters do not wear the hijab (headscarf), a few women wearing a hijab did appear on occasion in TV dramas, usually as victims of post-9/11 hate crimes. Two episodes of *7th Heaven* represent hijab-wearing Muslim girls and women as Americans who were subject to post-9/11 harassment. Similarly, on *The Education of Max Bickford*, a Muslim female student at the college receives a death threat. Perhaps the effort by TV dramas to create more complex characters led to complex terrorists but not complex victims. While "the oppressed Muslim woman" did not make compelling prime-time dramas, it did make for compelling news.

This chapter continues to outline post-9/11 representational modes and the role of emotion in representations of Arabs and Muslims after 9/11. It explores how affects evoked by stories about Arabs and Muslims can also contribute to such exclusionary logics. Arab and Muslim victims emerge as particularly important to simplified complex representations because they allow viewers to *feel* for a certain character type—a person who formerly was not seen as deserving of human feeling. The growth of this affect in turn comes to symbolize multicultural progress. Here, I examine another rendition of the victim: a Muslim woman who is brutalized by a patriarchal culture and needs to be saved.

A Vanderbilt Television News Archive search reveals dozens of news stories on Muslim women within a year after 9/11. A LexisNexis search reveals thousands of articles on Muslim women published within a year after 9/11 in major U.S. and world publications and thousands more during the subsequent seven years of the Bush administration's War on Terror. These stories include accounts of unbearable oppression, of the Arab and Muslim American plight as victims of hate crimes, and attempts to explain to Americans the veil and the status of women in Muslim societies.[3] Some stories sought to challenge the overwhelming focus on "the extreme cases of oppression against Muslim women" and to reveal that "there's another world out there."[4] Whether advancing or actively seeking to challenge the oppressed Muslim woman story, this narrative was repeatedly circulated after 9/11, and none was more powerful than this one. Despite an array of stories on Muslim women, the oppressed Muslim woman narrative derives its power from the strong emotions it provokes—pity and outrage.

Representations of the oppressed Muslim woman rely on an excess of affect—an explicit expression of outrage and sympathy—and representations of alleged terrorist men rely on the regulation of affect—a withholding of sympathy. The news media participates in policing the boundaries of feeling differently in the case of Muslim women and men in the War on Terror, resulting in a hierarchy of human life.

Sympathy is a key emotion that emerged in relation to Arabs and Muslims after 9/11. It is a key post-race emotion, as it importantly signals a capacity to have nuanced emotions toward the designated enemy. Rather than demonize all Arabs and Muslims, having sympathy for some of them illuminates an enlightened culture that can distinguish between the "good" and "bad" ones, the perpetrators and the victims. Sympathy can be manifested as the benevolent emotions explored in chapter 2—remorse and mourning—or as more active iterations of benevolent emotions—pity and outrage. Pity and outrage are two sides of the same coin. Pity is powerful, and also dangerous, because it implies that the person who has the emotion is more powerful than the person who is the object of the emotion. Empathy is not a relevant emotion here because it is built on a greater sense of equality between the two parties; the oppressed Muslim woman is figured as coming from a culture so different that it is difficult to understand or relate to. Pity makes outrage easy; feeling sorrow for someone's distress easily morphs into anger at the circumstances that caused the distress and thus outrage at the men, the culture, and the religion. Outrage emerges from the anger and shock when one's sensibilities or sense of right and wrong are offended. Pity and outrage lead to experiencing oneself as invested in justice.

The Arab/Muslim conflation has been advanced through stories about the oppressed Muslim woman in Pakistan, Afghanistan, Saudi Arabia, Nigeria, and other countries. Given the range of locations for this story, many of which are not Arab, my focus in this chapter is on Muslim women. The U.S. government has discovered that saving Muslim women is a compelling way to gain support for military intervention. Influential American women—conservative and liberal alike—have been among the relentless broadcasters of this story line. Former first ladies have authenticated the discourse on saving Muslim women by officially reproducing it as concerned American women. In Laura Bush's post-9/11 radio address, she states, "The brutal oppression of women is a central goal of the terrorists"; as a result, "the fight against terrorism is also a fight for the rights and dignity of women."[5] Hillary Clinton expresses a similar viewpoint in *Time* magazine where she makes a case for why women's rights in Afghanistan are an important issue in the War on Terror. She responds to critics who say that the West should not impose its values on other cultures: "A post-Taliban Afghanistan where women's rights are respected is much less likely to harbor terrorists in the future. Why? Because a society that values all its members, including women, is also likely to put a higher premium on life, opportunity and freedom—values that run directly counter to the evil designs of the Osama bin Ladens of the world."[6] These statements support a larger official narrative that the oppression of Muslim women and the likelihood of another terrorist attack on the United States are interrelated. The explanation that the tragedy of 9/11 occurred because "they hate us for our freedom" relies on the presentation of the oppressed Muslim woman as evidence of this hatred of freedom and also as a key to understanding and winning the War on Terror. It then follows in this paradigm that combating terrorism requires "liberating" Muslim women and punishing those responsible: namely, Muslim men or a "barbaric" Islamic culture more generally.

The problem I am seeking to highlight here is not that the viewer feels pity or outrage at these horrifying stories; such stories are indeed worthy of outrage. The problem, rather, is how these horrifying stories create a monolithic portrait of Islam that is then easily mobilized by the government to justify U.S. intervention in Arab and Muslims countries. Stories of oppression and violence within Islam are repeated to the point that the most brutal acts define Islam. In other words, the problem is not that a viewer feels pity and outrage that a Muslim woman has been stoned to death but that a viewer assumes that all Muslim men are capable of stoning their wives. The power of definition, or of associating violence and oppression with Islam, results not only from the repetition of such stories but also from the emotions they evoke. The heightened emotional state can turn the viewer into a political actor who participates in seeking to end the witnessed injustice. I do not mean that viewers become activists or politicians but that they become concerned and invested in alleviating the suffering of Muslim women and can do so by donating money, by signing petitions, or by speaking out.

The logics central to the War on Terror are not possible without their accompanying affects. The widely circulated narrative of the oppressed Muslim woman has an important affective dimension. During the War on Terror, in particular, it is powerful because of the argument it seeks to make about civilization and barbarism, wherein the United States represents civilization and Islam represents an inherently "barbaric" culture and religion in conflict with U.S. values. Affect has played a major role in media representations of the oppressed Muslim woman. Structures of feeling, in this case, the benevolent emotions pity and outrage, I contend, are culturally constituted and culturally shared in representations of the oppressed Muslim woman during the War on Terror.

TV and print news, especially in its commercial iterations, have increasingly taken on the elements of drama; perhaps to compete with the success of dramas, not to mention the booming new genre of reality television, news reporting has become increasingly sensationalized and often includes a hero or innocent victim, an antagonist, and a conflict arising from the interactions between the hero and the villain. The oppressed Muslim woman is the victim in this drama; Muslim men and Islam are the antagonists or villains. The United States figures as the hero who will save the oppressed Muslim woman from her culture. The *Oprah Winfrey Show* is a fascinating synthesis of news journalism and fictional drama. Winfrey underscores that what she discusses is "true" while relentlessly focusing on personal, tear-jerking narratives with dramatic presentations lifted from the realms of fiction. Ultimately, we must consider television and print news alongside TV dramas because the former, just like the latter, produce their own version of simplified complex representations, with their own consequences for how we perceive Islam.

In chapter 1, I defined simplified complex representations as the efforts by writers and producers of TV dramas to avoid stereotyping by portraying characters and events as multidimensional. Here, I examine three important iterations of simplified complex representations in television and print commercial news. In the first iteration, journalists use disclaimers to signal to readers that their news story about Islam and oppression should not be read as representing *all* Islam. In the second iteration, Muslim women who once faced gender oppression are portrayed as liberated and speaking of their former lives. They testify and authenticate the "barbaric nature of Islam," creating broad generalizations that nullify the aforementioned use of disclaimers. Third, both of

these representational modes of simplified complex representations are successful because of how they produce an excess of affect. Viewers are encouraged to
experience outrage at the injustice Muslim women face and an excess of sympathy and concern for them. This excessive affect is an important component
in simplified complex representational modes, particularly in creating the illusion of a post-race—and in this case, a post-feminist—society in which viewers
operate from a place of care and justice that enables and justifies the mistreatment of Muslim men and Muslim communities. My exploration reveals how
the media's use of these representational strategies tends to aid U.S. imperialism and advance the very problem of female oppression that they are purport-
edly trying to solve.

This chapter examines these three iterations of simplified complex representations by examining two sites. I first examine a sampling of commercial U.S.
media reports on the oppressed Muslim woman in order to scrutinize how
these stories are framed and what is strategically omitted to justify U.S. imperialist projects. Second, I examine the *Oprah Winfrey* episode, "Can We Save
Amina Lawal?," along with viewer responses to it.

Behind-the-Veil Exposés

I scoured news stories published in *Time, Newsweek, US News & World Report*,
as well as news shows aired on *CNN, ABC, NBC, CBS*, and *FOX*, with a focus
on the first year after the September 11 terrorist attacks. The result is an abundance of stories about the oppressed Muslim woman. Consider a sampling of
post-9/11 headlines: "Lifting the Veil," "Free to Choose," "Unveiling Freedom,"
"Under the Veil," "Beneath the Veil," and "Unveiled Threat."[7] Journalists promised to take viewers "behind the veil" to reveal a world—termed in varying
degrees secret, hidden, and mysterious—that would shed light on why Arabs/
Muslims are terrorists. Terrorism in these pieces is typically framed as without reason, through a standard omission of the social, historical, and political
conditions that produce terrorism (a topic I examine in chapter 4). Within this
framework—terrorism as incomprehensible—the oppressed Muslim woman
comes to offer a bizarre but very potent explanation. The oppressed Muslim
woman provides insight, a vital clue, into why terrorism occurs: Muslim men
oppress their women and regard the West with contempt for their equal gender
relations. As a result, they want to subjugate the rest of the world to impose
their way of life.

The commercial news media produces a mantra about Islam: veiled oppression, female genital mutilation, "honor" killings, and a lack of rights. "Behind
the veil," a reader or viewer is treated to an assault of evidence testifying to

the oppressive and backward nature of Islam, especially when it comes to women: story after story of Muslim women dying in "honor killings"; facing female genital mutilation; being beaten on the streets of Afghanistan and Saudi Arabia for violating the dress code by not wearing their veil properly; being sentenced to death for adultery; being buried alive and stoned to death; being beaten for disobeying their husbands; being raped by members of the husband's family; being unable to get a divorce or child custody; generally having no rights.[8] Images accompany these stories: a man whips a group of women and children on the street; a woman is in the hospital after being burned alive by her father-in-law for not doing the laundry properly. Other images of postliberation Afghanistan are juxtaposed to these horror stories: recurring favorites are images of wedding celebrations after the fall of the Taliban; men and women are celebrating together, and the women are not wearing burqas but high heels and makeup. Many news stories in the wake of the terrorist attacks in the aftermath of 9/11 contain references to the United States bringing "light" to the "darkness" that was Afghanistan. Many of these stories emphasize the horrors of women in Afghanistan under the Taliban; other stories take place in Iran, Yemen, and Pakistan, collectively stressing that the oppression of Muslim women is not an isolated instance but a widespread practice within Islam. These stories tend to evoke extreme and particular emotions: outrage and pity.

A November 2001 article in *Time* magazine, "The Women of Islam," by Lisa Beyer, is one example of how journalists use simplified complex representational strategies while advancing a monolithic image of Islam as brutal, violent, and oppressive.[9] The subtitle of the article reads: "The Taliban perfected subjugation. But nowhere in the Muslim world are women treated as equals." This article begins with a few concessions, stating that the prophet Muhammad was a feminist who improved the status of women in the seventh century. The author also writes:

> While it is impossible, given their diversity, to paint one picture of women living under Islam today, it is clear that the religion has been used in most Muslim countries not to liberate but to entrench inequality. The Taliban, with its fanatical subjugation of the female sex, occupies an extreme, but it nevertheless belongs on a continuum that includes, not so far down the line, Saudi Arabia, Kuwait, Pakistan and the relatively moderate states of Egypt and Jordan. Where Muslims have afforded women the greatest degree of equality—in Turkey—they have done so by overthrowing Islamic precepts in favor of secular rule. As Riffat Hassan, professor of religious studies at the University of Louisville, puts it, "The way Islam has been practiced in most Muslim societies for centuries has left millions of Muslim women with battered bodies, minds and souls."[10]

Journalists often begin with a disclaimer—"It is impossible to capture the diversity of the Muslim world," or "These are not Islamic practices"—before presenting an onslaught of evidence to prove the brutality of Islam. The disclaimer signals that the journalist is aware of the diversity of Muslim lived experiences and is making an effort to present a semblance of sensitivity and awareness. While lip service is paid to diversity and complexity, the vast majority of evidence supports the opposite idea.

The disclaimer in Beyer's report is followed by a portrait of injustice presented as inherent to Islam, information that provokes outrage in the ideal reader. She writes:

> Part of the problem dates to Muhammad. Even as he proclaimed new rights for women, he enshrined their inequality in immutable law, passed down as God's commandments and eventually recorded in scripture. The Koran allots daughters half the inheritance of sons. It decrees that a woman's testimony in court, at least in financial matters, is worth half that of a man's. Under Sharia, or Muslim law, compensation for the murder of a woman is half the going rate for men. In many Muslim countries, these directives are incorporated into contemporary law. For a woman to prove rape in Pakistan, for example, four adult males of "impeccable" character must witness the penetration, in accordance with Sharia.

Beyer also states that whereas women can marry only one man, men can marry up to four women. In addition, the legal age to marry is much younger for girls than for boys: the Prophet's wife was six years old when they married; in Iran the legal age to marry is nine for girls but fourteen for boys. The article reports that men can divorce easily, while women cannot; many women do not even attempt divorce out of fear of losing custody of their children. The denunciations continue: the Qur'an allows for the beating of an insubordinate wife: "Wife beating is so prevalent in the Muslim world that social workers who assist battered women in Egypt, for example, spend much of their time trying to convince victims that their husbands' violent acts are unacceptable." Beyer reveals that hundreds of women die each year in honor killings, and women are subject to female genital mutilation.

After this onslaught, Beyer inserts yet another disclaimer by stating that these are not necessarily Islamic practices. Regarding female genital mutilation, she writes, "Some Muslims believe it is mandated by Islam, but the practice predates Muhammad and is also common among some Christian communities."[11] Despite this disclaimer, the evidence continues to pile up, provoking outrage and pity in the ideal reader: The Qur'an instructs women to veil; in Saudi Arabia, women are beaten by the police if they violate the dress code. The author acknowledges that some women choose to wear the veil, but that hint of women's choice is quickly overwhelmed by a more ominous depiction:

In most Islamic countries, coverings are technically optional. Some women, including some feminists, wear them because they like them. They find that the veil liberates them from unwanted gazes and hassles from men. But many Muslim women feel cultural and family pressure to cover themselves. Recently a Muslim fundamentalist group in the Indian province of Kashmir demanded that women start wearing veils. When the call was ignored, hooligans threw acid in the faces of uncovered women.

The notion that wearing the hijab could be a choice is quickly undone by stressing the potential for violence. While the author underlines that it is impossible to capture the diversity of the Muslim world, she draws an incriminating portrait by overgeneralizing her evidence. Examples are often drawn from Saudi Arabia and Afghanistan under the Taliban—the most extreme examples—to support her depiction of Islam as a whole.

The article ends with a few concessions, acknowledging some improvements in the Muslim world: women have been elected to government positions in Syria and Iraq; four Muslim countries—Pakistan, Bangladesh, Indonesia, and Turkey—have been led by women; Bangladesh's legal punishments for crimes against women have become more severe; and Egypt has banned female circumcision and made it easier for women to divorce. After a long list of evidence of how unjust, unequal, and oppressive Islam is, Beyer writes that women in Iran "drive cars, buy and sell property, run their own businesses, vote and hold public office. . . . Still, Iranian women are—like women in much of the Arab world—forbidden to travel overseas without the permission of their husband or father, though the rule is rarely enforced in Iran."[2] It seems that Beyer makes an effort to end the article with simplified complex representations; she tries to complicate the article by acknowledging that her portrayal of life under Islam is not all-encompassing. Therefore, a few examples of Muslim women who do not fit the mold of the oppressed Muslim woman are tacked on at the end. Regardless of these gestures, Beyer's overwhelming message is that Islam is a violent and oppressive religion. Information regarding women's leadership roles cannot compete with the excess of outrage the story provokes.

Once again, the frame of these stories is crucial. As discussed earlier, the stereotype of the Arab/Muslim terrorist relies on framing violence enacted by Arabs and Muslims as working against democracy and freedom and therefore as reprehensible. Through omitting the context in which terrorism emerges— or the social, historical, and political conditions that produce terrorism— "terrorists" are framed as undeserving of human sympathy. Similarly, violence against women is framed as cultural, or as inherent to or mandated by Islam. Muslim women who are victims of violence are framed as deserving of sympathy, while Muslim men—who are explicitly or implicitly the agents of violence—are not. As Judith Butler argues, the media actively participates in a "strategy of containment, selectively producing and enforcing what will count as reality." In doing so, the frame is always "keeping something out, always de-realizing and de-legitimizing alternative versions of reality."[13]

What are the alternative versions of reality that stories about the oppressed Muslim woman omit? Among the alternative frames for understanding 9/11, the War on Terror, and the status of Muslim women that are de-realized and de-legitimized are the following: (1) the historical conditions that produced Islamic "fundamentalism" and "terrorism" are entwined with and not independent from U.S. involvement; and (2) Arab and Muslim feminists, intellectuals, and communities have long engaged in heated debates and reforms regarding gender roles in Islam. As for post-9/11 strategies of containment, this includes the U.S. government's co-optation of feminism. This kind of co-optation is not a new phenomenon but was central to European colonialism in the Middle East in the late nineteenth and early twentieth centuries.[14] Lord Cromer, a quintessential Victorian imperialist, saw veiling and women's seclusion as an obstacle to civilization in Egypt. Despite his opposition to Britain's suffrage movement and despite the fact that the women in his own country couldn't vote, Cromer and the British government co-opted feminist language to justify colonialism, arguing that women's progress in Egypt could be achieved only by abandoning the native culture. As Leila Ahmed has written, "The Victorian colonial paternalistic establishment appropriated the language of feminism in the service of its assault on the religions and cultures of Other men, and in particular on Islam, in order to give an aura of moral justification to that assault at the very same time as it combated feminism within its own society."[15] This colonial "feminism" had unintended consequences; for a broad swath of Muslims, Islam itself became a vehicle of dissent, a way to reject the West by embracing indigenous culture.[16] Minoo Moallem writes that the frequent binary framing in the West that positions fundamentalism as unique to Islam and modernity as unique to the West "makes various forms of fundamentalism and cultural nationalism attractive or appealing to the masses of people in the Middle East; in other words, it creates a situation where claiming an 'us' or making certain claims to authenticity becomes a site of resistance and identity formation."[17] Creating an Islam in opposition to the West has often occurred through women's bodies as symbols of cultural authenticity.[18]

Not only has European colonialism in the Middle East inspired unprecedented forms of Islam, including fundamentalism, as a strategy of resistance to Western interference and criticism, but U.S. interventions during the Cold War have further supported the growth of fundamentalism. This is one alternative version of reality that is often de-realized by the government and commercial media. As Mahmood Mamdani has shown, the terrorist attacks of 9/11 resulted from a complex confluence of factors, including U.S. covert operations and proxy wars during the Cold War era. During the Cold War, the U.S. government created and funded the mujahedeen to fight the Soviets; the mujahedeen would later become Al Qaeda and target their initial benefactors. Furthermore, the funding of Muslim religious extremists would set the scene for the Taliban's takeover of Afghanistan. Notably absent in helping the U.S. public understand the Taliban's emergence was the U.S. government's involvement. Charles Hirschkind and Saba Mahmood note how striking it was that many commentators "regularly failed to connect the predicament of women in Afghanistan with the massive military and economic support that the US provided, as part of its Cold War strategy, to the most extreme of Afghan religious militant groups."[19] Islamic fundamentalism, contrary to the U.S. government's and media's framing of it as being opposed to and incompatible with modernity, is a modern formation; Islamic fundamentalism is not an ancient or traditional phenomenon but rather a by-product of the ideological clashes of the twentieth century.[20] Mamdani argues that terrorism does not necessarily emerge out of religious tendencies, whether fundamentalist or secular. Rather, terrorism emerges out of political encounter. In this case, the West has played a central role in the political encounter with Islam that produced the terrorist attacks on 9/11.[21]

The media's framing of religious fundamentalism as unique to Islam and "Islamic fundamentalism" as a signifier for Muslim irrationality, moral inferiority, barbaric masculinity, and victimized femininity has several consequences. Moallem writes that "the association of fundamentalism with Islam undermines the powerful presence of various forms of fundamentalism in the West and disguises their relationship with liberal, democratic political orders." The impact of U.S. intervention in the formation of Islamic fundamentalism is notably absent from media reporting. Beyer's *Time* article exemplifies this failure to consider the role and impact of U.S. intervention in the history of these countries in order to portray Islam as always and already backward and oppressive. Furthermore, the U.S. government and media present U.S. military intervention as the solution to the oppressed Muslim woman, without noting how U.S. military intervention in the name of democracy and freedom has contributed to violence against Muslim women. The co-opted feminist focus on how women in Afghanistan are deprived of education and employment and forced to wear the burqa conceals how conditions of war, militarization, and starvation are harming women. To cite one example of overlooked consequences, the U.S. war on Afghanistan in the years after 9/11 led to starvation because U.S. bombing impeded the delivery of food aid.[22] The reductive framing of oppressed women creates a palatable narrative, where the blame can easily be placed on a people and a culture seemingly a world apart from Americans. Thus, the U.S. government (not to mention its citizens) need not be held accountable for its involvement in creating this modern conflict that contributed to the conditions of women's oppression.

In portraying Islam as always and inherently backward, another version of reality that is often de-realized by the government and media is the long history of Muslim intellectual writings or feminist debates within Islam.[23] As Moallem writes, "These totalizing discourses not only deny the presence of diverse social movements in the Muslim world, but also disregard lively discussions around the meaning of Islam taking place in many Muslim countries."[24] Islam, like any religion, is open to reinterpretation and change. Oppressive practices have resulted from patriarchal interpretations of the Qur'an as opposed to Islam itself. In the late 1800s, Muslim intellectuals, most notably Qasim Amin, called for reforms in polygamy and divorce to support women's rights, women's education, and the abolition of the veil. Furthermore, women's experiences under Islam vary widely depending on class, ethnicity, local culture, and historical-political context. A 2008 Gallup poll of fifty thousand Muslims from thirty-five countries has shown that the majority of Muslim women do not see Islam as an obstacle to their progress but as a crucial component.[25] Rather than attack Shari'a law, many Muslim women question whether or not a law that is discriminatory toward women is Shari'a compliant. In other words, many Muslim women assume that Islam is inherently equal and that inequality arises because of a patriarchal interpretation. Also lost to many Western observers, Muslim women tend to place the issue of women's rights in a context larger than their religion alone, and insist on examining a variety of factors, including human rights and harm caused by poverty, repression, and war. According to this same poll, the majority of Muslim women say that women deserve the same legal rights as men: to vote without influence from family members, to work at any job for which they are qualified, and to serve in the highest levels of government. Some Muslim women argue for gender equality but not for "the same" rights for men and women. These women argue for the same rights in terms of crime and punishment but different or "complementary" rights vis-à-vis the family, wherein a woman carries no financial obligation for the family and can keep her earned wages and property under her own name while having legal rights to her husband's property and earnings. These data stand in sharp contrast to how women's rights are conceptualized in the West and also to how Shari'a law is understood in the West.[26]

As a result of these frames, viewers and readers of the news have multiple opportunities to understand what barbaric Islam looks like and to feel outrage and anger at the religion's manifold injustices. Comparable opportunities to understand what the diversity or complexity of Islam looks like have less impact, partly because they are explored with less frequency and partly because they do not have the same emotional impact. There are not equal opportunities for audiences to explore internal debates and reforms regarding gender roles in Islam. Furthermore, viewers do not have comparable opportunities to feel outrage toward the United States for its involvement in creating oppressive conditions for these oft-lamented Muslim women.

Therese Saliba writes that Arab women are made invisible by the U.S. media in two ways: they are either not represented, or when they are it is to accentuate their invisibility and therefore to support "neocolonial interests of the new world order and the U.S. media's repression of the war's destruction."[27] Stories about the oppressed Muslim woman come to represent Islam and to explain why 9/11 happened and why the United States went to war in Afghanistan and Iraq. These stories have the impact of not only defining conversations about Islam/terrorism but also confining the conversation to these stories, what Amira Jarmakani terms "the politics of invisibility." She argues that the very categories that purport to give Arab and Muslim women visibility, such as the veil, actually render their experiences and their speech invisible because Arab and Muslim feminists are faced with continually responding to these categories rather than defining their own agendas.[28]

The media's relentless focus on Islam's violence against women also diminishes the occurrence of violence against women in the United States by giving the impression that violence against women is unique to Arabs and Muslims. Such absences not only imply that the United States is a bastion of gender equality but also that the United States has a monopoly on feminism, aligning the nation with freedom, equality, and civilization and positioning "the Muslim world" as its binary opposite. How these stories are framed, and what is absent and present in that framing, consistently positions the United States as a postfeminist nation. The problem I am seeking to highlight here is not that journalists are interested in reporting on stories of oppression and hardship but rather the cumulative effect of these stories, particularly on an emotional level. News stories have been published about successful Muslim women and advancements that Muslim women have made, but these do not have the same emotional impact and therefore social impact as stories about women subject to violence and oppression.

Earlier chapters explored the co-optation of multiculturalism by the commercial media and how this co-optation has participated in producing a postrace imaginary that stands in stark contrast to continued racist policies and practices. A parallel co-optation of feminism has occurred after 9/11 wherein a postfeminist imaginary is projected that purports that gendered violence is not a problem in the United States. Postfeminism is produced through projections of gender equality on television, particularly through televisual representations of powerful women as detectives, doctors, and presidents. It is advanced through representations of the "oppressed Muslim woman" that serves as a contrast to the "liberated American woman." Susan Douglas writes that a new form of sexism is covertly operating in the United States. What she terms "enlightened sexism" is the notion that American women have achieved full equality with men as the result of the feminist movement and therefore not only is feminism no longer needed, but advancing sexist stereotypes is seen as funny or harmless.[29] Enlightened sexism has the potential to undo feminist progress in a similar way that post-race ideologies have the potential to overlook and deny continued racist practices.

Many feminist scholars have written about how the U.S.-led war in Afghanistan and U.S. imperialism in the Middle East have been predicated on "saving the women."[30] The Bush administration co-opted feminist discourse and aligned itself with feminist organizations, such as the Feminist Majority Foundation, to garner public support for the War on Terror. Krista Hunt names this process "embedded feminism," that is, "the incorporation of feminist discourse and feminist activists into political projects that claim to serve the interests of women but ultimately subordinate and/or subvert that goal."[31] Embedded feminism, alongside enlightened sexism, constructs the United States as a postfeminist realm that is positioned for benevolent interventions abroad.[32] The oppressed Muslim woman supports U.S. interventionist projects through a particular conception of barbaric Muslim culture and through making absent alternate framings, in particular, the U.S. role in the formation of Islamic fundamentalists, the impact of U.S. interventions on Muslim life and livelihood, and the history of Arab and Muslim feminism.

Sherene Razack argues that stories about the "imperiled Muslim woman" who needs to be rescued by the "civilized European" from the "dangerous Muslim man," represent violence against women as unique to Islam and therefore "culturalizes" violence against women as an attribute of Muslim peoples. In addition to portraying violence and oppression as inherent and unique to Islam, I would add that the power of the figure of the imperiled Muslim woman is derived through structures of feeling—through defining the imperiled Muslim woman as necessarily provoking certain feelings, especially outrage and sympathy, and defining the dangerous Muslim man as unfeeling and therefore undeserving of human feeling.[33] Stories of Muslim women who are victims of a barbaric culture and religion and the emotions that accompany it are used to rationalize the need to expel Muslims from the political community, deny them human rights, and justify detentions, deportations, racial profiling, and prisoner abuse.[34] Concern or pity for the oppressed Muslim woman, in other words, is used to advance U.S. imperialism.

In addition to using disclaimers to signal that the news media does not intend to contribute to a monolithic portrait of Islam, and selectively including and excluding particular aspects of the context to understand the oppressed Muslim woman, an important simplified complex representational strategy is the use of native informants. Several Muslim women, including Ayaan Hirsi Ali, Nonie Darwish, and Wafa Sultan, have made successful careers as women who have defected from Islam and become spokespersons for the inherent backwardness of Islam. While the oppressed Muslim woman narrative has cross-ideological appeal and has been taken up as a cause by both the right and the left, these native informants collaborate with right-wing agendas that aim not only to help oppressed women but also to denounce Islam entirely. Nonie Darwish, an Egyptian, is the founder of Arabs for Israel, the director of Former Muslims United, and is the author of two books arguing that Islam is a retrograde religion.[35] Wafa Sultan, a Syrian, claims that Islam promotes violence; she is the author of a book titled *A God That Hates*.[36] Ayaan Hirsi Ali, a Somali, embraced atheism after 9/11; she has written numerous books as well as the film *Submission* and claims that Islam is incompatible with democracy.

Ayaan Hirsi Ali's story about being forced to have a cliterodectomy as a young child is cited in Robert Spencer and Phyllis Chesler's virulent pamphlet, "The Violent Oppression of Women in Islam," and David Horowitz's video based on this pamphlet is narrated by Nonie Darwish.[37] Both the pamphlet and the video argue that "the war we're fighting isn't just about bombs and hijacked airliners. It's also about the oppression of women—often in horrific ways. Nor is this oppression an incidental byproduct of terrorism. The Islamic law—Sharia—that terrorists are fighting to impose upon the world mandates institutionalized discrimination against women." These native informants use their own stories to authenticate the larger narrative produced by the right about the inherent evil of Islam and the need to defeat it in the War on Terror. Mohja Kahf writes that there are two kinds of stories about Muslim women that circulate and sell in the United States: a victim story or an escapee story.[38] Muslim women are portrayed as victims of a brutal religion or as having successfully escaped it. If a story does not fit one or both of these two molds, then it is unlikely to attract attention. While the often nameless, and seemingly endless, stream of oppressed women in news accounts occupy the former category, this much smaller but equally powerful group of native informants promote the narrative of the escapee. The U.S. media uses them to demonstrate that Muslim women's voices are indeed included in the presumed post-race era. However, beneath this seemingly enlightened perspective, their voices are often used to advance a particular framing of Islam that promotes Western imperialism.

On a guest appearance on CNN's *Anderson Cooper 360*, Hirsi Ali commented on a case in which a woman in Saudi Arabia was raped and punished with two hundred lashes. In response to a question about what life is like for women in Saudi Arabia, she said:

> For all women, the reality is stay in the house unless you have a pressing need to go outside. If you have a pressing need to go out you must wear the veil. If you marry, your husband can say three times, "I divorce you," and you are divorced. The other way around is not possible. The problem of child brides in Saudi Arabia is as common as drinking espresso coffee in Italy. It is because the Prophet Muhammad married a nine-year-old girl, every man in Saudi Arabia feels that he can marry a minor or he can marry off his daughter who is underage. You will be stoned, flogged if you commit or give the impression that you may have committed adultery. It is not nice being a woman in Saudi Arabia.[39]

Hirsi Ali reinscribes the mantra on Islam, solidifying the association of Islam with violence and oppression. Her insider status authenticates this narrative.

Cooper replies that he has been told that Islam means "peace" and asks her to comment on that.

> Well it depends on how you define peace. If you define peace as flogging a victim of rape with two hundred stripes because she was in the wrong place at the wrong time, then maybe that is peace. But that is not how we in the West or anyone who believes in the universal declaration of human rights believes to be peace. . . . In the West when we say peace, we mean something totally different from developing a bomb to eradicate Israel, or from flogging a poor young woman, a nineteen-year-old, with two hundred lashes of the whip.[40]

Hirsi Ali draws a clear distinction between East and West, claiming that in the East "peace" translates into a litany of unjust acts. Criticism of Israel (as I explore in chapter 4) becomes coded as one of many elements, along with oppressed women, that situate Islam as backward and terroristic. Moustafa Bayoumi writes that these Muslim women commentators are modern-day neo-Orientalists who narrate stories about Islam for Western consumption. The stories they tell are about Islam as a system of tyranny that defeats human liberty and the subsequent need to either renounce or drastically reform Islam to be more like Christianity, Judaism, or even atheism.[41] These female native informants are a version of the "good Muslim" who confirms to Western viewers that Islam poses a threat to women and to the West. Sunaina Maira writes, "By definition, 'good' Muslims are public Muslims who can offer first-person testimonials, in the mode of the native informant, about the oppression of women in Islam, . . . and the hatred, racism, and anti-Semitism of Arabs and Muslims. These Muslim spokespersons are the darlings of the Right-wing and mainstream media, publish widely distributed books, and have slick websites."[42] While there are male Muslim spokespersons, it is the women specifically who authenticate a Western co-opted feminist narrative about Islam. These female spokespersons are often regarded and praised by the news media as "moderate Muslims" while promoting racism and Orientalism through an authoritative voice as Muslim women who have escaped oppression.[43]

The inclusion of Muslim women as news commentators gives the impression that the news media is inclusive, multicultural, and not seeking to malign Islam. These native informants authenticate the Western mantra on Islam, and in doing so they also become symbols of Western feminism. They become feminist advocates by denouncing Islam and promoting Western values. Simplified complex representations provoke readers' and viewers' outrage at the oppressed Muslim woman, under the guise of disclaimers about the complexity of Islam, and through the inclusion of native informants. News stories on the oppressed Muslim woman shock and appall American readers: The brutality! The injustice! The ideal reader experiences outrage at the injustice, sympathy for the oppressed victimized women, and a desire for those responsible to be punished. Constructing emotive publics is central to gaining public support for the War on Terror.

Stories of the oppressed Muslim woman multiplied after 9/11. Jasmin Zine has written:

> As deplorable as the conditions faced by Afghan women were under the formerly US-backed Taliban regime, the fact that their plight became strategically positioned as being "prime-time worthy" only during the violent campaigns of the war on terror, reinforces their role as a political guise activated to engender sympathy for the military campaign as an act of "liberating" oppressed Muslim women from fanatical Muslim men. Through this process Afghan women's plights were reduced to a war against fundamentalism, erasing other important factors affecting their lives such as poverty, internal displacement and lack of healthcare and ability to meet even the most basic of needs, which the military campaigns were exacerbating.[44]

Although stories of oppressed Muslim women circulated in the U.S. commercial news media in the years before 9/11, they became part of the standard news cycle after 9/11. This repeated narrative and association with the War on Terror has coded Islam with a series of associations that include female genital mutilation, honor killings, public stoning, veiled oppression, unequal marriage and divorce rights. This mantra is produced through simplified complex representations—through providing disclaimers that signal sensitivity for diversity while adding fuel to the fire that is the War on Terror.

Saving Amina Lawal

On March 22, 2002, a Shari'a court in northern Nigeria sentenced Amina Lawal to death by stoning for having sex and a child out of wedlock. The father of the child did not face similar criminal charges because of a lack of evidence. The child served as evidence of Lawal's crime. The case drew international attention and outrage and became headline news in the United States; the oppressed Muslim woman so often referred to in the news since 9/11 finally had a name and a face.[45] The liberal organizations Feminist Majority Foundation and National Organization for Women protested at the Nigerian embassy to demand that the Nigerian government reverse the decision to stone Lawal.[46] A broad spectrum of organizations—liberal and conservative alike—urged letter-writing campaigns to the Nigerian government and donations to feminist organizations that help Muslim women around the world. *Ms. Magazine*'s website contained a link on how to take action: "Prevent Stoning Sentence Against Nigerian Woman Amina Lawal Kurami."[47]

The Nigerian government stated that the death sentence was not the decision of the Nigerian government but of the Shari'a court in the state of Katsina, and if appealed numerous times, it could make its way to the Supreme Court. The case did not make it to the Supreme Court. However, Lawal's lawyers appealed, and on September 25, 2003, the Shari'a Court of Appeals overturned the decision based on some technicalities in the application of Shari'a law. Lawal's confession was deemed invalid because it was not repeated four times, as required; one judge presided over the first trial instead of the required three; and Lawal was pregnant before Shari'a law was instituted in Katsina.[48] Amina Lawal was acquitted and went on to remarry.

On October 4, 2002, before the case was overturned, the *Oprah Winfrey Show* devoted an entire episode to Amina Lawal's case. "Can We Save Amina Lawal?"[49] is an emotive tour de force, an example of what Luc Boltanski terms "the politics of pity." Defined as "the ways in which television uses images and language so as to render the spectacle of suffering not only comprehensible but also ethically acceptable for the spectator," I argue that the politics of pity are crucial to news reporting on the oppressed Muslim woman.[50] Each society at a given historical moment delineates appropriate and inappropriate emotional responses that are constructed as natural or self-evident; emotions are cultural practices that contribute to giving various social formations their meanings and power.[51] Boltanski argues that television turns the suffering of others into a spectacle and in turn creates a relationship between the viewer and the distant sufferer. Pity is central to the process whereby sufferers are constituted "to engage spectators in multiple forms of emotion and disposition to action."[52] This spectacle is constructed as comprehensible and ethically acceptable for the spectator.[53] Pity is an important emotion in establishing the relationship between the viewer and distant sufferer and can inspire political action.

Winfrey, with her trademark penchant for pathos, constructs Lawal's case as a spectacle of suffering. In the opening segment, she frames her story:

> Why has 31-year-old Amina been sentenced to die this way? Because she did what millions of women in this country have done. She had a baby out of wedlock. And why should Amina matter to you? She's a human being, a mother, and this is how it starts. One woman, then many women, and before you know it, it's a way of life. It is barbaric, and all of us who consider ourselves civilized should not allow it to happen.
>
> Nigeria, where Amina lives, has not previously condoned stoning. It is a new development there. And as we know, it's not the only place where this is happening. Stonings take place in other Muslim countries like Sudan and Pakistan and Saudi Arabia. What you're seeing now is rare videotape of a stoning that was smuggled out of Iran. We cannot stand by and knowingly let Amina Lawal be stoned to death like this.
>
> Today we're going to tell you what you can do to help save this woman's life, Amina. It was no easy task to sit down and talk with her. She's soft-spoken, frightened. She has caused an international outcry.

Winfrey makes a case for caring about Lawal by establishing similarity and difference. Lawal has done what millions of American women have done; the difference is that she lives in a barbaric Muslim country. Winfrey appeals to viewers based on a sense of shared humanity, which only amplifies the outrage that we as viewers are supposed to feel. Winfrey then shows a harrowing clip of an unidentified woman in Iran being stoned. As always, she is skillful at connecting to her viewers on an emotive level. Winfrey compares and contrasts the contexts of Muslim women and American women as if they are supposed to be the same; the fact that they are so different produces outrage.

In addition to expressing emotions of outrage and compassion, delineating a dichotomy between civilization and barbarism, and encouraging her viewers to take action to prevent Lawal from being stoned to death, Winfrey portrays Lawal as the ultimate victim.

> **OPRAH WINFREY:** Amina Lawal does not have a clue about what is going on. She is uneducated and from a small village. . . . According to Hawa Ibrahim, an attorney now working on the case, Amina didn't stand a chance in court that day.
>
> **MS. HAWA IBRAHIM:** Amina cannot read. Amina cannot write. Amina is from a very small, tiny, little village. To me, she has been taken advantage of.
>
> **WINFREY:** Amina was forced to marry when she was just a child. After leaving her second husband, she became pregnant while in a relationship with a local man. She says he promised to take care of her and the new baby.

MS. LAWAL [THROUGH TRANSLATOR]: I have already cried out to Allah that even if justice does not take place here, Allah will be my judge.

The portrait of the victim is formed by describing Lawal as illiterate, from a small village, and not having "a clue about what is going on." By saying that Allah will be her judge, Lawal implies that she is resigned to the sentence and relies on her faith rather than questioning—as Winfrey so adamantly does— the injustice that has been done to her. Lawal's victimization is framed as requiring that she be saved and avenged for the injustice, the implicit assumption being that she needs to be saved by the West. What is oddly absent in this story of victimization—even while speaking to Lawal's lawyer, Ibrahim—is that even if Lawal is the ultimate victim, her lawyer is an accomplished Nigerian Muslim woman who would later succeed in representing her client and in overturning her death sentence. What is also absent is the outrage that Muslims expressed in relation to her story. Lawal received support from her own community, but such support goes unmentioned as it would suggest that Lawal does not need to be saved by the West.

Winfrey invites Professor Akbar Ahmed to serve as the scholarly voice on the topic. She asks him whether or not stoning is an Islamic practice; his voice operates like the journalistic disclaimers do, acknowledging that brutality is not unique to Islam while providing no visual or emotive evidence to corroborate this point.

WINFREY: Does the Koran say that you should be sentenced by stoning?

MR. AKBAR AHMED (AMERICAN UNIVERSITY): The Koran—it's very important, it's a very important question, Oprah, because the Koran, remember, is part of the Abrahamic tradition, which is the Judeo-Christian tradition, where punishments on the surface are very harsh. At the same time, remember they're reflecting a patriarchal society, a tribal society . . . Jesus pointed out that the first person to pick up a stone, to start stoning that woman, should be the one without sin. The prophet in Islam is the mercy to all mankind. This is the title he's given. So you have harsh punishments and you have the notion of compassion. What we are not seeing in the case of Amina and other cases like this is compassion.

Ahmed states that all Abrahamic faiths have harsh punishments but also encourage compassion. He attempts to establish that Islam has similarities to Christianity and Judaism and that this stoning sentence reflects a patriarchal interpretation of Islam. However, because there is no visual or emotive evidence to substantiate his claim, his comments become lost in a sea of emotive and visual evidence regarding the oppressive nature of Islam.

Like the news stories discussed earlier, story after story in this episode associates inhumane practices with Islam. Winfrey features the story of several other Muslim women who have been brutalized. In one example, a Pakistani woman, Ms. Sarfraz-Khan, appears as a guest and recounts a story about how she was educated in the United States and returned to Pakistan to get married. She was happily married to Fazal when one day a villager asked her husband to help him find his daughter who had run away trying to escape an arranged marriage. When Fazal found the runaway, her family arrived at the house with axes, planning to kill her for shaming the family. Fazal objected and said, "I didn't bring her back so you can slaughter her at my doorstep." He was struck by an ax and killed. Fazal's objection to killing the runaway is framed as exceptional in Pakistani culture and made possible only because he learned compassion while living in the United States.

> **WINFREY:** So what your husband did was not typical.
>
> **MS. SARFRAZ-KHAN:** No, it wasn't, especially from—coming from the tribal, feudal background. . . . This was Fazal's upbringing here in the US, where he learned his compassion, where he learned that you don't stand aside and watch a 15-year-old get slaughtered.

Winfrey's guests associate compassion with the West and a lack of compassion and barbaric practices with the East. Compassion is defined as a Western emotion that can be taught to Eastern peoples. Like the Muslim women discussed earlier who renounce their culture, Winfrey's guests function as native informants, reiterating the same narrow framing of Muslim women as either victims of or escapees from an oppressive religion and culture, the same narrow frame that is circulated and consumed ad nauseum.

Wendy Brown argues that in contemporary civilizational discourse, the liberal individual is uniquely identified with the capacity for tolerance and tolerance itself is identified with civilization. Tolerance becomes intertwined with civilization and intolerance with barbarism.[54]

> Nonliberal societies and practices, especially those designated as fundamentalist, are depicted not only as relentlessly and inherently intolerant but as potentially intolerable for their putative rule by culture or religion and their concomitant devaluation of the autonomous individual—in short, their thwarting of individual autonomy with religious or cultural commandments. Out of this equation, liberalism emerges as the only political rationality that can produce the individual, societal, and governmental practice of tolerance, and, at the same time, liberal societies become the broker of what is tolerable and intolerable.[55]

Tolerance here is invoked as a key value of liberal Western culture. Yet, paradoxically, maintaining a tolerant culture requires violence in order to root out intolerance. The parallel here is that Western individuals are identified as uniquely capable of compassion. As a result, compassion is invoked to root out those in whom it is absent. The news media's focus on oppressed Muslim women produces an excess of affect, an outpouring of outrage and pity that defines the United States and its citizens as uniquely compassionate. This compassion is a central component in post-9/11 representations of Arabs and Muslims and aids in producing the co-opted forms not only of feminism but also of multiculturalism.

Winfrey concludes her show with a powerful statement: "I continue to say if you're a woman born in America, you are one of the luckiest women in the world." This statement gives viewers, once again, the impression that violence against women is something that happens only beyond America's borders. Moral outrage, manifested in stories about the oppressed Muslim woman, reaffirms the myth of gender equality in the West and renews viewers' appreciation of the existing sexual, racial, and national imperial order in the United States.[56] Viewers are encouraged to feel assured that they are part of a collective of do-gooders battling a collective of dictators, oppressors, and barbarians—that they will help to bring justice around the globe. Winfrey herself embodies the possibilities of a postracial and postfeminist United States. Her identity as an extraordinarily successful (and extraordinarily wealthy) black woman symbolizes that the United States has overcome a history of racism and sexism. She now speaks as a privileged First World subject.

At the core of Winfrey's show is a call to action, a challenge that her viewers do something to prevent the death of Lawal:

> Right. Well, you can help save Amina Lawal from death by stoning by logging on to oprah.com. We have joined forces with Amnesty International. And we are urging—I am urging you personally to join our e-mail campaign. It takes just a few minutes, and it doesn't cost you anything. Amnesty International says this is the most effective way that we can put a stop to this stoning of Amina from being carried out. Over a million e-mails have already been delivered, and what I'm hoping from this show today, that we can send at least a million more. Two million people cannot be ignored. And five million would be even more powerful. So if you log on to oprah.com, all of these e-mails are going to be sent to the Nigerian ambassador here. And hopefully we'll make a difference in one woman's life.

Boltanski states that one common way in which viewers react to distant suffering witnessed on television is by following Winfrey's example and taking action; in the process, we become moral or political actors. Winfrey delineates three simple ways to help: donate money, sign petitions, and write letters to the Nigerian government. Winfrey's guest, Ms. Salbi, runs an organization that helps oppressed women. Salbi says that it only takes $25 to $100 per month to help a woman learn how to read and write and learn about her legal rights. Solving the world's problems, it seems, can be distilled into simple, feasible steps. We can help somebody on the other side of the world with a click of the mouse, a swipe of the credit card.

The politics of pity relies on this distance between the viewer and the viewed and the moral obligation that emerges from the sentiment of pity. Outrage can inspire action. Amina Lawal's story inspired over a million people to not simply turn off the television but to do something, to become invested, to take a moral or political stance, and to act. Boltanski states that in order for speech to transform a person into a political and moral actor, it must fuse an account of the suffering witnessed with a sense of how one felt while witnessing the suffering. When faced with the suffering of women in Afghanistan or Nigeria, a situation in which direct action is difficult, the spectator can maintain integrity by speaking to others about the outrage they experience when witnessing the oppression of women. Emotional or concerned speech turns the spectator into a moral and political actor.[57] Many viewers became moral and political actors after watching this episode of the *Oprah Winfrey Show* by taking action through emotive speech. Chain e-mail letters circulated urging recipients to visit the show's website to take action.

Winfrey's viewers and their contacts sent an estimated 1.2 million e-mails to the Nigerian government. In addition, thousands of viewers posted on Internet message boards. The *Dr. Phil Show* (produced by Oprah Winfrey's Harpo Productions) hosted a message board, "Can We Save Amina Lawal's Life?" for viewers to post their responses to the show.[58] The posts began immediately after the show was aired and continued for a year, until the sentence was overturned. Hundreds of viewers posted messages on a variety of themes, expressing outrage and encouraging action, debating the extent to which stoning is an Islamic practice, debating the extent to which adultery is a crime that should be punished by law, and debating whether the United States is a beacon of compassion and justice or a hypocrite for intervening in the laws of other countries. Some posters expressed outrage at Lawal's sentence and the lack of any punishment for the child's father. Other posters gave tips on additional ways to help, including signing other petitions sponsored by Amnesty International, and how to support Lawal in obtaining refugee status in the Netherlands or the United States. Some Muslim women testified to the oppression they faced in their own lives at the hands of brutal men; other Muslim women responded that that they are sick and tired of Islam being characterized as an oppressive religion.

Many posters to the online forum expressed gratitude to Winfrey for creating an outlet for activism and "bringing this outrage to the public."[59] Others encouraged prayer, letter writing, or fund-raising to help Lawal. Some announced the actions they had taken—"I cancelled my $25 a month tanning membership in order to sponsor a woman and hopefully change a life!" One poster stated that letter writing is useless and that the only way to save Lawal is by paying mercenaries to go into Nigeria and rescue her. He reasons, "This kinda of stuff happens all the time in 3rd world countries. The other famous one a few months ago occurred in a small village in Pakistan. A girl was caught sleeping with some guy from a 'royal' family—so the penalty was to have her gang raped by 12 men throughout a 24 period. Then of course is the common practice of genitilia burning for women so they aren't tempted to stray from their husbands in many middle eastern countries."[60]

The value of this message board emerges in the lively debates that the Lawal episode incited and that are inflamed by the anonymous nature of these postings. Here, I will briefly explore a sampling of posts on three of the most common arguments that emerged after the show—the barbarity of Islam, Lawal's victimhood, and the image of the United States. These exchanges hint at the competing moral frameworks involved and the tension between a reductive perspective, offered by the *Oprah Winfrey Show* and the commercial news media, and the challenge to that monolithic portrayal of Islam. Here is one exchange:

> christian views
>
> Posted by: *sbzlady*
>
> Posted on: 2002–10–09 18:34:23
>
> We have become a more humane people, we are in the United States, we have freedoms that the Muslim countries do not have. You say this should not be about religious views but this is exactly what it is. These horrible actions against women are in the name of the Muslim religion and Allah. Mohammed told them in the Quran that this is how they are to treat women. The Quran spells out that women are not worth much, that basically they are slaves to be used for sex. Get a hold of a book called titled 'Women in Islam' and you will realize this is a religious issue, at least for a Muslim.
>
> sbzlady—you just took wrong to a new level.
>
> Posted by: *real_talk*
>
> Posted on: 2002–10–31 02:23:41
>
> I don't know where you got your knowledge of the Koran, but you are way off base when it comes to women in the Koran. The book you mentioned . . . Women in Islam, that story came from a Saudi princess. You shouldn't believe everything you read . . . even Bio type books. It is true that certain countries go to extremes, but it is in NO WAY written that women be abused and used for just sex.
>
> There are religious crazies in ALL religions. Have you ever read a Koran?
>
> No one deserves to be mistreated or tortured in the name of ANY religion or politics. There are good and bad in all nations, religions, countries, cultures. It's up to us to educate ourselves on how to make sure the crazies are stopped . . . in ANY religion!

"Sbzlady" and "real talk" express outrage but disagree on its location: "sbzlady" is outraged by the brutality of Islam; "real talk" is outraged by "sbzlady's" outrage and sees her as gullible and uneducated.

Another common debate on the *Dr. Phil* message board was about Winfrey's portrayal of Islam.

> Its not just about Amina
>
> Posted by: *tahnya*
>
> Posted on: 2002–10–05 12:29:55
>
> Why did she not bring Christian horror stories or Jewish or Hindu, or why do we even have to state the religions of people, if you are trying only to reveal the people themselves and their pain. No religion preaches hate or injustice, yet many 'people' do, so shouldnt we keep the religion out of it and address all issues on a level of humanity and not religion. Shows like this may be preaching sympathy for victims but they are also breeding contempt for muslims. That is unacceptable.

> unbelievable
>
> Posted by: *all2gethor*
>
> Posted on: 2002–10–07 13:15:03
>
> I am shoked at the things that ppl are posting. I am a muslim woman and i have family who live in these types of countries, and non of them have ever faced these types of problem. Why do people always make Islam to be a bad religion, IT'S NOT. Howcome you never put on your show all these American fathers, uncles, grandfather etc, who rape their own sisters and daughters and wives. Yet you dwel on Muslim men instead . . . what about the mothers who beat their children to death and who throw them of the bridge in their cars . . . those people are never questioned, and if they are, they are only focused on for a day or two. I am not heartless, I do feel for those woman, whether they are Muslim, Christians, Jewish or anyother religion. However, since 9/11, the focus of the world has been on Muslims . . . Bush says that we are terrorist, but when he went into Afghanistan and killed thousands of innocent people, what does that make him? How come that is not an issue?

These posters criticize the monolithic indictment of Islam and the absence of a comparison with violence against women in the United States. "All2gethor" uses her own testimony as a Muslim woman to challenge stereotypes. She also charges the U.S. government's framing of terrorism as hypocritical. The difficulty in such challenging is highlighted in all2gethor's statement, "I am not heartless, I do feel for those woman." Her clarification here points to how any effort to broaden the context of this discussion, and move the focus away from an excess of affect for the oppressed Muslim woman, can automatically position one as unfeeling or as an apologist for brutality. She insists that her effort to advance a competing moral framework does not make her unfeeling.

Some posters express concern and outrage over how Lawal is being victimized and others question the extent to which Lawal is the ultimate victim as depicted on the *Winfrey Show*. Some posters claim that Lawal should not be perceived as a victim given that she knowingly broke the law in Katsina, Nigeria.

punishment

Posted by: *ccosmo*

Posted on: 2002–10–07 12:14:14

And why should either be punished for bringing a beautiful baby into this world . . . maybe that is the punishment for the baby . . . to be born into a world with such hate and crime . . . and unhumanity!

RE: punishment

Posted by: *fb6700*

Posted on: 2002–10–25 11:13:04

No one is being "punished for bringing a beautiful baby into this world." The mother is being (and the father OUGHT TO BE) punished for sexual immorality. Such immoral behavior does not even raise an eyebrow in our "enlightened" American society; and we'd love to force our (im-)morality on other sovereign nations as well. We decry the fact that this woman's children will be motherless as a result of this harsh punishment, but are we correct to blame the law rather than the violator of that law? Was she unaware that she could be executed for committing this crime? Would she not resist her selfish urges in order to see that her children were not left without a mother? Did she not love her kids enough to value them above a night's pleasure? There are always innocent victims when adultery is committed. Don't the guilty parties (and especially in this case, the woman with a family!) deserve any blame and punishment?? Here in America many people consider it an atrocity to execute someone for brutal rape, sodomy, cannibalism and murder. Not all cultures are as backward as ours. Some still recognize the necessity of appealing to a standard higher than human opinion, and reject the ignorance and foolish notions of humanism. If this woman was raped, let her accuse the rapist and let him be stoned to death. If she willingly engaged in the adultery, let the man be sought out and proved to be the father of this illegitimate child, and let him be stoned next to this adulteress. This is not a case of Nigeria engaging in genocide or war crimes. Let that nation enact its own criminal laws. And once enacted, let's respect their enforcement of such laws.

Amina Lawal

Posted by: *sea1982*

Posted on: 2002–09–29 19:43:17

I think it is terrible that this woman is going to be publically stoned. To think that such a barbaric act still exists in our world is astonishing and makes me sick to the stomach. My heart goes out to her and her children who will more than likely be orphaned. As much sympathy that I have for Amina, I can't help but blame her for her fate; if sex out of wedlock is such a no-no in her country, she should have known NOT to commit adultery. In the end, it really is her fault.

Two of these three posters question and reject Winfrey's portrayal of Lawal as the ultimate victim. They take moral stances on the case: Amina Lawal broke the stated laws in her country and must face the penalty. "Fb6700" challenges the moral framework offered by Winfrey even further by stating that adultery is a crime and should be punished. Similarly, "sea1982" openly blames Lawal for "her fate." These judgments, however harsh, are interesting in how they push against the common oppressed Muslim woman portrayal and toward an ideology of individual responsibility.

Finally, other posters reaffirmed or questioned how the *Oprah Winfrey Show* frames the United States as a beacon of compassion and justice. Some posters claimed that the United States is hypocritical for intervening in the laws of other countries and declaring them barbaric while still upholding the death penalty as legal in this country.

We Americans Can Intervene!
Posted by: *grw5459*
Posted on: 2002–09–30 13:03:03

This is a great opportunity as Americans to show the world we care about people other than ourselves!

We say "God Bless America", but God has blessed us! Let's share our blessings with others across the globe!

American Death Penalty
Posted by: *cncgandolf*
Posted on: 2002–10–22 18:03:32

Some states in the United States have the death penalty. Within those states acts have been identified with the consequence of doing those acts being the death penalty. The people who do the acts know the consequences they are risking. If another country refuses to send a killer back to the US because they don't have and don't support the death penalty, many Americans get very upset that they are imposing their anti-death penalty views on the people of the state attempting to try the killer. Is everyone in support of Amina also in support of other countries refusing to return people to the U.S. when our laws call for the death penalty for them? France doesn't have the right to tell the U.S. we can't have the death penalty . . . how do we have the right to tell another country they don't have the right?

Try respecting the laws of other countries maybe??

Posted by: *joeldg*

Posted on: 2002–10–23 11:44:18

    A friend forwarded me this absurd message about how the Oprah show was trying to save the life a criminal in another country. When you live in a country you generally know the laws and punishments of where you live. If you choose to break the law you in return choose the punishment. I thought this was a fundamental rule of living a society. Now, I understand that we don't stone people to death in this country, but we still electrocute people and inject them with poison often enough and don't have people in other countries send us letters asking us not to. This "world police" thing needs to end and I think that Oprah is just perpetuating it by praying on her audience who are mostly protected housewives in America with no idea about how the rest of the world works.

While some posters expressed support for U.S. intervention in the name of freedom, others expressed opposition not only to military intervention but also to moral intervention in other countries. Posters actively took moral stances by recounting the suffering they witnessed along with the outrage they experienced in the act of witnessing. This takes many forms, including expressing outrage at the media's stereotypical representation of Islam and outrage at U.S. intervention.

Outraged at Your Outrage

Both news reporting and TV dramas (and their perfect symbiosis, the *Oprah Winfrey Show*) operate as appendages of the War on Terror, by promoting acceptable emotional and intellectual responses to America's engagement with Muslims around the world. These myriad forms of representation—some fictional and others "real," some with clear ideological purpose and others unintentionally—shape the ways that we perceive our post-9/11 world. The government and commercial news media have defined a hierarchy of human lives in the War on Terror according to which certain people are deserving of spectators' emotions—especially sympathy and outrage—and actions whereas others are not. Who is worthy or unworthy of sympathy is not arbitrary; the boundaries of feeling are policed differently in the case of Muslim women and men. Government and media producers construct "regimes of pity" that determine whose suffering is dramatized and presented as worthy of a response.[61] Lillie Chouliaraki states that these regimes of pity suggest "that spectators do not possess 'pure' emotions vis-à-vis the sufferers, but their emotions are, in fact, shaped by the values embedded in news narratives about who the 'others' are and how we should relate to them."[62] The way we are encouraged to give and withhold support, in other words, and the way in which narratives and visuals of oppression are produced, is political.[63]

To restate the obvious: in the wake of 9/11, news reporting on oppressed Muslim women produced moral outrage. By "moral outrage," I mean the feeling of disgust that is often provoked by stories about the violent oppression of Muslim women. Readers and viewers are encouraged to feel outrage at the injustice and compassion for the women and to advocate correcting the injustice by saving these women and punishing the Muslim men who are presumably responsible. The *Oprah Winfrey Show* and media coverage on the oppressed Muslim woman both help to create an emotive public, that is, a segment of the public sharing in an emotion—outrage, pity, and so on—and the normalization of this sentiment in relation to Muslim women.[64] The emotive public created by the *Oprah Winfrey Show* shares feelings of outrage at the Amina Lawal case. But another emotive public—an oppositional one—is also created, reflected in how the outrage is fractured, sometimes directed not at the Lawal case but at those who represent the Lawal case or who respond to the Lawal case without questioning how it is represented.

Some posters became political and moral actors by means of relaying the suffering they have witnessed on television and the outrage they experienced while witnessing this distant suffering. Those who respond in the way intended by the show not only become political actors, they also become agents in the co-optation of feminism and the promotion of post-race racism. They express concern for oppressed women, but this supposed concern then becomes the root of an argument for intervention and war. They express concern for Muslim women, especially their treatment in the grip of brutal Islam, but then use that concern to support racist policies and practices against Muslims as a whole. This configuration of feeling is central to post-9/11 representations of Arabs and Muslims; the politics of pity makes it possible to deny or minimize racism directed at Arabs and Muslims during the War on Terror and also absolves the United States from its role in aiding numerous wars, the rise of fundamentalism, and the hardening of oppressive conditions for women.

Other segments of the public, however, refuse to participate in the emotive publics shaped by the media and the government. These people create an oppositional emotive public that expresses alternative emotional responses; these men and women are often "outraged at your outrage." These viewers of distant suffering question and criticize how the suffering is made meaningful to viewers. Reflecting an oppositional interpellation, these viewers express outrage at the assumptions embedded in this narrative—in the case of the *Oprah* episode, that Islam is barbaric, that Lawal is the ultimate victim, and that the United States as a compassionate and civilized nation must save her.[65] These posters also express outrage at those posters who express the outrage expected from the show's framing of the Lawal case. Some posters challenge the dominant framing of the oppressed Muslim woman through competing moral frameworks that challenge the notion that the United States is postfeminist by highlighting hypocrisy and through alternative testimonies by native informants. The politics of pity, therefore, has the unintentional side effect of inspiring viewer contestation and an insistence on alternative moral frameworks. These fractured responses demonstrate a challenge to the ways in which government and media discourses determine appropriate and inappropriate feelings in the War on Terror.

Outrage is an emotion that carries vast political potential. If we are outraged at the treatment of the oppressed Muslim woman, we are far more likely to support U.S. interventions in Muslim countries in the name of saving the women. The U.S. media participates in encouraging a particular form of outrage—outrage at the oppressive nature of Islam—while other forms of outrage are intentionally left absent, namely, that the United States has played a significant role in creating Islamic fundamentalism and current conflicts including 9/11 and the War on Terror. As Judith Butler has written:

> Open grieving is bound up with outrage, and outrage in the face of injustice or indeed of unbearable loss has enormous political potential. . . . Whether we are speaking about open grief or outrage, we are talking about affective responses that are highly regulated by regimes of power and sometimes subject to explicit censorship.[66]

The U.S. government and commercial media's selective framing of the War on Terror seeks to restrict outrage to narratives that absolve the United States from accountability and support its interventionist projects. This highly mediated evocation of outrage for the plight of the oppressed Muslim woman inspires support of U.S. interventions against Muslim men and barbaric Islam. War has been and continues to be made possible in part by the media's eager cultivation of pity and outrage.

4 Regulating Sympathy for the Muslim Man

We learned a good lesson on September 11: that there is evil in this world. And it is my duty as the president of the United States to use the resources of this great nation, a freedom-loving nation, a compassionate nation, a nation that understands values of life and rout terrorism out where it exists. . . . The evil ones have sparked an interesting change in America, I think. A compassion in our country that is overflowing. I know their intended act was to destroy us and make us cowards and make us not want to respond. But quite the opposite has happened. Our nation is united. We are strong. We're compassionate.
—President George W. Bush, The President's Remarks on the War on Terrorism

If we really want to stop terrorism, we have to get Muslim men laid. . . . We should hire women to infiltrate Al Qaeda cells and fuck them. Things would change quickly because young Muslim men don't really hate America. They're jealous of America. We have rap videos and the Hilton sisters and magazines with titles like *Barely Legal*. You know what's "barely legal" in Afghanistan? Everything! . . . But the connection between no sex and anger is real. It's why prizefighters stay celibate when they're in training, so that on fight night, they're pissed off and ready to kill. It's why football players don't have sex after Wednesday. And conversely, it's why Bill Clinton never started a war. . . . Forget the Peace Corps. We need a "Piece of Ass Corps"! Girls, there's a cure to terrorism, and you're sitting on it!
—Bill Maher, *Real Time with Bill Maher*

After 9/11 there were many attempts by government officials, journalists, scholars, bloggers, and citizens to explain why the terrorist attacks happened. The explanations ranged from the one offered by President Bush that there is evil in the world that must be fought by the good and compassionate United States to the one offered by TV show host Bill Maher that Muslim men simply need to "get laid." Bush's explanation relies on the notion that terrorism is an epic struggle between good and evil and that the terrorists hate us for our freedom. Maher's explanation for terrorism is a variation on that theme. As opposed to being jealous of our freedom of religion and the right to speak freely, vote, and assemble (as President Bush explained in other speeches), his explanation assumes that Muslim men (as a whole) are sex-deprived and therefore susceptible to anger, which begets terrorism. Although intended for comic effect, Maher's comment has a surprising resonance because he was not the only one to express such an idea. A professor of history wrote in the *Washington Post* shortly after 9/11 that "a kind of religion motivates the Taliban, but the religion in question, I'd say, is not Islam [but] insecure masculinity. These men are terrified of women." In other words, terrorism is not a political problem but a sexual one. Thus one possible solution to terrorism is war and murder; another solution is to encourage sexual liberation in Muslim countries. These popular explanations, not surprisingly, bypass the far more complex possibility of a root cause (or causes) for terrorism and the far more demanding possibility that the rest of the world could address the cause(s) by instituting economic, social, or foreign policy measures.

Such simplifications are not limited to describing actual people but extend to framing their actions. During the War on Terror, the government and media have used the term *terrorism* as a catchall for the endlessly complex realm of political violence; such terminology has in turn shaped the public discourse in at least three key ways. First, it tends to conflate all violence perpetrated by Arabs and Muslims as "terrorism" regardless of historical context or political grievance; such explanations are often depoliticized, dehistoricized, and decontextualized. The term *terrorism* has been used to describe an array of politically motivated violent acts, from anticolonial rebellion to Arab nationalists, from Palestinians' suicide bombings opposing Israeli occupation to the peaceful opposition of political Islamists to U.S. involvement in the Middle East.[2] The Bush administration, alongside Ariel Sharon's administration in Israel, has described Yasir Arafat and Osama bin Laden as terrorists without distinguishing between the actions and context of each. Such a conflation demonstrates "how easily the term can be abused to obscure the disparate histories of events that appear superficially similar."[3]

Second, the conflation of all Arab and Muslim violence under the rubric of terrorism masks terrorism perpetrated by people who are not Arab or Muslim. As Jasmine Zine has written, "the politics of representation in the 'war on terror' mask the fact that there are multiple and interlocking forms of 'terror' that need to be combated; the terror of neo-imperialism and global militarism, the terror of global corporate capitalism, the terror of poverty and starvation, the terror against the environment as bio-terrorism, racial terror, sexual terror, the terror of occupation and exile and the terror that is invoked in inscribing a Manichean world along racial and religious lines."[4] A central paradox operates in how violence is framed: violence is understood as bad; however, the violence of the United States is always framed as in the service of good. In other words, dominant discourses during the War on Terror position the United States as having the right to seek revenge for the violence experienced on 9/11, yet others do not have the right to seek revenge for violence they have experienced and in which the United States has played a role. The complexity of terror reveals how the U.S. government and media advance a restricted framing of terrorism.

Third, and most important for the current discussion, the reductive terminology (and the reductive discussions that follow) shapes our emotional response. Following the September 11 attacks, the government and media framed "terrorists" as not worthy of sympathy or understanding. Amy Kaplan states, "Often in our juridical system under the Patriot Act, the accusation of terrorism alone, without due process and proof, is enough to exclude persons from the category of humanity."[5] Exclusion from the category of humanity comes with a refusal to see from the point of view of the "terrorist" and therefore to investigate the root causes of political violence (and sometimes a refusal to even admit that such root causes might exist). This refusal provides the opportunity to advance dehistoricized and decontextualized explanations for terrorism and a portrayal of the United States as righteous, and even compassionate, in its efforts to destroy terrorism.

Sympathy, as discussed previously, is contested terrain. ABC canceled Bill Maher's talk show *Politically Incorrect* after Maher said that the terrorists who flew into the Twin Towers were not cowards, contrary to their typical depiction, since they were willing to lose their own lives. TV dramas, similarly, have been criticized by conservative critics for allowing viewers to see from the point of view of the terrorists and risk the possibility of garnering sympathy for their cause. Sympathy is regulated, not directly in the sense of government control, but indirectly by defining parameters around what should and should not be publicly spoken, heard, and felt. Crucial to this regulation is the notion—flawed but widely believed—that our emotions are "natural," that the way we respond to a situation is simply the way we feel and not subject to biases of one kind or another. However, emotions are at least partially constructed and shaped by media depictions.[6]

Chapters 1, 2, and 3 demonstrated how sympathy is an important representational device in our supposedly post-race era, because the emotion is central to depicting a group in a "positive" manner. Arabs and Muslims have been represented positively through the figures of the patriotic Arab American, the Arab American who is a victim of post-9/11 hate crimes, and the "oppressed Muslim woman." Despite an abundance of fictional characters (and of a character "type," in the case of journalistic accounts of the oppressed Muslim woman) who we are meant to feel sorry for, it is clear from government and media accounts that not all Arabs and Muslims are deserving of our sympathy. This chapter seeks to examine the parameters of sympathy. In chapter 3 I examined how the figure of the oppressed Muslim woman is narrated to solicit an excess of affect; here, as a counterpoint, I examine how the figure of the male Muslim terrorist is narrated with radically different framing parameters and how media discourses participate in regulating sympathy through particular explanations of how these men became involved in terrorism. Ultimately, the question I ask is, how is the regulation of sympathy inflected by race, religion, gender, and sexuality, and how does this regulation reinforce U.S. empire?

I investigate these complex issues first by examining news reports on the "root causes of terrorism" in order to delineate the ideological field of explanations harvested over the past decade. Second, I examine two case studies of figures who have made headlines during the War on Terror so as to assess the explanations offered for their involvement in terrorism: John Walker Lindh, the young white American from Marin County, California, better known as "the American Taliban" (note how the media seems compelled to give alleged criminals a dramatic name), and Jose Padilla, the Latino man from Chicago, better known as "the Dirty Bomber." Both made headlines within two years of September 11, 2001, and became a part of the War on Terror. Neither of them are Arab, and both were born in the United States. These cases emerged in the commercial news media as examples of non-Arab converts to Islam, as terrorists and alleged terrorists, and as examples of many (some would say endless) threats of radical Islam. I examine how the popular news media explains the trajectory into violence of non-Arabs who have converted to Islam (as opposed to examining the explanations for those who are Arab and/or Muslim) in order to explore the racialization of Islam during the War on Terror. Examining identities that are not implicated in the Arab/Muslim conflation from birth provides the opportunity to examine how Islam comes to be marked in the case of non-Arab/non–South Asian converts to Islam. Third, I examine iterations of the Lindh news story in one particular TV drama and the way that what he seems to represent has filtered into fiction.

As I discuss below, popular discourses can promote an absence of sympathy (versus an excess of sympathy in the case of the oppressed Muslim woman) by obscuring the "why" of the story so that political violence perpetrated by Arabs or Muslims is decontextualized and portrayed as senseless. As Barbie Zelizer and Stuart Allen have written, "Members of the public making their way through the September 11 coverage could learn much from what reporters told them about the 'who,' 'what,' 'where,' 'when,' and 'how' of the attacks. The matter of 'why,' however, remained elusive."[7] Obscuring the "why" is one of multiple ways the media regulates sympathy. What commonly stands in for the "why" is framing Islam as having a propensity for terrorism through a subcoding of race, gender, and sexuality.

My investigation into sympathy is not to suggest that the alleged terrorists examined in this chapter deserve this emotion. Their desire to kill civilians is abhorrent to me but no more or no less abhorrent than the killing of civilians by individuals and governments around the globe, and in our own backyards. Rather, I am seeking to highlight that the explanations offered for their involvement can lead to a narrow and inaccurate understanding of terrorism, one that benefits the endless aims of empire. Furthermore, the lack of sympathy extends to innocent Muslims, some of whom have been subject to torture and exempt from human rights.

Explaining Terrorism

In the weeks after 9/11 Prince Alwaleed bin Talal of Saudi Arabia wrote a check for $10 million to the city of New York to assist in disaster relief. When he stated that the U.S. government "should re-examine its policies in the Middle East and adopt a more balanced stand toward the Palestinian cause,"[8] Mayor Rudolph Giuliani refused the money, an act praised by many, including Thomas Friedman in the *New York Times*.[9] Examining the role of the United States in shaping the historical conditions that inspired the 9/11 terrorist attacks was off limits, and those who insisted on the need to examine U.S. foreign policies as a factor in the attacks were often met with hostility and accusations of justifying the attacks or sympathizing with the terrorists. Giuliani's refusal of $10 million epitomizes the ideological rigidity in post-9/11 thinking about terrorism. Since the terrorist attacks, multiple perspectives have indeed emerged across the United States on the possible causes of terrorism (including conspiracy theories accusing Jews and even George W. Bush of involvement). However, explanations that suggested any kind of U.S. accountability or involvement were criticized and marginalized.

Certainly some journalists were sincerely interested in exploring terrorism in its necessary complexity. In the years since 9/11, readers of the *New York Times*, for example, encountered a wide variety of scholarly opinions—poverty, lack of education, repressive regimes, human rights violations, social alienation, U.S. foreign policies—to explain what caused nineteen men to give their lives while taking the lives of approximately three thousand others.

In one such example, an opinion piece by the Pulitzer Prize–winning journalist Nicholas D. Kristof, the author searches through various explanations. Disagreeing with some of his colleagues, he argues that personal poverty has little to do with the causes of terrorism since bin Laden and other terrorists come from wealthy families: "Osama bin Laden's tricycle was probably gold-plated and we all know that the 9/11 hijackers came from privileged backgrounds. Look at ETA in Spain, Red Brigades in Italy, Aum Shinrikyo in Japan, the I.R.A. in Ireland or Timothy McVeigh: they suggest middle-class alienation rather than third-world deprivation." Instead, he cites three other factors as likely causes for terrorism:

> First, humiliation. "This word is extremely important in explaining why terrorists are so successful in recruiting large numbers of young men," said Jessica Stern, a Harvard scholar who has interviewed terrorists around the world. Indeed if we are to reduce terrorism in, say, the Middle East, then (as President Bush has suggested) it would help to reduce security arrangements that needlessly humiliate Palestinians.
>
> Second, economic isolation. Robert Lawrence, an economics professor, notes that the great majority of nations are members of the World Trade Organization, but that the few that are not include North Korea, Iran, Iraq, Syria, and Saudi Arabia. So trade promotion may help.
>
> Third, foreign policy. Anybody who has met Al Qaeda supporters know[s] that the terrorists are motivated in part by American foreign policy, principally the American military bases in Saudi Arabia and, to a lesser extent, Palestinian rights. But it's hard to make too much of the Israeli angle because Al Qaeda was planning the 9/11 attacks just as peace talks were proceeding unusually hopefully in 2000.[10]

Though Kristof seems to minimize the Israeli-Palestinian conflict in explaining U.S. foreign policy as a potential root cause for terrorism, he is wrestling with complex issues and bringing such issues to *New York Times* readers. This article suggests ways to reduce terrorism that stand in stark contrast to the Bush administration's measures, which focused on incarceration, militarism, and war.

Michael Elliot, in *Time* magazine, offers a corollary explanation that Islam acts as a refuge:

> But identifying terrorists is only half the job. The real challenge is to figure out why the Muslim community in Europe has become such a rich recruiting ground for Islamic extremists. Plainly, Islam exerts an appeal to those born into the faith who feel oppressed by societies that treat them like second-class relics of European colonialism. Islam also promises something to converts—like Reid and Courtailler—who feel marginalized by modern life.[11]

This line of investigation suggests that finding ways to reduce the marginalization and alienation of young men in postcolonial societies could reduce terrorism. While such articles do not provide a definitive explanation for terrorism, they do provide important opportunities for public debate.

Articles like these, however, that seek complex answers to a complex problem are outnumbered by articles that refute the notion that there are any root causes of terrorism worth considering. Quite a few journalists have challenged the notion that the causes for terrorism can be found in humiliation, the impact of U.S. foreign policies or European colonialism, and economic isolation. Instead, the cultural or civilizational argument is privileged. Claiming that there are no grievances worth considering, they contend that Islamic fundamentalism alone causes terrorism. Edward Rothstein, for example, writing for the *New York Times*, states, "It is remarkable how much agreement there is on the nature of these root causes. Many American intellectuals have cited American policy towards Israel, the poverty of Arab lands and inequalities and inequities reinforced by Western actions."[12] He characterizes these reasons as the "injustice theory" of terrorism and uses this classification to delegitimize possible root causes. Such "theories of injustice" assert that terrorism arises when people have a political grievance and have no recourse but violence. The grievance can be legitimate (i.e., one that many would agree on, such as the Israeli military occupation or apartheid in South Africa) or a "perceived injustice" (i.e., one that others might not agree constitutes an injustice, such as whether abortion constitutes murder).[13] Rothstein refutes this notion that terrorism is a result of a series of injustices, perceived or otherwise, experienced by those who carry out terrorist attacks; rather, he argues that the injustice theory is a double standard that is not applied equally across the board. To support his claim, he turns to the case of Timothy McVeigh: "No one suggested that his act had its 'root causes' in an injustice that needed to be rectified to prevent further terrorism. The injustice theory is apparently invoked only when one sympathizes with its conclusions." Contrary to Rothstein's claim, numerous news stories mentioned that McVeigh considered the U.S. government's massacre of members of the Branch Davidians at Waco, Texas, an injustice that he sought to avenge.[14] Such acknowledgment did not serve to justify McVeigh's actions but rather pointed to a root cause that for McVeigh was a perceived injustice.[15] More to the point, Rothstein's statement reveals the varied ways sympathy can be used—to promote the illusion of a post-race society or, in this case, to accuse liberals of supporting terrorism and to reframe the discussion around the need for military intervention. He accuses proponents of the injustice theory of sympathizing with the terrorists for considering the possibility that U.S. foreign policies could be a factor in the 9/11 terrorist attacks, suggesting that proponents of the injustice theory are trying to legitimize the identified grievance.

Rothstein goes on to say that terrorism and poverty are not interrelated and that the real cause for terrorism is religious fundamentalism: "The injustice theory, with its root causes, leaves no room for religious passion, irrational ambitions or cultural and tribal schisms. So it is unable to take into account the role played by fundamentalism. . . . Claims of 'root causes' are distractions from the real work at hand." It seems that, to Rothstein, anything that "distracts" from a militarized response is a waste of time.

Rothstein continues his argument in another article in the *New York Times*. Explaining how commentators have explained the root causes of Al Qaeda's violence, he states:

> In this view, terrorism is caused by social and economic injustice; it is an expression of political frustration and material desperation. The root cause argument invokes the grievance not to dismiss it, but to give it credence—and suggest unacknowledged guilt. But this notion, which has often been selectively applied to serve political purposes, fails to account for the lure of fundamentalist ideology or for the resentment of modernity that permeates Islamic terror. And poverty, the accumulating evidence suggests, far from causing terrorism, barely even correlates with it. So the empathetic invocations of "root causes"—a reflexive part of post-9/11 rhetoric—have become far more rare, particularly as it has become clear just what sorts of societies and values are championed by terrorism's practitioners.[16]

The search to understand why terrorism occurs and what would motivate someone to become involved in terrorist activity is reframed by Rothstein who though he offers various explanations bases them all in Islamic fundamentalism. Submerged in Rothstein's writings is a critique of the left for being too politically correct in their avoidance of maligning Muslims. He takes the position that Muslim societies are practicing indefensible values. According to Rothstein, legitimate explanations for terrorism include the notion that Muslim fundamentalism is a threat to the West; illegitimate explanations are those that explore in any depth the impact of U.S. foreign policies on human life, land, and resources in the Middle East. Interesting here is that Rothstein devotes nearly as much energy criticizing those people who seek root causes as he does attacking terrorists themselves. The consequences of such rhetoric are clear: in this line of conservative thinking, terrorists are often placed side by side with the liberals who seek to understand—that is, "defend"—them; both groups are a threat to the United States.

Rothstein's fundamentalism explanation for terrorism denies the complex convergence of factors that produce political violence. What makes this explanation so powerful is that it intersects with government discourses and the influential clash of civilizations theory that also explain terrorism through religious extremism and irreconcilable cultural difference.[17] While this article appears in the *New York Times* in the context of other points of view, the other points of view are not the ones most frequently echoed on TV and tabloid news—arguably the most important sources where most Americans get their news. The majority of journalism in America, in other words, doesn't even debate the importance of root causes; the majority of journalism pretends they don't exist.

The solution to terrorism, if understood as resulting from Muslim fundamentalism, is elimination of the terrorist through militarism, incarceration, and war, which has been the primary approach during the War on Terror. Advancing a series of possible root causes as an explanation for terrorism leads to very different, and far more difficult, solutions, which would require addressing the impact of U.S. foreign policies and which would likely diminish, rather than advance, U.S. power on a global scale.

Fundamentalism as the cause of terrorism has dominated discussion in the United States since 9/11. This rationale has set the terms of the debate and marginalizes the possibility of serious public discourse. The way in which Muslim fundamentalism is used to explain terrorism erases the complex political history that has led to authoritarian regimes and severe economic disparities. It also erases the ways in which Islamic militancy emerges from politics, not religion, even though it certainly converges with religion. Furthermore, it ignores the strong currents of secularism within Islam and suggests that the only path to democracy in Arab and Muslim countries is via secularism, as if democracy and Islam are incompatible.[18]

If such simplistic rhetoric had not achieved such a dominant position, then more Americans would discuss the ramifications of U.S. support for Israel against the Palestinians, or the polarizing role of U.S. military bases in Saudi Arabia, or the devastations caused by U.S. sanctions on Iraq between 1990 and 2003 (during which time between 170,000 and 1.5 million Iraqis, mostly children, died). Similarly absent from public debate is the U.S. role in the creation of Afghanistan's mujahedeen during the Cold War who were funded to fight a proxy war against the Soviet Union and whether mujahedeen (with American training and funding) fueled the rise of Al Qaeda. Such complexity, instead, seems distasteful to mainstream journalism. Such complexity requires too much explanation, especially for an audience raised on sound bites.[19] Rather the debate is over whether these stated grievances should be considered at all; the foundational premise, however, is more often than not just taken for granted: terrorism results from Muslim fundamentalism.

Journalists have used the life stories of particular individuals as another way to explain to the public why 9/11 happened, this time through the lens of biography.[20] John Walker Lindh and Jose Padilla became newsworthy for a variety of reasons. For one, they are not Arabs, raising the fascinating and deeply unsettling question for those who see Arab and American as irreconcilable identities of how Americans could fight for "the enemy." The ends of their stories (at least for our current narratives) are equally valuable: their capture and their failure to inflict harm became proof that the U.S. government is making the world a safer place. Below I compare two narratives that explain John Walker Lindh's trajectory toward violence: one in the commercial news media and one in a prime-time television drama. The stated objective of the majority of mainstream articles on Lindh, Padilla, and other figures in the War on Terror is to trace their biographic trajectories[21] in an attempt to explain what, where, how, and why these lives went wrong.

John Walker Lindh's Failed Heterosexuality

John Walker Lindh's trajectory goes as follows: he was born in Maryland in 1981 and raised in Marin, California, which is repeatedly described in news reports as a liberal town where Feng Shui, Buddhism, hippies, and vegans are commonplace. At age twelve, he became interested in Islam after watching Spike Lee's film *Malcolm X*. He attended an alternative high school where he designed his own course of study. Interested in religion and inspired by Malcolm X's autobiography and hip-hop music, he converted to Islam in 1999 and went to Yemen to study Arabic. In search of more rigorous study, Lindh left Yemen for Pakistan, where he was exposed to Islamic fundamentalism and began training as a soldier for Al Qaeda. In November 2001 he was captured and imprisoned by the Afghan Northern Alliance (a group that opposed the Taliban) and later found by the U.S. military. While two CIA operatives interrogated him, a prison uprising broke out, and one of the operatives was killed. Many news stories do not clearly state that Lindh was fighting with Al Qaeda for the Taliban against the Afghan Northern Alliance, not against the United States.[22] Regardless, the U.S. government charged him with conspiring to murder Americans and supporting a terrorist organization. The U.S. government and media have narrated Lindh as a traitor to his country; the U.S. government considered charging him with treason but instead charged him with the lesser crime of supplying services to the Taliban. He was convicted in October 2002 and sentenced to twenty years in prison.

The point is made endlessly: he was once a sweet, unassuming boy. The setup is obvious: How, then, did he become a Taliban supporter? The underlying question is, how did he go from living in "civilized" enlightened Marin, California, to living in "uncivilized" Mazar-e-Sharif, Afghanistan? How did he go from being a clean-cut, middle-class white boy to a man nearly unrecognizable, face blackened and bearded, clothes ragged and dirty, speech accented. How could he go from being a quintessential boy next door to being an alleged terrorist? Such questions imply that he "went Muslim"—that his conversion to Islam transformed him. His trajectory, which begins with his interest in Islam in liberal Marin, ends with him beaten, destitute, and a traitor to the United

States. His biography, in other words, functions as an explanation for terrorism. Lindh's alleged involvement with a terrorist organization is explained in terms of his interest in and conversion to Islam, or of "going Muslim."

I am using the phrase "going Muslim" to refer to a process whereby the discourse of "going native" has been recycled to fit a similar stereotyped notion of conversion to Islam. As colonizers in Africa or Native North America who adopted native culture were seen as having gone native, non-Arabs/Iranians/Turks/South Asians (those who are not associated with the Arab/Muslim conflation) who choose to convert to Islam are portrayed as having "gone Muslim."[23] Going native and going Muslim both signify a regression or the loss of a civilized state of being; a transformation from civilized to barbaric. The regulation of sympathy is inflected by the racial, sexual, classed, gendered, and religious identity of the alleged terrorist.

Going Muslim in Lindh's case resulted from a liberal upbringing gone wrong. According to *Newsweek*:

> The student was old for the madrasa, the primitive Islamic fundamentalist school in a remote corner of Pakistan. . . . He was a "model student," says his teacher, Mufti Mohammad Iltimas. The American had no interest in girls or parties or world events. His only real interest was studying. He seemed fixated, determined to memorize every word of the Quran, all 6,666 sentences of the ancient holy book that dictates every aspect of a devout Muslim's life, behavior and being. His only respite from studying apart from the occasional foray to the cyber tea shop in Bannu to ship e-mails home, was books on Islam. He slept on a rope bed in his teacher's study, in a place with no hot water, and no electricity after 10 p.m.[24]

Narratives like this create imagery of a privileged white boy who forgoes all luxuries as a result of his conversion to Islam. In tracking Lindh's transition from a "normal" American teenager to Muslim terrorist, *Newsweek* creates an implicit psychological profile for him, underscoring his "deviance" from normative (white, middle-class) masculinity. Through a curious number-crunching process that cites Lindh's devotion to the "6,666 sentences" of the Qur'an, the article evokes references to Satan's sixes in the service of painting a damning portrait of Lindh, when there are in fact 6,346 verses, 114 chapters, and 57,152 sentences in the Qur'an. The blatant misinformation of such a narrative emphasizes difference: he was like us, and then he became something vaguely sinister, involved in a numerological scheme that evokes the greatest enemy of Christianity. In this narrative, converting to Islam involves a transformation from civilized to uncivilized, marked by religious compulsion and rigidity.

Newsweek continues this portrait of Lindh's descent away from Americanness.

Most teenagers, when they rebel, say they want more freedom. John Walker Lindh rebelled against freedom. He did not demand to express himself in different ways. Quite the opposite. He wanted to be told precisely how to dress, to eat, to think, to pray. He wanted a value system of absolutes, and he was willing to go to extreme lengths to find it. Lindh, who grew up surrounded by upper-middle-class affluence in California, was determined to fit in at the Islamic religious school, an austere one-story building in a tiny village outside the town of Bannu in the Northwest Frontier Province of Pakistan. Speaking with Mufti Iltimas, Lindh was critical of America as a land that exalted self above all else. Americans were so busy preparing their personal goals, he said, that they had no time for their families or communities.[25]

Not interested in the opposite sex, rebelling against "freedom," and embracing a rigid structure, Lindh's conversion to Islam is portrayed as a trajectory away from his American identity. Going Muslim involves not only becoming un-American but also engaging in an auto-desexualization, a lack of interest in girls. According to *Esquire* magazine:

> The Koran asked him to quit the association with infidel friends, but in Abdulla Nana's memory there were no friends to quit. The Koran asked him to avoid women who were not devout, but in Abdullah Nana's memory there were no women, no girlfriends back in San Anselmo. There were only the trips to the mosque in Mill Valley and then other mosques in San Francisco, and the two- or three-hour discussions he and Nana and a few other strictly orthodox young Muslims would have after Friday prayers, sitting bearded and robed and shoeless in a circle on the mosque's carpeted floor.[26]

This part of the article delineates normative and non-normative teenage sexuality: the normal teenage boy is interested in girls, not in religion; the abnormal teenage boy lacks interest in girls and is interested in religion. While Lindh appeared to be a normal American, he was in fact already poised to convert to Islam given his non-normative sexuality.

In exploring the process of racial formations, David Eng claims that national subjectivity depends intimately on racializing, gendering, and sexualizing strategies.[27] Eng argues that white racial progress has relied on the presumed incivility of the figure of the primitive; a basic symptom of that incivility is a problem of sexual development.[28] In other words, civilizational discourses involve the casting of a primitive Other who is sexually perverse. This sexual perversion can take the form of a lack of control of sexual desires or control of sexual desires:

> For Freud, the fact that primitive societies have scrupulously regulated their sexual impulses does not function as collateral for their social restraint or as evidence of their civil progress. Rather, he reads this heightened sexual regulation back into

primitive societies as pathognomonic of their susceptibility to such temptations and consequently as further proof of their incivility.[29]

Lindh's control of his sexual desires, or rather, apparent lack of sexual desires, signals a loss of his coded white First World civility that turns him primitive.

References to Lindh's non-normative sexuality range from apparent asexuality to homosexuality. According to *Time*, Lindh had homosexual relations with a businessman while he was in Pakistan.

> Hayat met Lindh and took him on a tour of various madrasahs, searching for the perfect one from Karachi in the south to Peshawar in the northwest. The young American rejected them all and preferred remaining at Hayat's side. He helped Hayat at his store, a prosperous business dealing in powdered milk. Hayat, who has a wife and four children, says he had sex with Lindh. "He was liking me very much. All the time he wants to be with me," says Hayat, who has a good though not colloquial command of English. "I was loving him. Because love begets love, you know." Lindh's lawyers deny that their client engaged in homosexual relationships.[30]

The article then goes on to suggest the possibility of a sexual relationship with another man whom Lindh slept next to on a cot and with whom Lindh dreamed of opening an Islamic school in the United States. Added to allegations of his homosexuality are reports stating that when Lindh was a child, his parents separated and his father declared himself gay.[31] Lindh's father's homosexuality and Lindh's own alleged homosexuality operate to "queer" him but not necessarily as homosexual. Rather, this queering is the essential arc of his transition into someone unrecognizable and forges a link between the notion of Lindh's failed heterosexuality and his strange descent toward Islam.

According to *Time*, *Newsweek*, and other news magazines, Lindh's life trajectory toward terrorism can be explained by a falling away from normal American life. The steps along the way include being asexual or possibly homosexual, embracing a primitive lifestyle, and being critical of the United States. This failed life trajectory is framed—always loosely, never explicitly—as the result of liberal interests gone unchecked. Lindh is depicted as a child with a bright future who was corrupted by his interest in Islam, an interest that was not regarded as dangerous by his gay dad, hippie mom (who is cited as dabbling in Native American spirituality),[32] or liberal town. This indictment of liberal parenting, or liberal values, reflects conservative anxieties about American society being too permissive.

Lindh's trajectory from sweet and unassuming to American Taliban is depicted as a path from civilized to barbaric, reasonable to deranged, free American to Muslim fundamentalist, all explained by his conversion to Islam

Figure 4.1. John Walker Lindh as a youth. Image distributed to the media by the Lindh family. Obtained from www.time.com/time/2002/lindh/1.html.

and supported by a visual narrative (see Figures 4.1, 4.2, and 4.3). The photos that accompany the many articles about Lindh provide visual documentation of the going Muslim narrative.[33] The photo sequence begins with Lindh as a young American boy, continues through the beginnings of his conversion to Islam in which he wears Muslim clothing, and ends with him dirty and bearded in Afghanistan. This juxtaposition completes his transformation: not only does he appear dirty, unshaven, and therefore "primitive," but he is now one of "them."

In an episode titled "American Jihad," the TV drama *Law and Order* depicts two professors (husband and wife) at the fictional Stuyvesant College who are shot to death in their home. The detectives eventually discover that a young white man who has converted to Islam is responsible for their murders. He goes by the name Musah Salim, but his given name is Greg Landon (similarly, John Walker Lindh, while in Afghanistan, went by the name Sulayman al-Faris and

Figure 4.2. John Walker Lindh in Muslim clothing. Associated Press/ Wide World Photos.

later by Abu Sulayman al-Irlandi). Although the program opens with the text, "The following story is fictional and does not depict any actual person or event," it is clear that the episode is inspired by the story of John Walker Lindh and loosely based on the murder of two Dartmouth University professors in January 2001.[34] Further, the title of the episode, "American Jihad," resembles the sensationalized title given to Lindh by the news media, "American Taliban." The reference to Lindh is made explicit when at one point the police captain asks, "So you think we've got another John Walker Lindh on our hands?," and one of the detectives replies, "Yeah, but this one might have actually pulled the trigger." The character Greg Landon is a white nineteen-year-old who has grown a beard and wears Muslim clothing. He is facing serious legal charges after converting to Islam. However, the elements of Landon's going Muslim trajectory differ from Lindh's. Taken together, the news and TV drama narratives that explain Lindh's alleged involvement with terrorism imply a clear relationship

Figure 4.3. John Walker Lindh in Afghanistan, December 1, 2001. Associated Press.

between conversion to Islam and violence. The episode slowly builds a portrait of Landon, a convert from American Christianity to Islam, from citizen to murderer.

At the office of the slain female professor, the detectives learn that she held frequent open discussion sessions on a variety of topics, most recently on gender oppression in the Middle East. In her desk, they find a pamphlet from a Muslim bookstore that reads, "Men are commanded to whip their disobedient wives. Women are deficient in intelligence compared to men." This clue leads to the assumption that the murderer is Muslim, is extremely sexist, and might have targeted this feminist professor for advocating gender equality.[35]

When Landon is found and brought to court, the audience is told a tale of a Muslim convert who is led to murder: he is misogynistic, anti-Semitic, critical of American foreign policy, and convinced that America is part of a conspiracy against Islam. During court proceedings to determine his bail, he chants in Arabic, "Allahu Akbar, Allahu Akbar, I am a slave to Allah" (God is great, God is great, I am a slave to God), and demands a Muslim lawyer. "This prosecution is part of America's crusade against Islam. I want a lawyer who sees that," he declares. His hostile and inappropriate courtroom behavior positions him as a fanatic who is not in touch with reason. His ranting continues after he is appointed a Muslim American lawyer who plays the role of the "good Muslim" (consistent with the simplified complex representational strategies discussed earlier). In the middle of the court proceedings, Landon gets agitated, stands up, and says to his lawyer:

> Tell them about the U.S. government's crusade against Islam. They're trying to wipe us out. Three thousand killings on September 11th. Twenty thousand killed in Afghanistan. Your taxes pay for the bombs that kill Afghani children. You're the terrorists! They want me to shut up, that's why they're trying to put me in prison. Maybe send me to Cuba, like the others! They can't treat an American like a caged animal!

Landon is handcuffed and removed from the courtroom for his outburst. He grows frustrated with his lawyer, who refuses to argue that the American government is framing him because he is Muslim, and decides to represent himself. Although Landon is being tried for the murder of two professors, he behaves as if he is being tried for being Muslim. Landon advances some criticisms of the War on Terror and U.S. foreign policies. These criticisms, which could be presented as legitimate, are delegitimized in the mouth of a raving lunatic.

> **LANDON:** America has been trying to destroy Islam for years. It sides with the Jews against the Palestinians because America is a Judeo-Christian country. Since 1990, it has occupied our holy lands in Saudi Arabia. American women walk around with their faces uncovered in our holiest city. America doesn't respect any culture but its own.... You think that your way is the only way and feel that you have the right to invade anyone who disagrees. Bosnia. Somalia. Iraq. You try to assimilate the world. America is a country that was born out of the mass murder of Native Americans and built on the backs of Africans. If the Native Americans could have defended themselves by flying planes into buildings, don't you think they would have? If the slaves could have freed themselves by becoming martyrs, don't you think they would have? And it wouldn't have been terrorism; it would have been self-defense.
>
> **DISTRICT ATTORNEY:** So killing a woman who challenges your view of Islam is self-defense.
>
> **LANDON:** I didn't kill her.... It was a robbery....
>
> **DA:** But you're not sad she's dead.
>
> **LANDON:** She didn't know her place. Qur'an 4:34 says Allah made men superior to women.
>
> **DA:** Under your perversion of the religion.
>
> **LANDON:** You see this is what I'm talking about. Any religion that Americans don't understand, they call perverted.
>
> **JUDGE:** If we could get back to the homicides, Mr. McCoy.
>
> **LANDON:** Yeah, go ahead, Mr. McCoy. Go ahead. Listen to the lady.

JUDGE: Excuse me?

LANDON: No, I won't. I will not allow a female to judge me.

JUDGE: That's enough for today. We'll pick it up tomorrow at 9:30.

Landon critiques the way in which violence committed by anyone except Americans comes to be framed as terrorism. He also accuses the U.S. government of invading and occupying Muslim countries and draws a parallel to the oppression of African Americans and Native Americans. Landon's critiques of U.S. imperialism, however, are coupled with misogyny and thereby delegitimized. These elements not only position Landon as an unreliable speaker who is unworthy of human sympathy but also codes all elements of this ideology as beyond the realm of human sympathy. Landon's offensive disposition and personality preclude any of his words from being heard, most notably his critiques of the U.S. government and its destructive actions in Afghanistan and Iraq. This otherwise legitimate perspective, which has been made by many people around the world, is quickly rendered invalid.

Landon displays not only hatred for women but also hostility toward Jews. Later in the episode, representing himself, Landon questions the man who tested an audiotape and confirmed Landon's voice at the scene of the crime: "Are you Jewish? . . . As a Jew, isn't it your mission in life to destroy the lives of Muslims? You hate Muslims, don't you?" In Landon's character, critiques of U.S. government policies are impossible to hear for what they are; they are inevitably tainted by his misogyny and anti-Semitism. Landon represents Islam as fundamentalist, misogynistic, and anti-Semitic; the egregiousness of his character creates an easy source of shock for the audience, and an implicit contrast to the United States where anti-Semitism and sexism are unacceptable. Again, it is suggested that America is post-race and postfeminist, having happily thrown off the shackles of racism and sexism that burden Landon and his fundamentalist brethren.

Landon's conversion to Islam seems to explain why he murdered a feminist professor. However, the detectives' investigation, as is so often the case in *Law and Order*, reveals a twist, an underlying cause for his conversion to Islam. In a discussion after the court session, they try to figure out Landon's motive for converting to Islam:

LAWYER: If this had been about politics, he probably would have become an anarchist. If it was about music, he could have gotten into grunge or heavy metal. He picked religion, specifically Islam, for a specific reason.

DISTRICT ATTORNEY: Adolescent rebellion?

WOMAN: No, he could have bought a motorcycle or pierced his tongue. People who become fundamentalists do so because there is part of the dogma that resonates with them. There's something in their psyche that draws them to a distorted interpretation of an otherwise legitimate religion.

DA: There's a sect for every nut.

LAWYER: Exactly. But what is it about militant Islam that Landon finds so appealing?.... "Allah made men superior to women."

LAWYER: My guess is he's terrified of women. Militant Islam eases that anxiety by making women subordinate.

DA: Landon became a slave of Allah because he couldn't get a date?

LAWYER: It's not as simple as that, Jack. But I did see how he reacted to Judge Borke and I saw how his mother reacted to him.

DA: So mommy made him do it?

LAWYER: She walked out on him. Castration hurts, whether it's surgical or emotional. He can't confront his mother directly. I think he's scared to death of women, period.

The explanation provided by *Law and Order* is that Landon went Muslim because of symbolic castration. Using a Freudian pop-psychology perspective, his mother is blamed for Landon's "castration."

This symbolic castration narrative deepens when it is discovered that Landon used to have a girlfriend, Jennifer, who was a student of the professor he murdered. During a precourt meeting, Landon is informed that a new witness will be called to testify, and Jennifer is brought into the room. He is emotional and upset on seeing her.

JENNIFER TAYLOR: How could you, Greg? Did you do this because of me?

DA: Think about it, Greg. Think about what Jennifer will say on the stand. In front of your friends. The press. Your mother. The whole world.

GREG: Shut up! Shut up! You shut up because I am a man! I am a man no matter what she says about me. Okay? You laughed at me. You laughed! She laughed.

The exact details of their involvement are left ambiguous, but the script suggests that Landon was unable to perform sexually, or has a small penis, and Jennifer rejected him. Out of this rejection—another instance of symbolic castration—he began to resent women and was drawn to an ideology that would ease his humiliation. He eventually killed the mentor of the woman who rejected him. Landon's sexual failure as a man was so intensely traumatic for him that he needed an ideological justification for his hatred of women, which he found in fanatical Islam.

While deepening the fundamentalist-as-fanatic image, his back story has an unexpected side effect. The episode's final image of Landon, a man destroyed by sexual dysfunction, gives us an opening to sympathize with—or perhaps more to the point, pity—an otherwise unsympathetic character. In other words, tracing his actions to a root cause creates an opening for sympathy. Providing an explanation or attaching a "why" to his crime moves us away from simple demonization. The difference between this root cause—by definition, something that affects him alone, has no socioeconomic role, and demands no accountability from his nation—and the root causes of the terrorist attacks of September 11 are, needless to say, vast.

While there is no reason for Landon to have political motives, making him Muslim, anti-Semitic, misogynistic, and anti-American suggests that Muslim terrorists use politics merely as a front for their senseless violence. About this episode of *Law and Order*, Mucahit Bilici writes:

> The possible explanations offered to the episode's viewers do not help Islam's image as a religion. One implication is that Landon converted to Islam, a religion that allegedly considers men superior to women, but committed the crime because of his misogyny. The other implication is that he became Muslim and, because of his extreme Islamic beliefs, committed the crime. Apparently, both implications are negative for Islam. The show ends without giving the exact answer.[36]

Law and Order offers an alternative, albeit ambiguous, explanation for Muslim converts' violence in contrast to the corporate news media's going Muslim explanation. According to the news media, Lindh's conversion to Islam is interrelated with his deviation from normative heterosexuality. In contrast, according to *Law and Order*, Landon was drawn to Islam because he was symbolically castrated by his girlfriend. Both narratives involve a version of failed heterosexuality. *Law and Order* shifts the story line from portraying conversion to Islam as the cause of violence to revealing an individual with a pathological disorder who embraced a pathological ideology to justify his frustration. The root cause of violence is shifted from religion to psychological deviance. In shifting the cause of violence, adolescent white men who have not come to grips with their Oedipal complexes are to blame. Yet Islam remains central to understanding violence because it is the vehicle through which violence becomes justified. Islam is the enabler.

At the same time, since this young white man is granted a psychological explanation for his actions, he is afforded an opportunity for sympathy. Greg Landon's pop psychology explanation for becoming unhinged functions to redeem his whiteness, to shed his Muslimness, and to leave him with nothing more harmful than a wounded male ego. The news media's narration of Lindh, similarly, provides a small opening for sympathy. In general, we are discouraged from sympathizing with Lindh; there is no narrative offered in the standard accounts to explain what about Islam he connected with, and to what about the civil war in Afghanistan his "heart became attached."[37] *Esquire* notes that Lindh was the first person to be "Abu-Ghraibed": "The first to be denied medical treatment, the first photographed naked and bound, the first taunted while blindfolded, the first—certainly the first—to have SHITHEAD scrawled on his blindfold, the first whose digital photos made their way round the world as souvenirs, the first denied access to the Red Cross, the first to be ushered into a legal limbo created ex nihilo by the administration's notions of executive power."[38] The dehumanizing treatment of brown men that has become a signature of the War on Terror was also deemed suitable for Lindh; his privilege as a white male, his right to sympathy, was revoked when he went Muslim. However, sympathy enters from the edges of his story, as it were, because he was once an innocent and affluent white boy in a world of possibilities. Viewers can therefore mourn his tragic life, imagining what could have been had his parents steered him in the right direction.

Taken together, the explanations for Lindh's and Landon's turn toward violence is conversion to Islam. A string of biographic and psychological elements are merged to explain the process of going Muslim. For Lindh, it involves a lack of interest in girls, the possibility of homosexuality, criticisms of the United States, and an embrace of rigid fundamentalism. For Landon, a fictionalized Lindh, these formational elements include misogyny, anti-Semitism, and criticisms of the United States. From these trajectories emerge a generic portrait of Islam that is extremist, misogynistic, and anti-American. The implication of this portrait is that if one were to convert to Islam, these characteristics would inevitably be adopted.

While "going Muslim" operates as an explanation for violence, in both cases, a root cause is identified as an additional explanation. In Lindh's case, it is implicitly suggested that his liberal education is to blame for his involvement with terrorism. It was too open, too tolerant, too lax; it was a liberal education gone very wrong. In the case of Landon, it was symbolic castration that inspired him to look for an ideology that would legitimize his retaliation against female sexual rejection. Both the news and TV drama narratives contain a critique of liberal values and an enduring focus on sexuality. Sexual explanations, in other words, stand in for political explanations. The vast realm of political violence, whose complexity is already diminished through the use of the term *terrorism*, is now further depoliticized and portrayed as a mere cover for sexual problems. Landon's criticisms of the United States—for killing children in Afghanistan during the War on Terror, for imprisoning innocent Muslims at Guantánamo Bay, and for supporting Israel at the expense of Palestinians—are not unusual criticisms to hear from "liberals." However, the representation of such criticisms in *Law and Order* delegitimizes them as the ranting and raving of a lunatic murderer. Similarly, the common mention in media accounts of "liberal" Marin country, Lindh's ability to create his own course of study at an alternative high school, his mother's interest in Native American spirituality, and his father's homosexuality—all construct a portrait of the dangers of liberal ideology. A liberal upbringing is portrayed as dangerous, ruining Lindh's life chances and threatening U.S. national security.

Interrelated with this critique of liberals and depoliticizing of terrorism is a focus on sexuality. Lindh lacks interest in girls and is allegedly homosexual; Landon is a misogynist. Both the news and TV drama narratives involve emasculation. These individual stories—of non-Arab men who convert to Islam and become failed heterosexuals—support a larger narrative that terrorism is motivated by religious and sexual "deviation," as expressed by Bill Maher in the epigraph. On the one hand, Arab Muslims are narrated as jealous of U.S. democracy and sexual freedom. On the other hand, American converts are attracted to Islam because of their failed or non-normative heterosexuality. The explicit narrative is that converting to Islam causes terrorism, and the submerged narrative is that Muslims are sexually perverse. Thus terrorism, Islam, empty political rhetoric, and perverse sexuality are narrated as interconnected. These explanations marginalize a consideration of the political conditions that lead to political violence.

During the War on Terror, discourses on terrorism have redefined normative and non-normative sexualities. Jasbir Puar claims that homosexuality has been regarded in the United States as a non-normative sexuality but that this has changed through the War on Terror. Puar argues that certain homosexual bodies were folded into the national imaginary and national agendas during the War on Terror, producing what she terms "homonationalism"—the ways in which some homosexual identities came to inhabit a normative form that ultimately supported heteronormativity, as well as the national and transnational political agendas of U.S. imperialism.[39] Within this configuration of normative and non-normative homosexualities, the terrorist—and by default, gay or lesbian Muslims—are configured as improperly sexual, in contrast to the newly formed homonormativity:

> In the never-ending displacement of the excesses of perverse sexualities to the outside, a mythical and politically and historically overstated externality so fundamental to the imaginative geographies at stake, the (queer) terrorist regenerates the civilizational missives central to the reproduction of racist heterosexist U.S. and homonormative nationalisms, apparent in public policy archives, feminist discourses, and media representations, among other realms. Discourses of terrorism are thus intrinsic to the management not only of race, as is painfully evident through the entrenching modes of racial profiling and hate crime incidents. Just as significantly, and less often acknowledged, discourses of terrorism are crucial to the modulation and surveillance of sexuality, indeed a range of sexualities, within and outside U.S. parameters.[40]

Despite the critique of liberalism embedded in these biographic trajectories that explain one's involvement with terrorism, the United States is portrayed as liberal and progressive compared to Islam. Eng writes that the productions of queer liberalism, or normative homosexuality, and the discourse of racialized immigrant misogyny and homophobia are two sides of the same coin.[41] Presenting conversion to Islam as the cause of terrorism demonizes Islam "as illiberal, while masking the complicity of the neoliberal U.S. state in helping to engender the very homophobia that both the state and the larger public insist is imported part and parcel from these immigrants' home countries."[42] The narrative versions of John Walker Lindh operate to modulate and regulate sexuality by describing failed heterosexuality as a marker of terrorism.

Jose Padilla's Racialized Life

The story of Jose Padilla—a Latino man from Chicago—begins marked for failure. News accounts of Padilla unfailingly note the grimy underbelly of his early life: he was in a gang, a petty thief, and in and out of facilities for juvenile delinquency. As with the standard reductive explanations for terrorism, here too the typical media portrayal ignores larger, more complex environmental factors: Padilla went from a life of crime to terrorism. Different from the pitiable sexual pathology of Greg Landon, Padilla became a terrorist because at his core he is a menace to society; he was incapable of living a normative American life that includes holding a job, having a relationship and a family, and, most important, being a law-abiding citizen who does not commit crimes and end up in prison. Padilla is portrayed as part of a larger trend of men of color who fill prisons, convert to Islam while in prison, are released from prison only to commit another crime, and are sent back to prison. Islam here serves as yet another gang, but the severity of the crime goes from gang banging in the neighborhood to plots that threaten national security.

In contrast to Lindh, Padilla's life is void of promise from the start; he is not an iconic, middle-class, white teenager who makes a tragic decision to explore Islam but rather a small-time crook who fails at becoming a big-time terrorist. As a man of color with a minor criminal record, "going Muslim" becomes an obvious next step in a life of crime. According to *Newsweek*, Jose Padilla "wasn't one of those quiet, sweet kids the neighbors just can't believe got into trouble with the law. Growing up on Chicago's tough West Side in the late '70s and early '80s, young Jose was a known street thug and Latin Disciples gangbanger with an expanding rap sheet."[43] The recurring trajectory in Padilla's life involves a vacillation back and forth from prison for petty crimes and then conversion to Islam in 1994 while working at a Taco Bell. Mainstream news accounts explain that in 1998 he moved to Egypt to learn Arabic and later to Pakistan in search of a radical Islamic education. In 2002, after surfing the Internet and compiling information on how to make a nuclear bomb, he proposed his idea to detonate a radiological device in the United States to Al Qaeda. News reports claim that Al Qaeda leaders suggested he start smaller, with a radioactive bomb. While deplaning in Chicago—his first return to the United States in four years—the FBI arrested Padilla for his alleged plan to make a radioactive, or "dirty," bomb, and for conspiring with Al Qaeda to execute a terrorist act on U.S. soil. President Bush labeled him an "enemy combatant,"[44] a category created during the War on Terror to designate persons who would not be entitled to constitutional, international, or basic human rights; the creative terminology of the president has become a legal foundation for the U.S. government's logic of exception.[45] For the next three and a half years, he was held in a military brig in Charleston, South Carolina, as an enemy combatant, while the U.S. government sought to build a case against him more compelling than searching the Internet for a bomb recipe.[46]

Portrayed as a poor Latino from the barrio who had been in and out of prison and a gang member, Padilla's trajectory to potential terrorist is simplified through narrating him as a failure in life and menace to society. Converting to Islam, then, becomes an appealing option for menaces grappling with their failure in life. The author of an editorial in the *Providence Journal* writes:

> The Jose Padilla Show should have been closed down well before he started dressing his violent tendencies in the robes of radical Islam. Americans could have sealed his cell when he was just an ordinary criminal psychopath, but they missed the opportunity.[47]

The editorial writer delineates all the various crimes Padilla was involved in before he converted to Islam: robbery, road rage, and violence of various degrees. She claims that he is a "goon in exotic costume." In other words, Islam did not transform him, as some news reports indicate; rather, he found an ideological justification for his violent and pathological behaviors in Islam. Islam, she claims, is a "philosophic cover for [his] pathology," and law enforcement should have kept him behind bars to begin with. This narrative overlaps somewhat with the Lindh *Law and Order* episode, in the sense that Islam is not the cause of psychosis but a refuge for psychologically unstable men. This alternative perspective nonetheless maintains that Islam attracts the mentally disturbed, with the implicit—though never stated—hint that Islam itself is a pathological ideology.

Sexual perversion becomes intertwined in this narrative, as with Lindh. Some news reports mention that Padilla divorced his wife in the United States in March 2001 and later married a woman in Egypt. Pictures of his Egyptian wife published in multiple newspapers and news magazines show her wearing a

Figure 4.4. Jose Padilla's wife, Shamia'a, at the couple's home near Tanta, Egypt. Barry Iverson, for the *New York Times*, April 25, 2004.

niqab (a veil that covers the entire face, leaving only the eyes visible) (see Figure 4.4). His divorce from a presumably "normal" American woman and his marriage to a Muslim—who, according to dominant U.S. discourses, is oppressed by her patriarchal culture and religion—demonstrates Padilla's sexual perversion. The narrative emphasizes that his image of a "proper" woman fell in line with the restrictive, presumably misogynist attitude that we have come to expect from fundamentalist Muslims.[48]

In addition to being inflected by a narrative about non-normative sexuality, this narrative of Padilla as a psychopath in search of a legitimizing ideology has racial undertones. A Latino Studies professor, Ana Y. Ramos-Zayas, was contacted by a reporter to discuss Padilla:

> The reporter had read a few articles I had written about a popular education program directed by Puerto Rican nationalist activists in Chicago and she wanted to

know if I thought the reason why José Padilla was "so angry at the United States" had to do with his experience as "the son of a single mother, growing up in Chicago's Logan Square and being influenced by the barrio's nationalist activism and gang involvement." In this well-intentioned reporter's view, Padilla's involvement with the Taliban was almost explained away by his Puerto Ricanness. . . . More significantly, however, was the reporter's view of Padilla's involvement with the Taliban as a natural progression stemming from his "un-American" citizenship and from growing up in a social space that does not quite "exist" within the boundaries of how the US is imagined as perpetually prosperous and white. This of course is in stark contrast to how John Walker, the so-called "American Taliban," was portrayed: an unexplainable aberration, an exception to the otherwise normative whiteness emphatically represented in images of his upper-middle class professional suburban upbringing.[49]

Ramos-Zayas argues that the state has constructed a "politics of worthiness" in which U.S. citizens are deemed worthy of citizenship rights depending on race and a disavowal of radical politics that challenge U.S. mythologies of democracy and equality.[50] In Padilla's case, the root cause of his going Muslim is not a liberal education or symbolic castration but the fact that he is a Puerto Rican from the barrio.

In June 2004 the initial narrative about the ultimate loser who couldn't even plan a bombing properly drastically changed at a news conference held by James Comey, deputy attorney general for the U.S. Department of Justice.[51] After accusations from civil rights groups that the government was violating Padilla's rights as a U.S. citizen, the government held a press conference to release previously classified information. In the briefing, Comey reported that Padilla was in fact a key player in Al Qaeda and that his mission in the United States was to blow up high-rise apartment buildings in various cities. Padilla was then formally charged with providing material support to terrorists. With this revised narrative, the U.S. government was successfully deterring terrorism; the underlying hint was that the public should not question whom the government designates as an "enemy combatant" since the government is the ultimate authority in the War on Terror. Suddenly Padilla was no longer an incompetent terrorist; more valuable in 2004—as the protests against the "enemy combatant" designation grew—was that the machinery of Homeland Security was indeed working and that the United States had stopped a dangerous terrorist from striking. In January 2008 Padilla was sentenced to seventeen years in federal prison. Both narratives—of Padilla as a loser and as a danger—reveal his political usefulness to the broader narrative about the War on Terror. When he is portrayed as a failure, he delegitimizes Islam. And when he is portrayed as a danger, his arrest confirms the determination and success of the U.S. government in finding terrorists. Inderpal Grewal writes that "race and gender become modes of knowledge that produce the figures of danger and risk through technologies of surveillance, visibility, and, importantly, self-regulation."[52] Muslim men are figured as a risk to the nation—as threatening security, happiness, and freedom—and therefore figured by government and media discourses as requiring elimination through incarceration or death.

John Walker Lindh and Jose Padilla are archetypal figures of U.S. multicultural subjects who have converted to Islam, "gone Muslim," and become failed citizens. Both men embody American fears of the savage enemy within. Given, however, the racial differences between these men—one is white, one Puerto Rican—they do not "go Muslim" equally but to varying degrees depending on their race. The case of Lindh is the quintessential instance of going Muslim: a privileged white male from an upper-middle-class town converts to Islam and ends up a terrorist, dirty and destitute in a prison in Pakistan. The case of Padilla is not as shocking. As a Latino with a minor criminal record, he does not represent anything meaningful for America's self-image. He has already been written off as a racialized criminal or menace, so his descent into Islamic fanaticism is not as tragic or significant as that of Lindh.

In their explanations to the public for the criminal involvements of Lindh and Padilla, the media has made one thing explicit: both are converts to Islam. The media has focused on and sensationalized the stories of these two men, constructing a narrative that links violence, criminality, terrorism, and a delusional mental state to Islam; and more specifically, violence committed by Muslim converts is explained through an interlinked narrative of failed heterosexuality. Lindh and Padilla are not necessarily portrayed as homosexual; rather, their trajectory into terrorism is linked to failed heterosexual masculinity. And this supports the larger narrative that the causes of terrorism stem from sexual, as opposed to political, reasons.

The government and news media have constructed a politics of affective worthiness that delineates persons worthy and unworthy of human feeling, inflected by the politics of race, class, religion, gender, and sexuality. In particular, Euro-American subjects are granted a more thorough explanation than men of color. Their trajectories toward terrorism are punctuated with brief moments in which viewers can feel sympathy, based on the notion that they once had a bright future as white middle-upper class males. For Padilla and other men of color such small windows are not available because they never had a bright future to begin with. Race inflects sympathy as does gender and sexuality. Gender inflects sympathy by framing Muslim women as deserving of an abundance of sympathy and Muslim men as undeserving of sympathy. This is partly accomplished through narrating Muslim men as inhabiting a non-normative or perverse sexuality. Men who "go Muslim" are described as being asexual, homosexual, desiring a veiled (read: submissive) woman, abusing their wives, or lashing out against being symbolically castrated. Sexuality inflects the "going Muslim" narrative by coding Muslim men, not necessarily as homosexual, but as inhabiting a non-normative—and thus perverse—sexuality.

The elements identified in these biographic trajectories have bled far beyond the realm of newspaper articles and magazine profiles. They can be detected in the torture techniques, designed specifically to humiliate Muslims, used at Guantánamo Bay and Abu Ghraib prisons. Even James Yee, a Chinese American convert to Islam who served as the Muslim chaplain at Guantánamo Bay, was accused of being a traitor to the United States and charged with sexual perversion. In 2003, when Yee was returning to the United States from Cuba, a U.S. customs agent found a list of Guantánamo Bay detainees and interrogators in his belongings. Yee was arrested, detained, and charged with espionage and aiding the enemy. He made headline news as yet another Muslim convert who had become un-American. After being placed in solitary confinement for seventy-six days, he was released and the charges were dropped. Yee nevertheless faced lesser charges in the coming months and was portrayed as a sexual pervert: rumors circulated that he was storing pornography on his government computer and that he was an adulterer, tying Islam to sexual hypocrisy and deviance.[53] The case of James Yee is yet another example of how non-normative sexuality is used as a tool to mark Muslims as dangerous and perverse.

In a public lecture in 2008, following the publication of his 2005 book, *For God and Country: Faith and Patriotism under Fire*, Chaplain Yee argued that Islam was used against detainees by interrogators.[54] Female interrogators were told by command, Yee revealed, that the possibility of "creative approaches" made them particularly useful in intelligence gathering; they were encouraged to exploit "conservative Islamic etiquette" that segregated men and women and that regulated contact between men and women. Female interrogators, for example, stripped naked in an effort to frustrate the male detainees, rubbed their bodies on shackled Muslim prisoners, and grabbed Muslim male prisoners' genitalia. Male and female interrogators forced prisoners to shave their beards and disrespect the Qur'an by throwing it on the floor. Yee mentioned cases of interrogators dressing as priests and forcibly baptizing prisoners and also of wrapping them in Israeli flags, believing that this would agitate them to the point of making a confession.

Such treatment of Muslim male prisoners reveals a series of assumptions about Muslim men—that they are sexually repressed; that they are anti-Israel and anti-Semitic; that their faith is not worthy of respect. This ideology and practice, exemplified by the U.S. military's use of Rafael Patai's 1973 Orientalist book, *The Arab Mind*, as required reading, are accomplished through constructing Muslim men as practicing a non-normative religion and sexuality that automatically criminalizes them and exempts them from being the objects of sympathy.[55] The treatment of these prisoners is especially stunning when considering that the vast majority of prisoners have not been convicted of involvement in terrorism; many have not even been formally charged with a crime. Such treatment is only possible against people who are portrayed as *less than*— less than normal, heterosexual men—who inhabit a realm outside of normal human sympathy. Even if not guilty of terrorism, Muslim men are still framed as guilty: guilty of anti-Americanism, misogyny, sexual perversion, and therefore the potential for terrorism.

Simplified Complex Explanations

The commercial news media purports to search far and wide for an explanation for terrorism, yet the narratives explored here are another example of simplified complex representations. Media accounts suggest that they can explain what drove these men to violence, and yet they ultimately offer reductive explanations. Simplified complex explanations, as previously explored, decontextualize and dehistoricize terrorism while offering a root cause that signals complexity. "Going Muslim" stands in as a singular explanation for terrorism, marginalizing the gamut of political motivations for political violence. I am not arguing that these men deserve our sympathy. Instead, I am arguing that their portrayals in the media, and the media's implication that we should abstain from a sympathetic response, have two important consequences. First, "going Muslim" is not an adequate explanation for the actions of these men. Political violence at its core is not about symbolical castration, or sexism, or heterosexual failure, but rather about complex political and historical problems. Second, affect is configured to support empire. A lack of sympathy for supposed "terrorists" like these goes hand in hand with the delegitimization of any discussion of how U.S. foreign policies contribute to contemporary political problems.

This decontextualizing and dehistoricizing takes place through absence, that is, through the strategic omission of more complex root causes or grievances—the death of Iraqi children as the result of U.S. sanctions, for example, or U.S. support of Israeli military occupation—and the absence of opportunities to hear the "terrorists" speak and explain why they are involved in violent acts. The U.S. government even accused the Arab news station Al Jazeera of being a terrorist news network because it broadcasted tapes of Osama bin Laden speaking; even listening to perspectives that challenge the dominant narrative is framed as off limits. But what happens if we dare to listen to these voices of evil? What do terrorists sound like? What explanations do these men provide for killing or attempting to kill people?

In January 2003 the Jamaican Brit Richard Reid, known as "the Shoe Bomber," was given three consecutive life sentences in prison after he attempted to ignite explosives in his shoes on American Airlines Flight 63 from Paris to Miami on December 22, 2001. He explained his actions to Judge William Young:

> I further admit my allegiance to Osama bin Laden, to Islam, and to the religion of Allah. With regards to what you said about killing innocent people, I will say one thing. Your government has killed 2 million children in Iraq. If you want to think about something, against 2 million, I don't see no comparison. Your government has sponsored the rape and torture of Muslims in the prisons of Egypt and Turkey and Syria and Jordan with their money and with their weapons. I don't . . . see what I done as being equal to rape and torture, or to the deaths of the two million children in Iraq. So, for this reason, I think I ought not to apologize for my actions. I am at war with your country. I'm at war with them not for personal reasons but because they have murdered . . . many children and they have oppressed my religion and they have oppressed people for no reason except that they say we believe in Allah.

For a rare moment in post-9/11 America, a terrorist was given a chance to make a statement. The reaction to that statement is as telling as Reid's explication of his actions. Judge Young responded immediately:

> You are not an enemy combatant. You are a terrorist. You are not a soldier in any war. You are a terrorist. To give you that reference, to call you a soldier gives you far too much stature. . . . What your counsel, what your able counsel and what the equally able United States attorneys have grappled with and what I have as honestly as I know how tried to grapple with, is why you did something so horrific. What was it that led you here to this courtroom today? I have listened respectfully to what you have to say. And I ask you to search your heart and ask yourself what sort of unfathomable hate led you to do what you are guilty and admit you are guilty of doing. And I have an answer for you. It may not satisfy you. But as I search this entire record it comes as close to understanding as I know. It seems to me you hate the one thing that to us is most precious. You hate our freedom. Our individual freedom. Our individual freedom to live as we choose, to come and go as we choose, to believe or not believe as we individually choose.[56]

Though Reid's intention—to kill American civilians—is abhorrent, he has a very clear rationale for his actions. And yet Judge Young denies this rationale. He disregards Reid's statement and reinstates the official—and far simpler—post-9/11 rationale that Reid was motivated by a hatred of freedom. Even though directly confronted with a clearly articulated set of grievances, it is as if the judge has not even heard Reid, so quickly does he revert to the standard explanation of "unfathomable" hatred. The judge's dismissal of Reid's explanation—or rather, his refusal to even acknowledge Reid's reasoning—is significant. For if the judge—or most Americans, for that matter—took seriously the notion that Reid's actions were an attempt to avenge the death of many, many Iraqi children killed as a result of U.S. sanctions, the public discourse might be reframed about the U.S.-led war on Iraq, about the many nameless men held at Guantánamo Bay, about the astounding expenditure of American resources and life for the maintenance of "freedom" and "democracy." The clarity of Reid's thinking, and the complexity that inspired his actions were far from central to commercial news profiles of this terrorist. Absence, once again, is significant. The boundaries of perception, understanding, and emotion must be policed to maintain a particular narrative on the War on Terror, one that maintains the position that the U.S. is just and compassionate in order to support U.S. empire.

Advancing U.S. empire requires marginalizing alternate perspectives and feelings because they have the potential to be politically subversive. Similarly, Mumia Abu-Jamal, the journalist and death row inmate whose case has received international attention, offers a perspective on Lindh that challenges dominant narratives:

> "Johnny Taliban" *is* guilty—of rejecting his white-skin privilege, of betraying
> his class, and of converting from Christianity to the Islamic faith. He *is* guilty of
> fleeing the richest empire of earth, to seek spiritual solace in the dusty, wretched
> backwaters of empire. He *is* guilty of looking into the eyes of wrinkled sheikhs in
> Karachi, and seeing human beings instead of caricatures. He *is* guilty, of being a
> thinking, feeling human.[57]

Rather than frame Lindh as a traitor, Abu-Jamal challenges readers to see Lindh as someone whose values extend beyond his own white privilege, someone who feels sympathy—even empathy—for people who have been deemed unworthy by dominant U.S. narratives. Needless to say, this perspective was not part of the public discourse about Lindh; Abu-Jamal would likely be charged by many Americans, along with Lindh, as sympathizing with terrorists and with being un-American.

Emotions are always, at least in part, socially constructed, and yet a convenient fiction operates culturally that they are "natural" or precultural.[58] Such a fiction is far easier to maintain when public discourse is dominated by reductive narratives. These presumably natural responses, for example, that Muslim women deserve sympathy and Muslim men do not, create emotional hegemony: those who do not conform to the emotions designated as appropriate or inappropriate are marginalized for what Alison Jaggar terms an "outlaw emotion" and what Sunaina Maira terms "dissenting feelings."[59] Jaggar writes, "people who experience conventionally unacceptable, or what I call 'outlaw,' emotions often are subordinated individuals who pay a disproportionately high price for not maintaining the status quo."[60] Outlaw emotions have the potential to be politically subversive by questioning the seemingly obvious categories of who is and who is not deserving of sympathy and by unsettling the supposedly "natural" configuration of sympathy that aids the ongoing pursuit of U.S. empire.

5   Selling Muslim American Identity

Public diplomacy is the promotion of the national interest by informing, engaging, and influencing people around the world. Public diplomacy helped with the Cold War, and it has the potential to help win the war on terror.
— "Changing Minds, Winning Peace," Report of the Advisory Group on Public Diplomacy for the Arab and Muslim World

Do you really want to build a better understanding between Americans and Muslim? Or do you just want to win this campaign? We are not stupid or blind or deaf. . . . Be fair on the Palestinian issue, stop killing Iraqis and bombing their country, repair the destruction of what you did in Afghanistan, don't play tricks with the IMF.
—Comment posted by Aida in Indonesia, Shared Values Initiative website, Council on American Muslims for Understanding and the U.S. State Department

In the weeks after 9/11, patriotic advertising campaigns flooded highway billboards, radio, magazines, newspapers, and television. Many corporations directly or indirectly used the tragedy to market and sell their products. General Motors launched a campaign, "Keep America Rolling," offering zero percent financing deals on new cars and trucks. The New York Sports Club encouraged New Yorkers to "Keep America Strong" by joining the gym for a special discount rate.[1] Some corporations, such as AOL/Time Warner, MSNBC, Ralph Lauren, Sears, and Morgan Stanley advertised that they would not be advertising, instead buying advertising space on billboards and television and in print to offer their condolences, express their solidarity with America, and to extend an inspirational message.[2] Recovery from tragedy, in other words, came with a corporate sponsor; we were encouraged to practice citizenship through consumerism by both President George Bush and New York's Mayor Rudolph Giuliani, who encouraged citizens to fight terror and practice citizenship through consumerism—through visiting Disney World and visiting New York.

Corporations were not the only ones producing 9/11-specific advertisements in the weeks and months following: nonprofit organizations (most notably the Ad Council), civil rights groups (most prominently, the Council on American-Islamic Relations), and the U.S. government were also involved in post-9/11 advertising. The Ad Council created an extensive campaign aired on network television. There were ads that directed people who had lost family members to sources of financial assistance, others that alerted parents to possible child-rearing challenges in the aftermath of tragedy; some provided ways to get involved and help, and then there were those that aimed to unify the United States across racial lines and inspire patriotism.[3] More than an educational or emotional response to tragedy, post-9/11 nonprofit advertising sought to "sell" an imagined American community and in the process redefine American identity and citizenship.

Some PSAs attempted to create inspirational images of a united multicultural American citizenry, a response to hate crimes that targeted Arab, Muslim, and Sikh Americans. Hundreds of Arabs, Muslims, and those mistaken for Arab or Muslim were attacked or harassed, and people considering themselves patriots set fire to businesses and committed murder. Reports indicate that perpetrators of hate crimes said such things as "Go back to your country" or "I am an American" or made some kind of racial slur during the act of violence.[4] A 2004 nationwide survey conducted by Cornell University found that 44 percent of people in the United States favored some kind of restriction on the civil liberties of Arab and Muslim Americans—which included registering one's place of residence with the government and racial profiling. The poll also found that 74 percent characterized Islamic countries as oppressive to women; 50 percent perceived Muslims as violent, dangerous, and fanatical; and one-third indicated that a majority of Muslims are hostile to the United States. In addition, only 27 percent agreed that Muslim and Christian values are similar, and 47 percent indicated that the "Islamic religion is more likely than others to encourage violence among its believers." These figures indicate that at the time nearly half of U.S. citizens perceived Islam as both dangerous and as having values fundamentally different from those of Christianity.[5] Another study found that 49 percent of the general public supported surveillance of Arab Americans and 41 percent supported detaining Arab Americans without evidence. This study also revealed that only 38 percent believed that Arab Americans were doing all they could to help stop terrorism.[6] After 9/11, as Leti Volpp has argued, the category of the U.S. citizen went through a process of resignification, defined over and against the category of the terrorist.[7] The conception of the American citizen became suddenly and momentarily centered on opposition to Arabs and Muslims (who came to be marked as noncitizen terrorists), but this citizenry nevertheless took pride in its multicultural diversity. Post-9/11 hate crimes reflected a fault line in national unity; PSAs responded by projecting an imagined community that was both diverse and united.

In this chapter and the epilogue, I diverge from examining news reporting and TV dramas to examine challenges to the commercial media's representation of Arabs and Muslims. Here I turn to the ways that a nonprofit organization, a civil rights group, and a branch of the U.S. government represented

Arabs and Muslims. Dominant meanings about Arabs and Muslims during the War on Terror are not produced by one television drama, one government speech, one news report, or one nonprofit advertisement alone but through the ways in which multiple cultural productions and messages converge.[8] As Stuart Hall has written, "Ideas only become effective if they do, in the end, connect with a particular constellation of social forces."[9] What is particularly important about the PSAs is that they are not bound to profit-making. If they are not motivated by profit and the need to maintain the widest viewership possible, are they still subject to simplified complex representational modes, or do they diverge from the Arab American patriot and victim? I claim that after 9/11 an ideological moment emerged, supported by a range of individual and institutional discourses and practices, that reimagined U.S. citizens as diverse and united in the War on Terror. The imagined American community became carefully, intentionally multicultural—as if to make it clear that everyone was included.

Here I examine the ways in which PSAs narrated Islam and the United States as compatible in an effort to challenge ideas about their oppositional nature and inspire national unity during a time of crisis. I compare three advertising campaigns: the Ad Council's "I am an American," the Council on American-Islamic Relations' "I am an American Muslim," and the U.S. Department of State's "Shared Values Initiative." I argue that in an effort to deconstruct the opposition between American citizen and Arab Muslim terrorist, the PSAs reproduced restrictive representations of diversity—or what I term "diversity patriotism," that is, a version of American patriotism that glorifies the notion of a diverse citizenry and emphasizes America's multicultural unity. The PSAs that I examine here articulate three different versions of American diversity patriotism. The first version takes the form of ambiguous assimilative diversity. This is when diversity is defined through ambiguous representations that avoid Muslim or Sikh religious symbols after 9/11. The second version of diversity patriotism approximates patriotic sameness through the figure of the good Muslim. This involves representing Muslims as similar to Americans by articulating their service to the nation, legacy in the United States, diversity, and heterosexual family values. The third version is diversity patriotism gone global, in which the United States is represented as a land of opportunity, freedom, and equality for all. Muslims are represented to a global audience as prospering in the United States, and American values are sold to Muslims abroad. I conclude that in this post-race moment, attempts to produce inclusive images and discourses are predicated on minimizing difference and ultimately reproduce restrictive forms of inclusion.

"I Am an American"

The Ad Council started producing public service advertisements on behalf of the government and nonprofit organizations in 1942 to raise awareness of a variety of social issues. Topics have ranged from the prevention of child abuse to domestic violence, drug use, drunk driving, seatbelt safety, racism, and discrimination. The Ad Council's post-9/11 campaign, "I am an American," was created in direct response to the immediate surge in hate crimes against Arabs, Muslims, and Sikhs; it began airing on television ten days after 9/11 and ran for over a year. The thirty- and sixty-second ads featured a diverse group of approximately thirty people, seen one at a time, each staring at the camera and stating, "I am an American." This rainbow coalition of contemporary America included Latinos, Caucasians, African Americans, Caribbean Americans, South Asian Americans, Native Americans, Asian Americans, and the young and the elderly, as well as people in both urban and suburban environments, a fireman, and a woman who appears to be a nun. The advertisement ends with the written words, "E Pluribus Unum—Out of Many, One," followed by a young girl of about three or four who appears possibly to be Latina silently waving a U.S. flag and smiling (see Figure 5.1). The sound track, composed mainly of violins, sounds like an anthem in its solemn disposition.[10]

"I am an American" aims to discourage further attacks on Arabs, Muslims, and Sikhs by promoting unity through the marker "American," which is signified as a diverse designation. The ad appeals to viewers to accept people who look or sound different from themselves and to recognize them as "Americans." Some of the "Americans" featured in the PSA have accented English, signaling that English is not their first language and thus that they are first-generation immigrants (nevertheless, everyone is speaking English). As the Ad Council's website explained, "Diversity is what defines America. In the wake of this national tragedy, it is time to embrace our differences and celebrate that diversity, rather than let it divide us. Our nation's motto sends a message that has never been more appropriate—E Pluribus Unum, or Out of Many, One. We are all Americans and our differences create the very foundation and spirit that define this nation."[11] One version of diversity patriotism is articulated here: difference is identified as defining the nation; American identity is defined as diverse; and national unity is the objective of the message. But what kind of diversity is acceptable? How is diversity defined?

Diversity patriotism is here articulated through ambiguous assimilative diversity. Despite seeking to deconstruct the binary citizen/terrorist, Arabs, Muslims, and Sikhs are not included in this diverse display. There are no visible markers of anything Arab, Muslim, or Sikh in the ads—no veil, no mosque,

Figure 5.1. Still from the Ad Council's PSA, "I Am an American." Created pro bono by GSD&M for the Ad Council.

no turban, no beard; no distinctive Arab, Muslim, or Sikh clothing; and no Arab accent. There is an African American man wearing a suit and bowtie in the advertisement who could possibly be a member of the Nation of Islam, but such identification is ambiguous. There is one young woman who appears to be South Asian American, and a young man who might be South Asian American or Arab American, but there is no clear indication of their identities. The young man who might be South Asian or Arab American has a difficult time articulating that he is an American because he is overcome with emotion. All the other individuals clearly state, "I am an American," distinguishing this ambiguously Arab man as someone for whom it is especially meaningful to be an American. The fact that Arabs were blamed for the 9/11 terrorist attacks but South Asians were also subject to attacks, harassment, deportation, and surveillance demonstrates that the U.S. public conflates these identities. The Ad Council continues this conflation through the ambiguous representation of this Arab/South Asian man as an American.

In addition, this conflation exists side by side with a curious absence. Those who were most frequently targeted after 9/11 were persons who wore religious symbols, such as veils and turbans; the conspicuous absence of any religious identification, other than the presumably Catholic nun, raises serious questions. Why is Islam ignored in this ad? Why the ambiguity? What purpose is served by not making it clear that Arab and South Asian Americans are included in the lineup? Why are these groups seemingly unrepresentable in a mainstream campaign that promotes a vision of a proudly diverse American citizenry?

The ad responds to national crisis through diversity patriotism, with racialized groups eagerly (though perhaps temporarily) incorporated into the imagined community of "Americans." Amid legislation to deport Arabs, Muslims, and South Asians and end affirmative action, the idea (and the perhaps impossible ideal) of diversity is mobilized by this PSA urgently and expediently, motivated in response to trauma. Despite the fact that U.S. citizenship has been historically defined as white—and repeatedly redefined as such through immigration policies, attacks on affirmative action, and other legal and governmental mechanisms—hegemonic whiteness is temporarily suspended in the national imaginary and replaced by diversity as the paradigm of American citizenship. Latinos, Asian Americans, and African Americans are refigured as "American" alongside whites. The ambiguous assimilative diversity patriotism that is mobilized by the Ad Council, best captured in the vague representation of Arabs and Muslims within this multicultural panoply, provides unintentional evidence of the widespread binary between the ambiguously diverse U.S. citizen and the presumably unambiguous Arab/Muslim terrorist.

Who does and does not count as an American, particularly in relation to race and religion, has long been contested. Though until 1952 citizenship laws that mandated whiteness as a prerequisite to U.S. citizenship were unevenly applied and wrought with contradictions, they contributed to defining American identity as white and Christian.[12] The civil rights movement of the 1950s and 1960s marked a move away from the construction of white national identity toward a more inclusive, diverse, and imagined national identity that continues to be contested and remains incomplete. One significant moment in defining a diverse and unified U.S. citizenry, particularly in relation to the Middle East, was the 1991 Gulf War. In this case, highlighting previously neglected though always historically important African American soldiers helped erase the imagined imbalance of a white U.S. military attacking a nonwhite populace in the Middle East. Both Melani McAlister and Wahneema Lubiano have written about the centrality of narrating African American soldiers as heroes of the 1991 Gulf War to redefining a diverse U.S. citizenry.[13] But there were very clear limits to the representation of an inclusive U.S. force: McAlister notes that during the Gulf War "the images of diversity and strength of U.S. armed forces simply did not include Arab Americans."[14] At the time U.S. diversity was defined in opposition to the Arab/Muslim enemy.

In the post-9/11 context, a diverse body of U.S. citizens is also imagined in opposition to the Arab/Muslim enemy; however, the representation of Arab/Muslim American victims and patriots complicates this binary.[15] "I am an American" does not directly or clearly represent Arab and Muslim Americans as victims and patriots. However, the PSA is informed by the notion that all U.S. citizens are united by their experience of being victims of the 9/11 attacks and overcoming being victims through their identity as patriotic Americans. The Ad Council should be commended for not including Arab and Muslim Americans in the imagined U.S. community merely as victims or patriots; instead, however, they emerge as an ambiguous part of the diverse nation.

As a direct response and challenge to the Ad Council's incomplete projection of a diverse U.S. citizenry, Cynthia Weber, professor of politics and international relations, produced a series of videos titled *"I Am an American": Video Portraits of Unsafe US Citizens*. The main video takes the same form as the Ad Council's PSA, featuring each subject talking directly into the camera and with the same music playing in the background. Instead of each repeating the same "I am an American" phrase, however, these "Americans" proclaim a very different truth about themselves and thus about their identity as Americans (see Figure 5.2). One boy says, "I am the son of an immigrant without papers. I am American"; an army veteran who refused to serve in the Iraq War and became a political refugee says, "I am a political refugee from the United States and I am an American"; Muslim chaplain James Yee, who served at Guantánamo Bay prison and was wrongly accused of being a terrorist spy, says that being a patriotic American means speaking out against the injustices he witnessed at Guantánamo. Rather than end the film with the U.S. motto, Weber ends it with a black screen that reads *Ex Uno, Plurus* (From One, Many), which Weber believes is "a phrase that more accurately captures the always fractured U.S. and the plurality of the citizens who compose it."[16]

Weber critiques how the Ad Council's PSA "organizes the U.S. national imaginary by disavowing many differences in the name of one national ideal of tolerance and censuring many differences in the name of one national idea of justice."[17] It not only forecloses a range of possible expressions of humanity but also, as demonstrated by Weber, forecloses the possibility of considering the experiences of unsafe Americans, whether those who are innocent and have been accused of terrorism, or those who are undocumented and treated as if guilty of terrorism, or those who conscientiously objected to serving in the Iraq War and became political refugees, or those who are human rights activists and have been arrested for assisting migrants to the hospital for heath care. Weber highlights the discrepancy between the ideal of diversity and tolerance expressed in the Ad Council's PSA and the reality for some Americans who are

'I am a human rights activist, and I am an American.'

—Shanti Sellz, No More Deaths activist arrested for transporting dehydrated migrants to hospital

Video Portraits of Post-9/11 US Citizens Series 1 by Cynthia Weber
©Pato Productions 2008

Figure 5.2. "'I Am an American': Video Portraits of Unsafe US Citizens," by Cynthia Weber.

unsafe and at risk of being criminalized. This version of diversity patriotism, while appealing to notions of inclusivity, ultimately limits who can be imagined as a legitimate American. As with previous chapters, my critique is not to say that the Ad Council or other organizations examined here failed in their ad campaigns. Rather, my focus is on tracing the contours around how American-ness and Muslimness are conceptualized at this historical moment. These public service announcements offer a portrait of what constitutes an American and how that notion remains very rigid despite ideals of diversity.

"I am an American Muslim"

While the Ad Council does not directly address the relationship between Arab and Muslim Americans and American citizenship, the Council on American-Islamic Relations—the largest Muslim civil liberties and advocacy organiza-tion in North America—does. CAIR's mission is "to enhance understanding of Islam, encourage dialogue, protect civil liberties, empower American Muslims, and build coalitions that promote justice and mutual understanding."[18] Since its establishment in 1994, CAIR has sought to promote a positive image of Islam and Muslims in the United States, through media relations, lobbying, education, and advocacy. Among its many post-9/11 initiatives are the "National and Worldwide Condemnation of Terrorism" and "Not in the Name of Islam" campaigns—both of which denounce terrorism as part of an effort to correct public assumptions that Muslims support terrorism. CAIR was among 120 Muslim groups to support a fatwa, or Islamic religious ruling, against terrorism and extremism.

Despite CAIR's work in condemning terrorism and educating the public about Islam, conservatives have attacked the group, accusing them of being a front for terrorism, specifically for Hezbollah and Hamas. CAIR officials have stated that such accusations stem from the group's differing perspectives on particular issues. While they are critical of Hamas and Hezbollah, they refuse to join in the Bush administration's blanket condemnation of these groups. In addition, they have urged the U.S. government to stop shipments of weapons to Israel and have opposed the pro-Israel lobby in Washington. Such stances have sometimes made it difficult for CAIR to work with government officials. Senator Barbara Boxer of California, for example, in December 2006 revoked a certificate of appreciation that she had issued to the group a month earlier, in order not to be perceived as supporting terrorism.[19]

One of CAIR's post-9/11 initiatives was an advertising campaign, "Islam in America," to foster understanding of Islam in the United States and to counter anti-Muslim rhetoric. The campaign consisted of one television PSA and six print advertisements.[20] Compared to the Ad Council, which broadcast its PSA repeatedly on network television for months after 9/11 and for weeks after the first and second anniversaries, CAIR, with a much smaller budget, had each of its PSAs printed in the *New York Times* only once (first on Sunday, February 16, 2003), a total of six times. CAIR's television PSA was shown on network television only once, during the fourth season of *24*, when the plot centered on Arab terrorists seeking to destroy the United States. CAIR lobbied for fair representation. The producers of *24* and executives at FOX agreed to air the PSA on the same day as the program. Given its many prime-time spots, it is likely that hundreds of millions of viewers saw the Ad Council's "I am an American" PSA, many of them more than once. In contrast, CAIR estimates that one million people might have seen its ads in the *New York Times* and that approximately six million have seen their other campaigns on CAIR's website or in local newspapers.

Each of the six ads is designed to address one aspect of Islam and to educate the public about it. Seeking to move away from the Arab Muslim villain made popular by Hollywood and the government and journalistic framing of a clash of civilizations between the West and the East, the ads attempt to redefine Islam and its relationship to America. Through the slogan, "I'm an American Muslim," CAIR tries to break down the constructed opposition between American and Muslim, to include Muslims in the imagining of America, and to draw a parallel between the diversity of America and the diversity within Islam. Through the language of diversity, CAIR's PSA emphasizes the compatibility between Americans and Muslims and the possibility of a patriotic American Muslim identity. In other words, it presents another version of diversity patriotism. Rather than the ambiguous assimilative diversity of the Ad Council, CAIR articulates a different version of diversity patriotism: it accentuates similarities to "American values" through the figure of "the good Muslim." The advertisements assert that "American" and "Muslim" are compatible by articulating a number of discourses, including a Muslim legacy of military service to the U.S. nation, to replace the notion that Muslims are violent fanatics who hate the United States.

The television PSA takes place indoors against a gray background, and the synthesizer music creates a hopeful atmosphere. The four Muslim speakers featured in the thirty- and sixty-second versions appear to be in their twenties, thirties, and forties. They appear, as in the Ad Council's PSA, one at a time, staring at the screen.

> **NARRATOR:** America is the land of diversity and service.
>
> **AFRICAN AMERICAN MAN:** I am an African American. My forefathers overcame the trials of slavery.
>
> **NATIVE AMERICAN WOMAN:** I am Native American. I'm a journalist, wife, and mother.
>
> **WHITE MAN:** I am of European heritage. One of my ancestors was a member of the Continental Congress.
>
> **LATINA (WEARING A HEADSCARF):** I'm Hispanic American. I've been a Girl Scout since I was six years old and now I'm a troop leader.
>
> **AFRICAN AMERICAN MAN:** I served in our nation's armed forces, as have many of my relatives.
>
> **NATIVE AMERICAN WOMAN:** My father served two terms of duty in Vietnam.
>
> **WHITE MAN:** Another fought for freedom at Gettysburg.
>
> **LATINA:** Two of my uncles fought for our country in the Korean War.
>
> **AFRICAN AMERICAN MAN:** And I am an American Muslim.
>
> **NATIVE AMERICAN WOMAN:** And I am an American Muslim.
>
> **WHITE MAN:** And I am an American Muslim.
>
> **LATINA:** I am an American Muslim.
>
> **NARRATOR:** Muslims are part of the fabric of this great country and are working to build a better America.

This advertisement relays three interrelated messages. First, it seeks to delink Islam from Arabs. By not representing any Arabs in its multiethnic display of

"American Muslims," it serves to correct the common conflation that all Arabs are Muslim and all Muslims Arab. Second, by invoking slavery, representing a Native American, and speaking of ancestors, the notion that Muslims are "foreign" or "new" immigrants—and therefore un-American—is challenged. Instead, the PSA establishes a narrative of a Muslim legacy in the United States. Third, Muslims are represented as productive citizen-patriots who serve their country by being Girl Scouts, by fighting for the nation, and by having ancestors who also fought for the nation. Thus this advertisement claims that Muslims are American by virtue of their legacy of patriotic service to the nation, and patriotism is defined by one's willingness to fight and risk his or her life for the United States. The discourses that are mobilized to include Muslims within American cultural citizenship[21] are centered on notions of the United States as a melting pot nation and on service to the nation and are expressed in a variety of ways for men and women and for U.S.-born and foreign-born citizens. Diversity is expressed through representing Latinos, African Americans, Native Americans, and European Americans as Muslim Americans (or rather, as "American Muslims"). Service to the nation is articulated for men through military service as the quintessential enactment of patriotism and for women through being a Girl Scout or participating in volunteer or relief work. American identity is further established by mentioning the length of time one has lived in the United States.

While a simple declaration is enough to establish one's American identity in the Ad Council's PSA, in the case of CAIR, action—like military service—and even oath taking are required. One print ad features Muslim American girls taking the Girl Scout oath, pledging to serve their country as well as God (see Figure 5.3). Beneath an image of eleven girls posed for a class photo, each with the signature three-finger Girl Scout salute, the advertisement reads as follows:

"We're Americans and we're Muslims."

"On my honor, I will try: To serve God and my country. And to help people at all times."

The members of Santa Clara Muslim Girl Scout Troop #856 have made a pledge to serve their community, their country, and God. The American values that all cherish—like service, charity, and tolerance—are the same values that Muslims are taught to uphold in daily life.

Muslim life and worship are structured around the Five Pillars of Islam—faith, prayer, helping the needy, fasting, and pilgrimage. The third pillar teaches that all things belong to God and are only held in trust by humans, so as Muslims we are expected to share a percentage of our wealth every year to help the poor.

Devotion to God and the teachings of Islam strengthen our commitment to community and country. Like Americans of all faiths, we use the principles of our

WE'RE AMERICANS AND WE'RE MUSLIMS

On my honor, I will try:
To serve God and my country.
And to help people at all times.

The members of Santa Clara Muslim Girl Scout Troop #856 have made a pledge to serve their community, their country and God. The American values that we all cherish—like service, charity and tolerance—are the same values that Muslims are taught to uphold in daily life.

Muslim life and worship are structured around the Five Pillars of Islam—faith, prayer, helping the needy, fasting, and pilgrimage. The third pillar teaches that all things belong to God and are only held in trust by humans, so as Muslims we are expected to share a percentage of our wealth every year to help the poor.

Devotion to God and the teachings of Islam strengthen our commitment to community and country. Like Americans of all faiths, we use the principles of our religion to guide us in an ever-changing world, and we teach our children to respect the values that make our country a secure place for all Americans.

WE'RE AMERICAN MUSLIMS

CAIR

Number two of fifty-two in the Islam in America series.
To learn more about the series, visit www.americanmuslims.info

Figure 5.3. Islam in America Series, 2 of 5, Council on American-Islamic Relations.

religion to guide us in an ever-changing world, and we teach our children to respect the values that make our country a secure place for all Americans.

"We're American Muslims."[22]

The advertisements produced by the Council on American-Islamic Relations, as well as by the Ad Council, take the form of a performative speech act. Defining the self becomes a means for inclusion in the imagined diverse U.S. nation. With the declaration of oaths, and declarations of their identity, the speakers not only illustrate that they are "good Muslims" but also display to other Muslims how to be a credit to one's race. In the case of CAIR, the emphasis is not only on speaking, declaring, or taking an oath but also on articulating enactments of service to the nation. American values are defined as "service, charity, and tolerance," and these are situated as identical to Muslim values. American and Muslim values are revealed through the PSA to be the same. In addition, we are told Islam teaches its adherents to be patriotic and creates charitable, tolerant citizens who serve their community and country. Interest in the security of the United States is expressed by the oaths that Muslims take from a young age to serve their country and God.[23]

Though serving the nation takes precedence in the articulation of American Muslim identity, other ways to serve the nation are also identified in these ads. One ad features a photo of a family—husband, wife wearing a headscarf, and two children who are probably four and six years old (see Figure 5.4).

> My name is Aminah Kapadia, and I'm a wife, a mom, and a student. I'm studying for a master's degree in education, and I volunteer at our children's school, where I'm also active in the PTA. I was born in Philadelphia, to Puerto Rican parents, and have lived in the United States my entire life. My husband, Zubin, is from India, but has called America home for more than thirty years. He's an attorney and former economic officer for the U.S. Department of State. Now he spends his time running a consulting firm and coaching our son's T-ball and soccer teams.
>
> Like many Americans, my husband and I face the challenges of raising our children in an unpredictable world. That's why the basic principles of our religion, like tolerance, justice, and devotion to family, are a central part of our lives. As the Prophet Muhammad told us, "The best of you is he who is best to his family. None of you will have faith until he wants for his brother what he wishes for himself."
>
> We believe the security of our nation is dependent upon the strength of our families, and Islam teaches us the values that provide that strength.
>
> "We're American Muslims."[24]

This advertisement demonstrates the convergence of a variety of discourses through this multicultural Muslim American family. Readers are informed that the Puerto Rican woman was born in the United States while her Indian husband was not. Nonetheless, his legitimacy as an American is claimed by virtue of the length of time he has been in the country and his patriotic service. Furthermore, he is a successful, middle-class family man and thus a productive and desirable citizen-patriot. And he participates in quintessential American activities.

Meanwhile, although the woman was born in the United States, her identity challenges what the general public purports to "know" about Islam and Muslim women; she is of Puerto Rican descent. Thus we learn that Muslims can be of any background and that not all Muslim women are oppressed or confined to the home. Although she is married and a mom and has many home and family responsibilities, she still pursues a master's degree. Finally, by affirming that "the security of our nation is dependent upon the strength of our families, and Islam teaches us the values that provide that strength," the ads link Islam, heterosexual family values, and national security.

Needless to say, American values and the qualifications for citizenship changed after the 9/11 tragedies. According to polls, the primary reason Bush's

WE'RE AMERICAN AND WE'RE MUSLIMS

MY NAME IS AMINAH KAPADIA, and I'm a wife, a mom and a student. I'm studying for a Masters degree in education, and I volunteer at our children's school, where I'm also active in the PTA. I was born in Philadelphia, to Puerto Rican parents, and have lived in the United States my entire life. My husband, Zubin, is from India, but has called America home for more than thirty years. He's an attorney and former economic officer for the U.S. Department of State. Now he spends his time running a consulting firm and coaching our sons' T-ball and soccer teams.

Like many Americans, my husband and I face the challenge of raising our children in an unpredictable world. That's why the basic principles of our religion, like tolerance, justice and devotion to family, are a central part of our lives. As the Prophet Muhammad told us, "The best of you is he who is best to his family. None of you will have faith until he wants for his brother what he wishes for himself."

We believe the security of our nation is dependent upon the strength of our families, and Islam teaches us the values that provide that strength.

WE'RE AMERICAN MUSLIMS

CAIR COUNCIL ON AMERICAN-ISLAMIC RELATIONS

Number five of fifty-two in the *Islam in America* series.
To learn more about the series, visit www.americanmuslims.info

Figure 5.4. Islam in America Series, 5 of 5, Council on American-Islamic Relations.

supporters voted to reelect him in 2004 was "values." These values were not the constitutional foundations of freedom of speech and freedom of religion but rather "moral" values such as the prioritization of the heterosexual family unit, belief in God, and opposition to abortion.[25] According to the CAIR PSAs, Muslim family values are not that different from how President Bush might define American values. Such similarity is especially significant given the past decade's controversy over gay marriage. Though CAIR does not make an explicit statement against homosexuality, its PSAs accentuate its support for the heterosexual family as the foundation for a secure nation. The organization seeks to connect with other Americans under the rubric of tolerance and diversity. These advertisements target other religious Americans, presumably the majority of Americans, and in doing so seeks to place Islam on the same level and within the same value structure as other faiths, Christianity and Judaism in particular.

While some of CAIR's advertisements stress similarities between Islam and America, others explicitly seek to correct misperceptions of Islam. Since dominant narratives in the West often revolve around "the oppressed Muslim woman," CAIR seeks to counter such a stereotype by showing hijab-wearing Muslim women as active in the public sphere. One ad offers a portrait of a Muslim American wearing a headscarf above the following text (see Figure 5.5):

> My name is Manal Omar. I've earned a Master's degree from Georgetown University, and I've won several national public speaking awards. I'm a development researcher for an international corporation. I vote. I'm active in politics, and I belong to several civic organizations.
>
> I am an American Muslim woman and I wear hijab.
>
> I choose to wear hijab—a headscarf and modest attire—because the practice is integral to my religious beliefs, and because I am proud to be a Muslim woman. In Islam, both women and men are encouraged to dress modestly, thereby allowing a person to be judged on the content of his or her character, and not on physical appearance.
>
> To me, hijab is a symbol of my confidence and self-respect.
>
> I'm an American Muslim.[26]

This Muslim American woman is a model citizen: educated, professional, and involved in politics. Challenging the image of the Muslim woman oppressed beneath her hijab, Omar is not hidden away at home but actively participates in the public sphere and is even an awarded public speaker. The hijab is explained: it is asserted as her choice and as an expression of her beliefs. Her statement that dressing modestly allows one to be judged by character as opposed to appearance resonates with Martin Luther King Jr.'s "I Have a Dream" speech, in which he dreams of a day when people will be judged by the content of their character and not by the color of their skin. Evocative of the inspiring message of the civil rights movement—a message that now, in our multicultural era, is firmly in the mainstream—the statement invites other Americans to practice tolerance and diversity.

The main message these ads seek to convey is that Muslim values are compatible with American values, even—and especially—conservative American values. A variety of dominant discourses are mobilized to make this possible: on diversity, legacy, patriotism and national service, belief in God, and the significance of the heterosexual family unit. Just as the United States is a diverse nation, so too is Islam an ethnically diverse religion, according to the PSAs. The PSAs tell us that Muslims are not foreign invaders but have a long history in the United States; they have served and contributed to the nation for more than a hundred years. In addition to their rich legacy, like the rest of America, Muslim Americans today are concerned about national security and are patriotic.

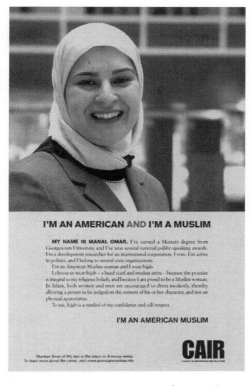

I'M AN AMERICAN AND I'M A MUSLIM

MY NAME IS MANAL OMAR. I've earned a Masters degree from Georgetown University, and I've won several national public-speaking awards. I'm a development researcher for an international corporation. I vote. I'm active in politics, and I belong to several civic organizations.

I'm an American Muslim woman and I wear hijab.

I choose to wear hijab – a head scarf and modest attire – because the practice is integral to my religious beliefs, and because I am proud to be a Muslim woman. In Islam, both women and men are encouraged to dress modestly, thereby allowing a person to be judged on the content of his or her character, and not on physical appearance.

To me, hijab is a symbol of my confidence and self-respect.

I'M AN AMERICAN MUSLIM

CAIR

Number three of fifty-two in the Islam in America series.
To learn more about the series, visit www.americanmuslims.org

Figure 5.5. Islam in America Series, 3 of 5, Council on American-Islamic Relations.

Ultimately, we are told, Muslim Americans—like Americans of all stripes in this era of diversity patriotism—have their priorities straight: they are American first and Muslim second. The PSAs all end on the identical note, driving the same message home over and over: "We're American Muslims." "American" is the privileged identity here, and "Muslim" is packaged, marketed, and sold in ways that emphasize its subservience to that first, dominant identity. In their likeness to their fellow Americans, American Muslims are model American citizens who are interested in national security; they are productive citizens who possess high moral values and promote a middle-class heterosexual family structure. Islam, in other words, is palatable; its adherents serve America. In articulating a version of diversity patriotism that is built on sameness, CAIR reinscribes the figure of the "good Muslim." CAIR's ad campaign falls within the "good Muslim/bad Muslim" paradigm in which what makes a Muslim "good" or "bad" is not his or her relationship to Islam but rather his or her relationship to the United States.[27] Similar to the TV drama version of a "good Muslim," the PSA version is an über-patriot.

These specifications effectively lead to other exclusions. What about those who do not actively serve the nation through military service, who do not work for the government, are not heterosexual, or are not religious? Are they not equally American? In contesting the exclusion of Arabs and Muslims from the U.S. national imaginary, CAIR ends up relying on other narratives of exclusion. As Akhil Gupta and James Ferguson have written, strategies of resistance can be complicit with strategies of power: "Practices that are resistant to a particular strategy of power are never innocent of or outside power, for they are always capable of being tactically appropriated and redeployed within another strategy of power, always at risk of slipping from resistance against one strategy of power into complicity with another."[28] While the Ad Council and the Council on American-Islamic Relations clearly aim at producing a more inclusive framework for U.S. citizenship, their public service announcements participate in the formation of a particular exclusionary version of diversity that requires individuals to approximate a patriotic sameness in order to gain access to cultural citizenship.

Regarding a comparable historical phenomenon—Judaism in the United States—Laura Levitt argues that "tolerance works to both regulate and maintain a deep ambivalence."[29] She states that acceptable Jewish difference has been defined as religious difference—that is, they simply go to a different "church" in order to be accepted as Jews in U.S. culture. As a result Jews have had to remake their Jewishness into a bastardized but comprehensible version of Christianity.[30] Levitt claims that the remaking of Jewishness into an acceptable form demonstrates the failed promise of liberal inclusion. A similar process is taking place in these CAIR advertisements, which reveal (albeit unintentionally) the particular form in which Islam must be represented in order to fall under the umbrella of liberal multicultural inclusion and tolerance. Islam cannot be included in liberal multicultural society in just any form: it must take the form articulated in the PSAs—emphasizing likeness to and compatibility with a dominant, and conservative, American culture. Both versions of diversity patriotism—ambiguous assimilative patriotism and approximating sameness through the figure of the "good Muslim"—rely on diminishing difference in order to sell inclusion.

As Muslim as Apple Pie

Using advertising for the purpose of nation building and patriotism is certainly not unique to the United States. Communist countries, for example, are known for their noncorporate advertising. The streets of Havana have been lined with billboards of Cuban flags and statements such as "Hasta la Victoria Siempre" (Always until Victory) and "Viva la Revolución" (Long Live the Revolution), that seek to promote patriotism and nationalism, to inspire hope for and commitment to revolution, and to promote pride in being Cuban. Similarly, England's "Cool Britannia" campaign, pursued by Tony Blair after his Labor Party won the 1997 election and launched in a Ben and Jerry's ice-cream flavor of the same name, was used to sell an updated national image.[31] The objective of the campaign was to modernize England's sense of self, from a place of imperialism and monarchy and old, white, stuffy traditions to "a young, stylish, post-imperial nation with leading-edge creative cultural industries"; the new "Cool Britannia" national slogan was far breezier, and with far fewer negative historical connotations, than the former "Rule Britannia." Promotional videos of "New Britain" and a pop version of "God Save the Queen" were used to sell Britain's remade image as a multicultural modern nation, both internally and externally.[32] "Cool Britannia," however, was criticized for seeking to create a multicultural image without addressing the legacy and remaining reality of racism. It was also disparaged for seeking to narrowly define a national culture that is broad and complex. In early 2002 the British Tourism Authority restrategized its public relations campaign and began using the far tamer "UK OK," invoking Britain's monarchic past and present and allowing for a range of possible meanings.[33]

Cuba's patriotic billboards and England's Cool Britannia campaign are just two of many examples of nations marketing themselves like products for both internal and external consumption. Governments use public relation campaigns to perform the ideological work of (re)defining a national image and the ideas associated with that nation. As Mark Leonard writes, "Today all modern nations manage their identities. They use logos, advertising campaigns, festivals and trade fairs to promote a national brand."[34] In the case of the United States, "public diplomacy" emerged as an important form of "political warfare" during the Cold War, and such efforts have been revived in the War on Terror.[35] Penny Von Eschen writes that between the 1950s and the 1970s the U.S. State Department sent African American jazz musicians abroad to "win the hearts and minds" of the Third World and to counter the country's racist image with a depiction of the United States as a color-blind democracy. Like many attempts to re-create one's self-image, this diplomatic effort was built on a deep contradiction: while African American culture was being promoted abroad, at home racial segregation and inequality persisted.[36]

Just a month after 9/11 the Department of Defense sought to manage its identity abroad by establishing the Office of Strategic Influence. The effort to market America's War on Terror was short-lived. In February 2002, just four months after opening, the office closed in the wake of a media scandal in which classified information was leaked to the *New York Times*, alleging that the Office of Strategic Influence would be manufacturing support for U.S. policies through the dissemination of misinformation to foreign governments and media sources.[37] Donald Rumsfeld, then secretary of defense, denied the allegations and claimed that the objective was to circulate important information to its allies, such as radio broadcasts to let the Afghan people know that the U.S. government was not waging war against them, or dropping leaflets to inform them of the difference between cluster bomb packages and food packages.[38] He stated that the media scandal made it difficult for the Office of Strategic Influence to fulfill its objectives and thus had to close down but that those objectives would be carried out by different offices.

In early 2003 the White House created the Office of Global Communications, in response to President Bush's executive order on the need for strategic communications to promote the interests of the United States abroad.[39] The Advisory Group on Public Diplomacy for the Arab and Muslim World was established to advise the government on how best to propagate their influence in the Middle East. In its report, issued in October of that year, the advisory group outlines a strategic plan to initiate a public relations arm for U.S. policies. Its recommendations are varied, yet all are tied to a central effort of ideological influence abroad: greater funding of public diplomacy efforts; an increase in staff training in the Arabic language and recruitment of Arab and Muslim American government employees; the establishment of "American corners" (resource centers for information on American culture), "American Knowledge Libraries," and American studies centers in the Middle East; the strengthening of American universities in the Middle East; a publication initiative in which American books are translated from English into Arabic; technology initiatives; educational fellowships and exchanges; and the establishment of a think tank; among other initiatives.[40]

This extensive campaign makes clear that winning the War on Terror requires not only military and financial strength but also ideological hegemony. In other words, the levels of warfare are many, and ideological engagement is often as crucial as drone strikes or forward operating bases. As Tucker Eskew, director of the White House's Office of Global Communications, has stated, "We're fighting a war of ideas as much as a war on terror,"[41] explicitly referring to both the ideological and violent state apparatuses that are central to the U.S. imperial project.[42] The report makes the importance of ideological gains clear and thus argues for increased funding for public diplomacy initiatives abroad:

The United States today lacks the capabilities in public diplomacy to meet the national security threat emanating from political instability, economic deprivation, and extremism, especially in the Arab and Muslim world. Public diplomacy is the promotion of the national interest by informing, engaging, and influencing people around the world. Public diplomacy helped win the Cold War, and it has the potential to help win the war on terror.[43]

As Liam Kennedy and Scott Lucas have written, "In the promoting of 'freedom' to foreign audiences, public diplomacy is inextricably connected with the development and implementation of U.S. foreign policy, charged with the awkward task of reconciling interests and ideas."[44] In other words, winning the War on Terror and ending the presumed crisis in national security depend on influencing people around the world by promoting American national interests, particularly through popular culture and advertising campaigns. Public diplomacy has "politicized the international spread of American popular culture."[45]

The U.S. Congress, even before the recommendations of the advisory group, had already begun several forays into a popular culture campaign in the Middle East after 9/11. Radio Sawa (Radio Together), located in Dubai and launched in March 2002, broadcasts pop music in English and Arabic (from Britney Spears to Amr Diab) and news from an "American" perspective in several Arab nations, including Jordan, Iraq, Morocco, Sudan, Yemen, and Qatar.[46] The Broadcasting Board of Governors decided to focus on music with sporadic news interludes after research indicated that music would be the most effective way to attract listeners. Alhurra Television (The Free One), launched in February 2004 and broadcast out of Virginia to counteract the purported negative light cast on the United States by Al Jazeera, features a mix of news and popular culture, including magazine shows with segments on exercise, fashion, technology, and movies, twenty-four hours a day.[47] *Hi Magazine*, launched in 2003 and suspended at the end of 2005, was an Arabic-language monthly magazine sold in Lebanon, Jordan, the West Bank and Gaza, Israel, Algeria, Egypt, Cyprus, and several Gulf nations.[48] The articles were written by Arab Americans and strove to highlight similarities between youth in the United States and the Middle East. These initiatives all sought to produce and package a particular version of U.S. national identity for consumption by Arabs and Muslims in the Middle East and Southeast Asia. Its stated objective was to influence the "hearts and minds" of the opposition and to reduce hatred of the United States. President Bush, for his part, exclaimed that Alhurra Television would "cut through the hateful propaganda that fills the airwaves in the Muslim world."[49] The combined annual budget for these three public relations campaigns were initially $100 million in 2003; two years later, even though *Hi Magazine* had failed, federal expenditures had grown to $100 million just for Alhurra alone.[50]

Like the use of jazz musicians to promote an idealized vision of the world, these initiatives are built on their own contradictions. Two criteria were established by Congress for Alhurra: the television station would promote U.S. foreign policy objectives and practice professional journalism. William Youmans argues, however, that these two criteria pose an "existential dilemma": how can professional journalism be practiced if it is tied to promoting a specific goal? Youmans shows that such a contradiction creates incongruence between American policy and rhetoric and helps explain why Alhurra's credibility has suffered across the Middle East.[51] Public diplomacy efforts seem by definition to come with constraints that compromise their credibility.

In addition to the aforementioned projects, the U.S. government—through the Department of State and the Council of American Muslims for Understanding (created after 9/11 and funded by the State Department)—spent $15 million on the "Shared Values Initiative."[52] Charlotte Beers, a corporate advertising executive who created the Uncle Ben's campaign, was hired by the State Department to market and sell the nation abroad. The campaign, "meant, in part, to correct a mistaken image of U.S. hostility to Islam that research showed was prevalent in the Arab and Muslim world," included Internet videos and television ads, newspaper ads, and radio spots seeking to "establish a recognition that Americans and Muslims share many values and beliefs [and] demonstrate that America is not at war with Islam."[53] The U.S. media dubbed the advertisements the "Muslim-as-Apple-Pie" campaign.[54]

The ads were aired between October 28 and December 10, 2002, during the Muslim holy month of Ramadan, in Pakistan, Malaysia, Kuwait, Saudi Arabia, the United Arab Emirates, Bahrain, Oman, Qatar, and Indonesia. They were refused by the state-owned television stations of Egypt, Lebanon, and Jordan because they were perceived as contradictory: they portrayed Muslims testifying to the freedom and respect they experience living in the United States while failing to acknowledge the detentions, deportations, and racial profiling Muslims have been subjected to since 9/11.

These ads produce an iteration of diversity patriotism gone global. In this global version, the U.S. is represented to Muslims abroad as the land of opportunity and freedom, despite post-9/11 policies that have restricted Arab and Muslim immigration to the United States. The ads aim to demonstrate to Muslims abroad that Muslims in the United States live prosperous lives free of harassment and therefore that there is no need to hate the United States. Five print ads were produced for both radio and video, each featuring the story of one U.S. Muslim with a banner headline. Devianti Faridz, an Indonesian graduate student of broadcast journalism at the University of Missouri, testifies, "The values that I was taught as a child in Bandung are the values they teach here in America." Another ad featured Farooq Muhammad, a paramedic with the New York Fire Department, who states, "We are all brothers and sisters. Here I am one human being taking care of another." Dr. Elias Zerhouni, director of the National Institutes of Health from 2002 to 2008, is featured in another ad, saying, "I am basically an immigrant here, and the tolerance and support I have received myself is remarkable." Abdul-Raouf Hammuda, a bakery owner in Toledo, Ohio, states, "Religious freedom here is something very important. Muslims are free to practice their faith in totality," (see Figure 5.6). The text that accompanies his advertisement reads as follows:

I was born and raised in Tripoli, Libya. I came to America to go to school. After I graduated, I really saw the opportunity this country would have for me as a businessman.

I went through four or five businesses that failed before I succeeded with the Tiger Lebanese Bakery. We make the greatest pita bread in the nation. I added some dishes from the African nations of Libya, Morocco, and Tunisia, we put a deli in, and it was received very well. My wife is my right-hand person, and I have been very fortunate to have my children help me part time at the bakery.

My customers are probably 75% non-Muslims, 25% Muslims. Since 9/11, we've had an overwhelming sense of support from our customers. I believe Americans in general respect the Islamic faith. Religious freedom here is something very important, and no one has ever bothered us.

I was also one of the co-founders of the Toledo Islamic Academy, the first school of its kind in the state of Ohio. We started with about 50 students, and now we are from pre-K through high school and bursting at the seams.

America is a land of opportunity, of equality. My children converse in Arabic, they can read Koran, they know the Sunnah, we're free to worship in mosques. We are happy to live here as Muslims and preserve our faith.

Hammouda's narrative affirms several nationalist tropes, particularly the United States as a land of opportunity and a land of (religious) freedom and equality. His biographic arc—coming to the United States to go to school and staying to open a now-successful business—hints at abundant educational and financial opportunities in the United States. His narrative stresses that non-Muslims are supportive of his business, signifying that anti-Muslim discrimination is not a problem in his adopted country. He furthermore states that he is not only able to practice his religion, but he is actively involved in a Muslim community and in creating future generations of Muslims. The advertisement contains an image of him praying outdoors at an amusement park, presumably with three of his sons. While Muslims praying in public is a far from ordinary occurrence in the United States, it is pictured as if it is, symbolizing public acceptance of Islam. Hammouda's narrative thereby

Figure 5.6. "Open Dialogue—Hammuda," Council of American Muslims for Understanding. Produced in collaboration with the U.S. government in 2002.

revives age-old nationalist tropes in the service of denying discrimination or hatred against Muslims.

This ad is certainly a vast improvement over the notion of postwar American Jews who had to explain themselves by saying they just "went to a different church." The depiction of praying in public and mention of the Toledo Islamic Academy reveals a different era compared to the pressures to assimilate that earlier groups faced. Advances in diversity in the United States can be seen in all the public service announcements examined in this chapter. However, at the same time they also reveal that prerequisites to acceptance remain, the most significant of which is demonstrating that one is a "good Muslim"—one who demonstrates patriotism by working with the U.S. government and by not having any overt criticisms of the United States. Furthermore, the Muslims who participated in these ads embrace this discourse and strategy of the "good Muslim" themselves. Their participation demonstrates how Muslims have adopted this particular strategy in seeking greater integration in U.S. society.

Another ad, featuring Rawia Ismail, a teacher, paints a similarly rosy portrait (see Figure 5.7):

> I'm a schoolteacher in a public school in Toledo, Ohio, in the United States of America. I also teach my own children in Saturday school, Islamic school.
>
> I was born in Beirut, Lebanon, and came to the United States in 1984. I have four beautiful children. I decided to become a teacher because I enjoy working with children more than anything.
>
> At the Islamic Center I teach the kids about an hour of religion, an hour of Arabic, they have some lunch in between, and then we all do prayers together. This is something I have found to be the only way of life for me and my family. Being a Muslim means everything to me.
>
> In my neighborhood, I see that all the non-Muslims care a lot about educating their children and family values, just as much as I do. I didn't see any prejudice anywhere in my neighborhood after September 11. My neighbors have always been supportive, truly.
>
> I wear a hijab in the public school classroom where I teach. Children ask me a lot of questions. I have never had any child that thought it was weird or anything like that. And they like the fact, both them and their parents, that they're introduced to a different culture.
>
> I work a lot at getting the kids to understand that the most important thing is that we should work on our similarities rather than our differences.

Ismail's involvement in an Islamic school, like Hammuda's, signifies that she is involved in creating future generations of Muslims. Her involvement in the public school illustrates that her life in the United States is not restricted to a Muslim enclave but rather that she is part of an American public—a middle-American public, no less—where her difference is valued. Photos of her teaching at the public school provide visual evidence to support her narrative. She also states that non-Muslims in America care about family values, and she insists that her neighbors have always been friendly and supportive of her as a Muslim. Her final statement about the importance of similarities over differences seems like a message to Arabs and Muslims not to hate the United States for differences but to embrace similarities in values and in humanity. Furthermore, Ismail's generalizations seem eager to provide a perfect (and as a result, one-dimensional) image of America, one that is hard to believe. Blanket statements like "I didn't see any prejudice anywhere" are perhaps one reason why these campaigns have not worked well with Muslims abroad; they can be easily dismissed as propaganda.

Figure 5.7. "Open Dialogue—Ismail," Council of American Muslims for Understanding. Produced in collaboration with the U.S. government in 2002.

These ads collectively seek to prove that Muslims live prosperous lives, are not marginalized, and are included as part of the core of U.S. society—in leading government positions, as paramedics, students, teachers, and business owners with predominantly non-Muslim clients. These Muslim immigrants in the United States portray themselves as raising their children speaking Arabic, as involved in Islamic schools, and as able to assert their Muslim identity without obstruction. The ads draw on discourses of the United States as a land of opportunity, freedom, equality, and diversity. The message is that people of all religions get along in the United States and Islam is respected; Muslims can be themselves here without barriers. The campaign seeks to remake America into a nation that is not against Islam, despite waging war against Arabs and Muslims at home and abroad. Unlike the CAIR ads that seek to demonstrate that Islam shares values with America, these ads from the Shared Values Initiative seek to prove that U.S. values do not conflict with Muslim values. With a different target audience from the CAIR ads, Muslims abroad as opposed to non-Muslims in the United States, these ads assert that American values, namely freedom, equality, and respect for diversity, provide Muslims with opportunities for a prosperous life in the United States; they are values that not only benefit Muslims but also from which they can learn. This version of U.S. diversity patriotism gone global presents itself as an example for others to follow.

The U.S. Shared Values campaign emphasizes that Muslims are recent immigrants and are treated fairly in a country in which they are foreigners, while the CAIR ads emphasize that Muslims are not recent immigrants and therefore are part of the U.S. nation. While these campaigns are commendable in their efforts to promote cross-cultural understanding, it is more significant that they reveal the contradictions within America's presentation of Muslims. If Muslims were truly part of the U.S. national community in the way that the government claims in their Shared Values campaign, then there would have been no need for CAIR to produce their "I am an American Muslim" ads, with their message to non-Muslims that Muslims are American too. While CAIR seeks to alter material reality through an ideological product, the U.S. government ads seek to cover material reality through an ideological campaign. This is not to say that some Muslims do not live prosperous lives free of harassment in the United States, but rather that hate crimes against Muslims persist even a decade after 9/11.[55]

Following the Ramadan ads, in 2002, a web survey was conducted in Indonesia, which "determined that 63 million Indonesians learned that 'Islam is not discriminated against' and is given equal treatment with other religions in the United States."[56] In addition, the website (which has since been taken off line) displayed viewer responses to the ads of the Shared Values Initiative.[57] The responses ranged from praise and appreciation to skepticism and rejection. Some expressed a desire for peace and harmony; others described the absence of discrimination during their visits to the U.S.; some expressed comfort that the U.S. government cares and is multicultural; while others charged the campaign with being patronizing and reductive, with missing the complexities of being Muslim in America, and for only showing "good Muslims." The most significant critique that emerged was that the ads would not solve policy issues, particularly regarding Iraq and Palestine. Here is a selection of the displayed comments:

From Ahmad in Indonesia

> This Web site is very good progress for cross-cultural understanding and hopefully it will make a contribution to establish world peace. This is a good example for all of us that we are able to cooperate though we have different faith.

From Arif-ur in Pakistan

We all need to pray for one another, and to love one another. We need to pray for a world full of love and without hatred or fear; a world where we can join hands together and accept one another, regardless of our skin color, ethnic divisions, religion or nationality. If we don't unite as a human race, then we have condemned the future generations of children to a dark and very grim future. Our survival depends on our unity. Without unity, there will be no human race in the future. We will be as extinct as the dinosaurs.

From Aida in Indonesia

Do you really want to build a better understanding between Americans and Muslim? Or do you just want to win this campaign? We are not stupid or blind or deaf. We read your intention not by what you say but what you do. We are not easy to believe you anymore after so many disinformations by your politicians, mass media and others. This won't work if you see us as an object. Be fair on the Palestinian issue, stop killing Iraqis and bombing their country, repair the destruction of what you did in Afghanistan, don't play tricks with the IMF. Do you want us to suffer more? Do you hope us to be tender of this situation?

From Omer in Pakistan

You are only highlighting the cases of Muslims in American where things are going right. I request that you also highlight the cases of arrest and torture of the Muslim population in American after Sept. 11. They are tortured mentally everywhere they go, or if they have a visa problem or there is a security concern. Have a look at that as well.

Dadi Darmedi, Center for the Study of Islam and Society, Jakarta

Washington is not the enemy or Islam. But it overlooks the fact that there are flaws in the U.S. foreign policies with respect to Muslims.

Din Syanmuddin, Secretary-General of Indonesian Council of Ulemas Jakarta, Indonesia

I don't think this kind of propaganda will significantly change the image that some Indonesians have of America. What needs to happen is a change in U.S. policy toward Muslim governments. The U.S. war on terrorism is one example of Muslims being blamed for too much of the violence.[58]

Many web posters, along with journalists and academic critics, raised the same crucial question: how could the U.S. government believe that a media campaign would solve problems arising from foreign policy? If the government wants to change opinions about the United States in Muslim countries, this critique went, then the way to do so would be through changing foreign policies. That the media is being used to cover up a policy problem merely garners greater suspicion and animosity toward the United States for presuming an ignorant audience. As one journalist wrote:

> Middle Eastern papers were nearly unanimous in arguing that American support
> of Israel and its occupation of Iraq are the issues that fuel anti-American senti-
> ment—and Alhurra can do little to disguise this. The *Jordan Times* put it in terms
> even an American could understand: "No amount of sweet words and pretty
> pictures will change the reality of an Israeli occupation, soon in its 37th year, or the
> chaos in Iraq, both of which can be directly attributed to American policy. No one
> here is going to be convinced of America's benign intentions as long as these issues
> remain unresolved. It all seems so obvious, at least to most of the people of this
> region, that, to borrow the phrase of an American cultural icon, 'doh!'"[59]

The U.S. message of freedom was met with suspicion and seen as propaganda
by many. "Freedom," as Kennedy and Lucas assert, has become a signifier of
American imperialism—"the empire for liberty."[60]

Even the Advisory Group on Public Diplomacy for the Arab and Muslim
World began its recommendations with the concession that the problem is
based in U.S. foreign policy:

> We fully acknowledge that public diplomacy is only part of the picture. Surveys
> indicate that much of the resentment toward America stems from real conflicts and
> displeasure with policies, including those involving the Palestinian-Israeli conflict
> and Iraq. But our mandate is clearly limited to issues of public diplomacy, where we
> believe a significant new effort is required.[61]

The Bush administration's use of used popular culture (advertising, pop music,
etc.) to sell ideology and brand national identity like a commodity raises questions about the way in which this ignores serious policy issues. The quote above
seems typical of American initiatives. Even in those moments when members
of the government acknowledge that there are problems with the government's
approach, there remains an unshakable faith that other, simultaneous efforts
will somehow override decades of policy. The government effort also raises
important issues about the reception of such initiatives, especially since this
particular campaign was deemed a failure. In 2005 Charlotte Beers resigned
from her position at the helm of the Shared Values Initiative. That same year
the government suspended production of *Hi Magazine*. Shortly thereafter, the
Shared Values campaign was removed from the Internet.[62] Viewers in the Middle East and elsewhere made it very clear that they were not likely to confuse
the rhetoric of U.S. respect for Islam with the realities of U.S. foreign policy.

The Limits of Diversity Patriotism

It is not unusual for the rhetoric of diversity to be mobilized during an era in
which the United States is least multicultural, or rather most discriminatory.
The shiny veneer of diversity can be a deceptive palliative, an optimistic balm

to soothe the harsh reality of racist policies and practices. The War on Terror, because it is so explicitly anti-Arab and anti-Muslim requires the rhetorical production of diversity. Some civil rights groups and nonprofit organizations responded to material realities (i.e., hate crimes) by promoting the ideology of diversity to encourage racial harmony among the public. The U.S. government, by contrast, sells the ideology of diversity to conceal the blatant discriminatory practices it enacts daily.

While the PSAs actively sought to promote a social message about American ideals of diversity, they reveal that there are limits to conceptualizing Arab and Muslim identities, even when profit is not a key motivator. They sell an inclusive vision of American society, yet rely on the narrow trope of the "good Muslim." In addition, they do not necessarily respond to views held by the majority of the U.S. public but react to and make visible the discourses of ideological hegemony. The Ad Council challenges the notion that only whites are American. CAIR challenges the notion that Muslims are violent and have incompatible values. The Shared Values Initiative challenges the notion that the United States is at war with Islam. Ultimately, these campaigns reveal that ideological meanings, in particular as they relate to U.S. national identity, are constantly being reworked. The election of the first-ever African American president in 2008 generated enormous hope for innumerable reasons, including President Obama's potential to inaugurate a more diverse image of the U.S. citizenry. The actual effects of his presidency, however, are far less clear than the hope inspired by his election campaign. From the perspective of post-9/11 ideological formations—in which we are still mired, despite our multiracial president—the terms within which Muslim-American citizenship can be articulated are restricted to the rigid discourses of the War on Terror that position Muslims as a threat to the nation. Thus while CAIR responds that Muslims are not a threat to the nation, the Ad Council leaves this question ambiguous by excluding Muslim and Sikh religious symbols from its PSA. In contrast, the U.S. government's message to Muslims abroad is that Muslims are safe in the United States and that the United States is not a threat to Muslims worldwide. These different approaches, and the pitfalls of each, reveal that even efforts to promote diversity can fall into simplified complex representational modes.

The three versions of diversity patriotism explored in this chapter project an inclusive portrait of U.S. citizenship, one that is multicultural and includes Muslims. However, they are predicated on a restrictive kind of inclusion, one that minimizes rather than relies on difference. Despite the buoyant optimism of these ideological campaigns, U.S. Muslims after 9/11 must nevertheless prove their loyalty to the nation for a chance to be imagined as part of the diverse national community. Inclusion of Muslims in diversity patriotism comes in the form of either ambiguous representations or the tried-and-true stereotype of the good Muslim. Jasbir Puar has argued that it was not only multicultural/ multiracial subjects who were incorporated into diversity patriotism but also homosexuals. She claims that the U.S. nation-state temporarily suspended its heteronormative imagined community after 9/11 in favor of a more inclusive imagined national community. She notes, however, that the inclusion of homosexuals in the national imaginary after 9/11 was limited to specific forms of homonormativity. Puar writes that the state manages and appropriates difference—ethnic and sexual difference—in order to produce complicity: "Part of the trappings of this exceptional citizen, ethnic or not, is the careful management of difference: of difference within sameness, and of difference containing sameness.... [W]hat little acceptance liberal diversity proffers in the way of inclusion is highly mediated by huge realms of exclusion."[63] Arab and Muslim Americans are included up to a point, so long as they comply with acceptable forms of sameness and difference. While the commercial media tends to represent Arab and Muslim identities as terrorists, victims, and patriots, nonprofitt advertising tends to represent Muslims as able to assimilate into U.S. society by virtue of possessing compatible values, patriotic devotion, or toning down visual differences and accentuating ambiguous assimilative diversity, revealing the limits of diversity at this historical juncture.

Epilogue

The thing that frustrates me is when I see us on TV nowadays. Who do they always show? They always show the crazy dude burning the American flag going: "Death to America!" Always that guy. Just once I wish they would show us doing something good, man. Right? Just once, right? Yeah, man! Right? Show us doing something good, like you know like baking a cookie or something, right? Cause I've been to Iran. We have cookies. Just once I want CNN to be like, "Now we are going to Mohammed in Iran." They go to some guy who's like, "Hello, I am Mohammed and I am just baking a cookie. I swear to God. No bombs, no flags, nothing. Back to you, Bob." That would be the whole news piece. They're never going to do that. Even if they ever did that, they would follow it up with another news piece: This just in: A cookie bomb just exploded.
—Maz Jobrani, *The Axis of Evil Comedy Tour*

Post-Race Racism in the Obama Era

During the 2008 U.S. presidential campaign, right-wing activists accused Barack Obama of being a closet Muslim, a secret Muslim, and a sleeper cell agent.[1] "Once a Muslim, always a Muslim," declared the conservative political commentator Debbie Schlussel.[2] The proof, critics claimed, was everywhere: Obama's middle name, Hussein; the fact that he spent some of his childhood in Indonesia, allegedly attending a Muslim school; the fact that his father was Muslim.[3] E-mails circulated accusing Obama of not wearing an American flag pin (which had, in recent presidential elections, become ridiculously reductive "proof" of one's patriotism). Some e-mails circulated photos of Obama that made him look like Osama bin Laden; others associated him with an often vague but always ominous Islamic threat [see Figures 6.1–6.3]. Other widely circulated e-mails stated that he would take his oath for political office on the Qur'an, would side with Muslims over Americans, and is anti-Israel— all signifiers of being un-American, anti-American, or a threat to the United States.[4] One such e-mail stated, "The Muslims have said they plan on destroying the US from the inside-out, what better way to start than at the highest level—through the President of the United States, one of their own!!!!"[5] The Clarion Fund, a right-wing nonprofit organization whose mission is to educate the public about the radical Islamic threat, distributed 28 million copies of a film, *Obsession: Radical Islam's War against the West*, months before the election in an attempt to associate Obama with terrorism.[6]

Figure 6.1. Example of images circulated by right-wing activists accusing Barack Obama of being Muslim.

Figure 6.2. Example of images circulated by right-wing activists accusing Barack Obama of being Muslim, implying dangerous radicalism.

Figure 6.3. Example of images circulated by right-wing activists that likened Barack Obama to Osama bin Laden.

Obama had to "go stealth" with whatever associations he had with Islam or risk his chance at the U.S. presidency. On the campaign trail, Obama repeatedly asserted his commitment to Christianity, repeatedly assured the American public that he is not nor has he ever been Muslim.[7] He distanced himself from his father's Islamic faith, his Muslim relatives in Kenya, his childhood in Indonesia. He did not visit mosques despite invitations. The efforts were clear: as long as he could convince voters that he was not Muslim, he was acceptable as a U.S. presidential candidate.[8] Despite these numerous attempts to discredit Obama—by turns inventive, amusing, and repugnant—he was elected president.

The election of Barack Obama takes post-race racism to a new level. Many people considered Obama's successful bid for the presidency the crowning evidence of a post-race era, an era in which the United States is finally a color-blind democracy and meritocracy. Claims to a post-race society became more widespread and popular across party lines than ever before. What could be better evidence of a post-race era than the election of the first African American as U.S. president? However, Obama's presidential campaign, while celebrated as evidence of racial progress, revealed continued strains of anti-immigrant, anti-black, anti-Arab, and anti-Muslim sentiment.

A few years into Obama's presidency, these strains only seem more prominent. The persistence of racism is evident in public opinion polls, hate crimes, and right-wing activism against Islam. Accusations of his hidden Muslim life did not disappear on Obama's election. A Pew Forum poll in August 2010, a year and a half into his presidency, revealed that 18 percent of Americans believed that Obama is Muslim, compared to 12 percent in March 2008. When asked, "What is Obama's religion?," 34 percent answered "Christian," compared to 47 percent in 2008, and 46 percent said they did not know, compared to the prior 34 percent. Not surprisingly, the poll indicates a correlation between those who believe that he is Muslim and those who oppose his presidency. According to the poll, "Beliefs about Obama's religion are closely linked to political judgments about him. Those who say he is a Muslim overwhelmingly disapprove of his job performance, while a majority of those who think he is a Christian approve of the job Obama is doing. Those who are unsure about Obama's religion are about evenly divided in their views of his performance."[9]

Politicians and aspiring politicians alike—from Andy Martin and Orly Taitz (leader of the "birther" movement) to Donald Trump—accused Obama before and after his election of not being a U.S. citizen, questioning his place of birth, highlighting that his father is from Kenya, and claiming that he is not a "real" American.[10] Though nearly a decade after 9/11, the flames of fear and suspicion are easily stoked. With the slander that prominent public servants voice—with great pride—is it any surprise that hate crimes and discrimination against Muslims continue? In August 2010 a passenger stabbed a New York City cab driver after confirming that he was Muslim.[11] A few months later, slices of bacon arranged spelling "pig chump," were left on the tile walkway to a mosque.[12] In March 2011 a Muslim woman wearing a hijab was removed from a Southwest Airlines flight because the stewardess deemed her suspicious.[13] And in May 2011 two Muslim clerics traveling to North Carolina for a conference on Islamophobia were escorted off an Atlantic Southeast Airlines flight in Tennessee after the pilot expressed discomfort at their presence.[14]

Right-wing anti-Muslim activism—well coordinated and often well funded—has likewise continued. On February 13, 2011, the Islamic Circle of North America Relief Organization held a charity dinner in California. Their aim was to raise money for their programs that provide shelter and support for homeless Muslim women in the United States. This charity event was protested by several hundred people, many affiliated with Tea Party groups such as the North Orange County Conservative Coalition and ACT! for America, who picketed the event holding American flags, booing and shouting. Organizers of the dinner reported hearing a vast array of anti-Muslim slogans: "Go back home!" "Mohammad was a pervert!" "Mohammad was a child molester!" "Mohammad was a fraud!" "Mohammad was a false prophet!" "You're a stupid terrorist, go home!" "Why don't you go home and beat your wife as you do every night and then have sex with a nine-year-old?" "One nation under God, not Allah!" "Go home, we don't want your Sharia law!"[15] Villa Park councilwoman Deborah Pauly told protesters that what was going on at the charity event was "pure unadulterated evil" and that she knew some Marines "who would be very happy to help these terrorists to an early meeting in paradise." One of the protest organizers, Steven Amundson, said, "It's not right for terrorism to come to Yoruba Linda. I always stress the need to be peaceful and positive."[16]

Right-wing and Christian-right activists have protested Muslim events, the religion of Islam as a whole, and the building of mosques and Muslim community centers. Plans to build Muslim mosques and community centers have led to a wave of hate crimes against Muslim individuals, mosques, and Muslim-owned businesses around the country.[17] A church in Gainesville, Florida, planned to commemorate the ninth anniversary of the September 11 attacks by hosting a Qur'an-burning ceremony. Pastor Terry Jones of the Dove World Outreach Center's International Burn a Koran Day told CNN, "We believe that Islam is of the devil, that it's causing billions of people to go to hell, it is a deceptive religion, it is a violent religion and that is proven many, many times."[18]

Most notorious were protests against the Cordoba Initiative's plan in 2010 to build a Muslim community center in an abandoned building two and a half blocks from ground zero in New York City.[19] The term *ground zero mosque* was coined by the right-wing activist Pamela Geller soon after the plan was announced. It was then picked up and used by the news media, giving the impression that the combined mosque and community center would literally be built on the site of the former World Trade Center. President Obama supported the construction of the community center based on the argument that Muslims have a right to religious freedom under the First Amendment, stating, "As a citizen, and as president, I believe that Muslims have the same right to practice their religion as anyone else in this country. That includes the right to build a place of worship and a community center on private property in lower Manhattan, in accordance with local laws and ordinances."[20]

The controversy surrounding the "ground zero mosque" is part of a larger debate about the place of minorities in U.S. public life, revealing that a particular kind of discriminatory logic—whether based on race, religion, or the racialization of religion—is alive and thriving in the Obama era. Obama's election, while celebrated as signifying racial progress in the United States, reflects a new era that has emerged since the multicultural movement in the 1990s in which explicit racism, a denial of the persistence of racism, and a celebration of the end of racism operate simultaneously. These three strands can be seen throughout a disturbingly large segment of American life and in one of the prominent arguments against building the Muslim community center near ground zero.

The argument that acquired perhaps the most sympathy and support was that the Muslim community center, if built on the proposed site, would disrespect the memory of the three thousand people who died on 9/11.[21] This claim makes use of a powerful rhetorical strategy, redirecting the intellectual debate on religious freedom to an emotional plea to respect the victims of the terrorist attacks. Evoking the memory of those who died effectively shuts down the conversation, since virtually all agree that those who died should be respected.[22] No one wants to be perceived as insensitive to the victims' memory or to the grief of their loved ones. However, following this logic, we can argue that no Catholic churches should be built near schools because this would mean disrespecting children who have been abused by priests. U.S. Representative Peter King (R-NY) has stated, "It is insensitive and uncaring for the Muslim community to build a mosque in the shadow of Ground Zero. While the Muslim community has the right to build the mosque, they are abusing that right by needlessly offending so many people who have suffered so much."[23]

This argument is distinct from the common right-wing argument for national security over political correctness—in this case that if the mosque/community center were built, then it would mean the terrorists had won. Rather, it is one that claims to not seek to discriminate, yet nonetheless expects Muslims to willingly subvert their identity and rights in favor of some unarticulated "greater good." Furthermore, assuming a stance of antiracism and sensitivity, this argument nonetheless operates from the presumption that Islam and terrorism are synonymous. This logic maintains that the issue at hand is not Islam, and not even national security, but rather the protection and respect of the memory of 9/11 victims and their families. The popularity of this argument is no surprise, as it exemplifies the denial of racism that accompanies explicit racism, a denial that enables a far more insidious form of discrimination, in the name not of race but of sensitivity, and that argues for First Amendment rights, not against them.

The ground zero mosque controversy reveals the ways in which the boundaries of American identity continue to be policed, often through struggles over who counts as a "real" American. It demonstrates the extent to which Islam is figured as un-American and terroristic and also the extent to which all Muslims are required to account for the actions of those who commit violence in the name of Islam. More than anything, it reflects the state of public discourse in "post-race" America: racism can persist even through arguments that advocate civil rights for all. The furor over the ground zero mosque reveals an enduring theme in American life—that race and racism are far from settled national issues. These three simultaneous trends in U.S. public debate—the persistence of overt racism, denials of the persistence of racism, and celebrations of the end of racism—underscore this book's main claim that positive representations do not signal the end of racism. Rather, the expression and articulation of racism in government, media, and civic discourses has become more varied, subtle, and diffuse.

As this book has demonstrated, positive or sympathetic representations of Arabs and Muslims in government discourses and media representations during the War on Terror do not necessarily signify a new era of multicultural sensitivity. Rather, they can and often do reproduce logics and affects that legitimize exempting Arabs and Muslims from rights. Archetypical images of Arab and Muslim Americans confine the range of possibilities of what it is to be a Muslim or an Arab in America. Such archetypes participate in the seemingly endless—and varied—history of human racism. To cite one of many other examples, Patricia Hill Collins argues that African American women are stereotyped as the mammy, the matriarch, the welfare mother, or the Jezebel:

> These four prevailing interpretations of Black womanhood form a nexus of elite white male interpretation of Black female sexuality and fertility. Moreover, by meshing smoothly with systems of race, class, and gender oppression, they provide effective ideological justifications for racial oppression, the politics of gender subordination, and the economic exploitation inherent in capitalist economies.[24]

Similarly, the images of patriotic Arab/Muslim Americans, victimized Arab/Muslim Americans, oppressed veiled Muslim women, and terrorist Muslim men control how Arab and Muslim identities can be thought of and understood, revealing the limits of representations at this historical moment. Some images, logics, and feelings remain outside the realm of acceptable representations because they threaten the project of U.S. empire. Can we imagine Arab and Muslim characters that do not fit the mold of the patriotic American, the Arab American victim of hate crimes, the oppressed Muslim woman, or the lunatic terrorist man? Can we imagine a version of diversity that does not require downplaying difference and accentuating heternormativity (or even homonormativity), patriotism, and one's contribution and service to the nation? Can we imagine ordinary Arab and Muslim characters that, as Maz Jobrani hopes, do nothing more remarkable than bake cookies?

The revolutions in Tunisia, Egypt, Libya, and Bahrain in 2011, referred to as the Arab Spring, proved that Arabs want democracy. These mass demonstrations demanding democracy posed a clear challenge to widespread assumptions in the West that "they" are against democracy and freedom and "hate us for our freedom." It is too soon to predict whether these revolutions will affect how Arabs and Muslims are portrayed in the U.S. media, but the potential for change is ripe.

Challenging Simplified Complex Representations

The ideological work produced by the media during the War on Terror has had profound effects on human lives, as evidenced by the way in which 24 has contributed to shifting public opinion on the torture of Arab and Muslims at Abu Ghraib, Guantánamo Bay, and a number of other unnamed prisons. At the same time, as shown throughout this book, audiences have launched effective challenges to the commercial media's production of archetypes. Internet fan sites, where viewers discuss and respond to TV shows, are increasingly popular and an important element in an emerging interactive economy. Such participation demonstrates that viewers are not passive consumers who merely imbibe dominant images but are actively creating a community of viewers who serve as virtual production assistants.[25] In addition to watchdog groups that lobby TV shows to urge them to make changes to their scripts, fan sites now also have the potential to make TV producers more accountable to viewers.

Viewers are not the only emergent actors signaling potential change. Arab and Muslim American writers, artists, organizations, and even a few mainstream sitcoms, have sought to challenge dominant images of Arabs and Muslims. For example, Arab and Muslim American organizations have been actively monitoring the media for instances of Islamophobia, promoting Arab and Muslim American political participation, and expanding popular understanding of Arabs and Islam in the United States. Such organizations include the American-Arab Anti-Discrimination Committee (ADC), the Arab American Institute (AAI), the Council on American-Islamic Relations (CAIR), and the Muslim Public Affairs Council (MPAC). CAIR has prepared a guide to understanding Islam for journalists, and MPAC opened a Hollywood bureau in April 2007 that offers consulting services, reviews scripts for film and television, hosts film screenings, and also holds an awards ceremony to recognize achievements in challenging stereotypes. Edina Lekovic, the communications director, has stated, "MPAC doesn't want to be a watchdog. . . . It wants to be an ally in helping tell better stories about Muslims."[26] Important alternative media outlets have also emerged, such as Bridges Television (the only Muslim television station broadcasting in English in the United States) and Link Television (an independent media organization that broadcasts voices underrepresented in commercial media).

Arab and Muslim Americans are also producing creative work to challenge stereotypes and hegemonic meanings about Arabs and Muslims after 9/11. Similar to the "vibrant black public spheres" that Herman Gray has described, "whose cultural transactions unsettle and challenge traditional representations and meanings of blackness," Arab and Muslim American artists and writers are articulating new possibilities for representing Arab and Muslim identities. This includes but is not limited to stage productions by Leila Buck, Heather Raffo, Betty Shamieh, Najla Said, Laila Farah, Najee Mondalek, Arab Theatrical Arts Guild, Golden Thread Productions, and the Nibras Collective; the art collectives Other and Sunbula; independent filmmakers, including Rola Nashef, Cherien Dabis, and Jackie Salloum; novelists like Mohja Kahf, Randa Jarrar, Diana Abu-Jaber, Laila Halaby, Laila Lalami, and Alia Yunis; poets such as Khaled Mattawa, Naomi Shihab Nye, Lisa Suhair Majaj, Suheir Hammad, Natalie Handal, Hayan Charara; the blogs Kabobfest, Angry Arab, Progressive Arab Woman's Voice, and Baheyya; hip-hop artists, including the Iron Sheik, Excentric, Omar Offendum, the Philistines, and the N.O.M.A.D.S; DJs like Sultan32, Emancipation, and Mutamussik; and stand-up comedians such as Ahmad Ahmad, Aaron Kader, Maysoon Zayid, Dean Obeidallah, Maz Jobrani, Ray Hanania, Azhar Usman, Preacher Moss, Mohammed Amer, and Shazia Mirza.[27] These organizations and artists have, in ways subtle and absurd, comic and devastating, challenged the commercial media's limited representations of Arab and Muslim identities. They are going beyond the monochromatic representations of Arabs and Muslims in the media, showing Arabs and Muslims in their full human complexity as intellectuals, poets, teachers, artists, and family members, as people affected by war and U.S. racism, as people who face the challenges of life by laughing and by crying, with desperation and with faith and optimism.

If the representational strategies identified in this book fail at humanizing Arabs and Muslims, then what strategies might prove more successful? My contention throughout this book is not that these simplified strategies such as flipping the enemy, diversifying Muslim identities, and sympathizing with the plight of Arab Americans are simply useless. Rather, the problem is that these representations are chained to the War on Terror, thereby associating Arab and Muslim identities indelibly with terrorism, extremism, and oppression. My hope is to see Arab and Muslim characters in contexts that have little to do with terrorism, or extremism, or oppression; characters that break out of the good/bad Muslim dichotomy; and characters in more leading and recurring roles. In digging through the mire of post-9/11 popular culture, we actually find a few mainstream productions that have been trying all three of these things. Interestingly, these shows—*Whoopi!*, *Aliens in America*, *Community*, and *Little Mosque on the Prairie*—are all sitcoms. Although they refer to the context of the War on Terror, they do not take it as their central subject.

Whoopi Goldberg's sitcom *Whoopi!* (2003–4) premiered two years after 9/11 and centers on Mavis Rae, a former singer and one-hit wonder who opens a small hotel in New York City. Much of the humor centers on her interaction with her Iranian handyman, Nasim, played by Omid Djalili (the first Iranian in a recurring role on U.S. television). Nasim is the butt of jokes about terrorism, his experiences with racial profiling are highlighted, and he is fearful of deportation. In one scene, Mavis complains that her unemployed brother is driving her crazy and jokes that if he does not find a job soon, she will kill him. Nasim replies, "It's a shame you live in America. You don't have a secret service where they can just come in, bash him on the head, put a hood over it, take him away, and then get him in a cell and place two electrodes . . . "[28] Nasim is a humorous and likable character whose life as a handyman is affected by 9/11 in ridiculous ways. *Whoopi!* favors a representational strategy that challenges stereotypes and diffuses racial tension by using humor to accentuate stereotypes to demonstrate their absurdity. Though nominated for an Emmy award, it lasted for only one season on NBC.

Aliens in America (2007–8) also lasted only one season, this one on the CW network. It is about the Tolchucks, a middle-class white American family in Wisconsin with two children in high school: a daughter who is popular and a son who is awkward and unpopular. The mother comes up with a scheme to popularize her son by signing up for a foreign exchange student from Norway. She assumes that he will be blond and gorgeous and therefore make her son immediately popular. Instead, they receive a Pakistani Muslim named Raja Musharaff who they initially try to get rid of, since his presence would ruin the popularity plan. However, the Tolchucks end up raising Raja as their own after they discover that his parents died. Raja is an offensively one-dimensional character: he speaks with an accent, wears traditional Pakistani clothing, has strange customs, and is very naive and square. He is a caricature. On first meeting the Tolchucks, he says, "You are such good people to open your home to me. Thank you Allah for the Tolchucks."[29] He believes in dating only if chaperoned, will not kiss until married, does not lie, and is extremely honest and giving of himself. In one episode, he works at the convenience store and refuses to sell alcohol to his classmates with fake IDs.[30] His host brother pleads with him to sell them alcohol so that they could have a chance at becoming popular, but Raja is unyielding; he does not care about being cool and

Figure 6.4. Promotional ad for *Aliens in America*, CW, 2007–8.

subscribes to higher principles. Raja is not alone in being stereotyped: Americans are depicted as ignorant and racist, but the Tolchuck family is trying to rise above their surroundings.

Despite the stereotype, the sitcom is notable for having this character in a leading role, and the focus of the show is ultimately about two misfits—the white American boy who does not fit in at school and the Pakistani Muslim who does not fit into suburban American culture. The representational strategy is to parallel these two outcasts to accentuate their similarities while still exploring cultural and religious differences. Like *Whoopi!*, the show tries to diffuse post-9/11 tension about Muslims through humor, reveling in the ordinariness of daily life, reminding viewers of how much of life is *not* about terrorism, or September 11, but rather about petty squabbles, social anxieties, and the other mundane dilemmas of being human.

Community (2009–present), currently in its third season, is a sitcom on NBC about students at a community college who have formed a study group. Danny Pudi plays Abed Nadir, a Palestinian American student who is obsessed with popular culture and socially awkward. Abed is a weird guy, but his weirdness has nothing to do with his ethnic or religious identity. Despite references to his obligation to take over the family falafel business and a stereotypical appearance

Figure 6.5. Abed, played by Danny Pudi, in *Community*, NBC, 2009–present.

by his father, Abed is a refreshingly original character, unlike any other portrayal of Arab Americans on network television to date.

Finally, *Little Mosque on the Prairie* (2007–2012), winner of numerous awards, has been broadcast for five seasons by the Canadian Broadcasting Corporation and is slated for a sixth and final season. Created by Zarqa Nawaz, a Muslim Canadian woman of Pakistani descent, it is about Muslims in a small Canadian town who start a mosque and community center for Muslims. Nawaz began the sitcom with an explicit teaching mission: to bring the lives of ordinary Muslims to North American viewers and to educate viewers about who ordinary Muslims are. Beneath the laughs, it is about two communities colliding and learning to live together and also about the internal dynamics and struggles within the Muslim community. In an interview, Nawaz stated:

> I think people are assuming because of the title and the subject matter that it's going to be really controversial and political. But it's just a comedy that happens to

Figure 6.6. Promotional ad for *Little Mosque on the Prairie*, CBC, 2007–2012.

have Muslim people in it, and it's meant to make people laugh. It's about relationships and human interactions and life in a rural setting. But it's really the first comedy of its kind in North America, and that's why it's so intriguing.[31]

The uniqueness of the show is evident throughout. As a sitcom, it is successful because it is at heart about what all good comedy is about—relationships and human interactions—universal conditions that are explored through a very particular, and often revelatory, situation. The show thus immerses us in the specifics of observant Islamic life and focuses on internal debates between conservative and liberal Muslims. The result are discussions that are both hilarious and unprecedented, including how to determine when Ramadan officially begins (does one spot the new moon with a telescope or with one's eyes, or follow what is determined in Saudi Arabia?); whether there should be barrier between men and women at the mosque; whether Muslims can celebrate Halloween; what a Muslim-compliant bachelor party should look like; and whether Muslim women can take a swimming class if the instructor is a gay man. Nawaz says, "We try to find the hilarity in every scenario. . . . Muslim women cover their hair because they're worried men will be attracted to it. But what if the guy is gay and isn't attracted to it? Does that count?"[32] In addition to internal debates, the series also addresses issues external to the community, such as racial profiling and assumptions by the public that Muslims are terrorists. The representational strategies used include humanizing Muslims by featuring them as lead characters and depicting the differences among them, showing that Muslims are not monolithic but have diverse perspectives and varying degrees of religiosity. What is especially notable about *Whoopi!, Aliens in America, Community,* and *Little Mosque on the Prairie* is that the story lines do not revolve around terrorism or homeland security. They are about a boutique hotel, a high school, a community college, and a community center. Not only do the story lines represent a departure from prior tropes, but the characters also deviate from the standard patriot and victim molds. What makes these programs notable in challenging simplified complex representational strategies is that characters are not measured in relation to terrorism; they are people with varied lives. At times these shows contain elements of the stereotyping and simplified representations common to TV dramas. But at other moments they use this common reference point to push it to its extreme, creating characters and situations so absurd that they highlight the problem of racism itself.

Little Mosque on the Prairie has been broadcast in France, Switzerland, Francophone African countries, Israel, Gaza, the West Bank, Dubai, Finland, Turkey, and the United Arab Emirates. FOX planned to adapt the show to an American setting, but those plans have not come to fruition.[33] Nawaz speculates why the show was a success in Canada but not in the United States: "I think Canada, you know, we were one step removed from 9/11 so that rawness wasn't there in the country. The networks were more willing to take a chance on a subject like this. Also, the network is the CBC [Canadian Broadcasting Corporation], which is a publicly owned and funded television station. It's a not-for-profit station so they don't have to worry about profit-making as much as representing the diversity and the regionality of the country."[34] The lack of success of three out of four of these sitcoms in the United States could be interpreted as another common sitcom casualty or as another instance of the country's resistance to diverging from co-opted versions of multiculturalism.

Television has participated in the co-optation of multiculturalism by portraying limited and acceptable versions of diversity, thus demonstrating again and again that an increase in diverse representations of Arab and Muslim identities does not in itself demonstrate a victory over racism. Gray has written that the evolving strategy of television networks since the 1980s—from containing the many difficult questions of race to superficial support of liberal pluralism—has had a nasty side effect: the elimination, repression, or incorporation of difference as part of the co-optation mechanism.[35] Similarly, Hall has written that the spaces "won" for difference are "very carefully policed and regulated. . . . [W]hat replaces invisibility is a kind of carefully regulated, segregated visibility."[36]

This careful regulation can be seen with the limiting representations of patriotic and victimized Arab and Muslim Americans and the carefully managed efforts to humanize terrorists, and reference terrorist motives, while restricting audience sympathies or identification to veer toward "the terrorists." The four sitcoms discussed above, however, offer an intriguing alternative. They seem to incorporate some elements of media co-optation of difference by including elements of caricaturing yet at the same time offer possibilities for future diversions from representing all Arab and Muslim characters in contexts exclusively focused on terrorism and solely in supporting or inconsequential roles. As Hall writes of black identities, "What is at issue here is the recognition of the extraordinary diversity of subject positions, social experiences and cultural identities which compose the category 'black.'"[37] These sitcoms help construct a different field of representation that produces diverse meanings about Arabs and Muslims and hints at the potential for a more diverse field of representations in the future.

If more and more Americans were to see more and more complex portrayals of Arabs, Muslims, Arab Americans, and Muslim Americans on television and film, who knows what the effect would be. Racism is endlessly flexible; resentment of the Other can be easily stoked; stereotyped assumptions are difficult to overcome. Perhaps the emergence of honest, and varied, and *human* portrayals of Arabs and Muslims would make little difference in a country, and a world, attuned to prejudice. At the same time, television can have a surprising effect on its viewers. Television shows, as these few comedies demonstrate, have the potential for more complexity than we often give them credit for. Perhaps, en masse, they could compel an audience to reject the logics that legitimize the denial of human rights.

Needless to say, we should be wary of believing too much in the promise of any one medium, particularly a medium shaped by advertising dollars and therefore governed by the unyielding pull of the lowest common denominator. The problem of legitimizing the denial of rights to any group of people is larger than the question of representations. We are not even close to resolving terrorist threats to the United States by Muslim extremists; the impact of U.S. foreign policies on Muslim lives around the world, perceived by many outside the United States as a different, and unacknowledged, form of terrorism; racism directed toward Arabs and Muslims under the guise of national security and a feminist imperative; or violence against women around the globe. So long as Muslim grievances resulting from U.S. foreign policies go unrecognized; so long as the solution to terrorism perpetrated by Muslim extremists is explained away through a simplified depiction of religion and culture and resolved through war; so long as discourses and representations produce a mirage of harmonious multiculturalism; and so long as U.S. imperial power is prioritized over the value of human life, a solution to these serious concerns will remain out of reach. What will not remain out of reach, however, are justifications for the United States to abuse its power and deny human rights to Arabs and Muslims under the banner of multiculturalism.

Notes

NOTES TO INTRODUCTION

1. Throughout this book, I use the term *American* to refer to citizens of the United States; it does not include other North Americans or South or Central Americans.

2. Here, I use "9/11/01" to mark this particular crisis in the United States and acknowledge that there are other 9/11's, namely, in Chile in 1973. In the rest of the book, however, I use "9/11" since I have already established which September 11 is the subject of this book.

3. For a comprehensive summary of how Arabs and Muslims have been represented in Hollywood Cinema during the twentieth century, see Jack G. Shaheen, *Reel Bad Arabs: How Hollywood Vilifies a People* (Northampton, MA: Interlink Publishing Group, 2001). Also see Shaheen's *The TV Arab* (Bowling Green, OH: Bowling Green State University Popular Press, 1984) and *Guilty: Hollywood's Verdict after 9/11* (Northampton, MA: Olive Branch Press, 2008).

4. George W. Bush, "Address to a Joint Session of Congress and the American People," September 20, 2001, www.whitehouse.gov/news/releases/2001/09/20010920–8.html (accessed September 8, 2008).

5. Nacos and Torres-Reyna note an increase in Arab and Muslim American perspectives in the media immediately after 9/11. See *Fueling Our Fears* (Lanham, MD: Rowman & Littlefield, 2007).

6. This episode was written and aired during the period in which some cafeterias in government buildings and restaurants in the United States altered their menus, replacing "french fries" with "freedom fries," in an act of protest against France for not supporting the U.S. invasion of Iraq.

7. *7th Heaven* followed up on Ruthie and Yasmine's friendship and explored their religious and cultural differences in "Peer Pressure," Season 7, Episode 8, WB, November 11, 2002.

8. "Chapter Seventy-Four," *Boston Public*, Episode 74, FOX, December 19, 2003.

9. "Save the Country," *The Education of Max Bickford*, Season 1, Episode 11, CBS, January 13, 2002. For additional examples, see *Jack and Bobby*, "A Man of Faith," Season 1, Episode 4, WB, October 3, 2004; "The New Normal," *Judging Amy*, Episode 617, CBS, March 22, 2005; "Profiles in Courage," *George Lopez Show*, Season 2, Episode 18, ABC, March 12, 2003; and Whoopi Goldberg's sitcom, *Whoopi!*, which included an Iranian supporting character played by Omid Djalili, NBC, September 2003–April 2004.

10. TV shows like *7th Heaven*, *Boston Public*, and *The Education of Max Bickford* stand out from many of the others because of their explicitly educational message. *The West Wing* attempted to be educational in its post-9/11 special episode, "Isaac and Ishmael," but was met with much criticism for seeking to educate rather than entertain. In contrast, because these programs are either aimed at a younger viewing audience or take place in educational institutions, they were able to take on an educational thrust without much of a backlash from viewers and critics. My focus in this book is on TV dramas with an adult viewing audience, as opposed to those aimed at youth.

11. Marcy Kaptur, "Kaptur Bill Safeguards Civil Liberties for All: H. Res. 234 Seeks to Protect against Religious, Ethnic Persecution," Press Release, Rep. Marcy Kaptur (D-OH), May 15, 2003, www.adc.org/index.php?id=1803 (accessed August 23, 2010).

12. American-Arab Anti-Discrimination Committee, "Report on Hate Crimes and Discrimination against Arab Americans: The Post-September 11 Backlash," Washington, DC: American-Arab Anti-Discrimination Committee Research Institute, 2003, www.adc.org /hatecrimes/pdf/2003_report_web.pdf (accessed January 30, 2008). For additional information on hate crimes, the experiences of Arab Americans, and government measures after 9/11, see Arab American Institute, "Healing the Nation: The Arab American Experience after September 11," AAI's first anniversary report on Profiling and Pride, 2002, www.aaiusa.org/issues/1639 (accessed September 30, 2008); and Human Rights Watch, "We Are Not the Enemy: Hate Crimes against Arabs, Muslims, and Those Perceived to Be Arab or Muslim after September 11th," *Human Rights Watch Report* 14, no. 6 (G), November 2002, www.hrw.org/reports/2002 /usahate/ (accessed September 30, 2008). Also see Louise Cainkar, "The Impact of 9/11 on Muslims and Arabs in the United States," in *The Maze of Fear: Security and Migration after September 11th*, ed. John Tirman (New York: New Press: 2004); Louise Cainkar, *Homeland Insecurity: The Arab American and Muslim American Experience after 9/11* (New York: Russell Sage Foundation, 2009); and Anny Bakalian and Mehdi Bozorgmehr, *Backlash 9/11: Middle Eastern and Muslim Americans Respond* (Berkeley: University of California Press, 2009).

13. American-Arab Anti-Discrimination Committee, "Report on Hate Crimes and Discrimination against Arab Americans," 134–35.

14. For reports on the government's practice of detaining and deporting Arabs and Muslims after 9/11, see, for example, American-Arab Anti-Discrimination, "ADC Fact Sheet: The Condition of Arab Americans Post-9/11," March 27, 2002, www.adc.org/index.php?id=282 (accessed March 7, 2007); "Equal Employment Opportunity Commission (EEOC) Fact Sheet," January 13, 2003, www.adc.org/index.php?id=1682 (accessed March 7, 2007); and "America's Disappeared: Seeking International Justice for Immigrants Detained after September 11," January, 26, 2004, www.aclu.org/FilesPDFs/un%20report.pdf (accessed March 7, 2007). For the impact of 9/11 on Arab and Muslim communities, see Nadine Naber, "The Rules of Forced Engagement: Race, Gender, and the Culture of Fear among Arab Immigrants in San Francisco Post-9/11," *Cultural Dynamics* 18, no. 3 (2006): 235–67; Cainkar, *Homeland Insecurity*; and Bakalian and Bozorgmehr, *Backlash 9/11*.

15. For a summary of government initiatives, see Cainkar, *Homeland Insecurity*. A summary of all government initiatives after 9/11 can be found in Bakalian and Bozorgmehr, *Backlash 9/11*, 253–65. Also see Sally Howell and Andrew Shryock, "Cracking Down on Diaspora: Arab Detroit and America's 'War on Terror,'" *Anthropological Quarterly* 76, no. 3 (2003): 443–62.

16. *Enemy combatant* is a term created by the Bush administration to justify the suspension of human rights for people associated with Al Qaeda, a non-national military organization.

17. Council on American-Islamic Relations, "The Status of Muslim Civil Rights in the United States 2002: Stereotypes and Civil Liberties," Civil Rights Report, 2002, www.cair .com/CivilRights/CivilRightsReports/2002Report.aspx (accessed May 9, 2011).

18. Nancy Chang, *Silencing Political Dissent: How Post–September 11 Anti-Terrorism Measures Threaten Our Civil Liberties* (New York: Seven Stories, 2002).

19. Tram Nguyen, *We Are All Suspects Now: Untold Stories from Immigrant Communities after 9/11* (Boston: Beacon Press, 2005).

20. Louise Cainkar, "Post-9/11 Domestic Politics Affecting U.S. Arabs and Muslims: A Brief Review," *Comparative Studies of South Asia, Africa, and the Middle East* 24, no. 1 (2004): 245–48.

21. See American Civil Liberties Union, "Blocking Faith, Freezing Charity," *ACLU Report*, June 16, 2009, www.aclu.org/human-rights/report-blocking-faith-freezing-charity (accessed August 18, 2010).

22. Bakalian and Bozorgmehr, *Backlash 9/11*, 168–71.

23. For an account of the impact of 9/11 on Arab Americans and Muslim Americans, see Nadine Naber and Amaney Jamal, eds., *Race and Arab Americans before and after 9/11* (Syracuse, NY: Syracuse University Press, 2007); Cainkar, *Homeland Insecurity*; Sunaina Maira, *Missing* (Durham, NC: Duke University Press, 2009); Bayoumi, *How Does It Feel to Be a Problem*; and Junaid Rana, *Terrifying Muslims: Race and Labor in the South Asian Diaspora* (Durham, NC: Duke University Press, 2011). Also see Wayne Baker et al., *Citizenship and Crisis: Arab Detroit after 9/11* (New York: Russell Sage Foundation, 2009).

24. For more on the psychological impact of 9/11 on Arab Americans, see See Wahiba Abu-Ras and Soleman H. Abu-Bader, "The Impact of the September 11, 2001, Attacks on the Well-Being of Arab Americans in New York City," *Journal of Muslim Mental Health* 3, no. 2 (2008): 217–39.

25. Junaid Rana, "Tracing the Muslim Body: Race, US Deportation, and Pakistani Return Migration," in *The Sun Never Sets: South Asian Migrants in the Circuits of US Power*, ed. Vivek Bald, Miabi Chatterji, Sujani Reddy, and Manu Vimalassary (New York: New York University Press, forthcoming).

26. Naber, "The Rules of Forced Engagement."

27. Michelle Malkin, "Racial Profiling: A Matter of Survival," *USA Today*, August 16, 2004, www.usatoday.com/news/opinion/editorials/2004-08-16-racial-profiling_x.htm (accessed August 15, 2010).

28. John Carter, "Political Correctness Kills," *Washington Times*, December 11, 2009, http://carter.house.gov/index.cfm?sectionid=104&sectiontree=6,104&itemid=1110 (accessed August 16, 2010).

29. See Mahmood Mamdani, *Good Muslim, Bad Muslim: America, the Cold War, and the Roots of Terror* (New York: Pantheon Books, 2004).

30. See Ella Shohat and Robert Stam, *Unthinking Eurocentrism: Multiculturalism and the Media* (New York: Routledge, 1994); and Ella Shohat, "Gender and the Culture of Empire," in *Visions of the East: Orientalism in Film*, ed. Gaylyn Studlar and Matthew Bernstein (New Brunswick, NJ: Rutgers University Press, 1997).

31. For a comprehensive examination of representations of Arabs in Hollywood cinema, see Shaheen, *Reel Bad Arabs*. Examples of films that represent women in harems and as slaves are *The Lad and the Lion* (1917); *The Lady of the Harem* (1926); *Kismet* (1920, 1930, 1944, 1955); and *Road to Morocco* (1942). For more on representations of women in Hollywood films, see Tania Kemal-Eldin's film, *Hollywood Harems* (1999). For a critique of Orientalist imagery, see Elia Suleiman and Jayce Salloum's film, *Introduction to the End of an Argument* (1990). Also see Nadine Naber, "Ambiguous Insiders: An Investigation of Arab American Invisibility," *Racial and Ethnic Studies* 23, no. 1 (2000): 37–61; Ella Shohat, "Gender in Hollywood's Orient," *Middle East Report*, 162 (January–February 1990): 40–42; and Amira Jarmakani, *Imagining Arab Womanhood: The Cultural Mythology of Veils, Harems, and Belly Dancers in the U.S.* (New York: Palgrave, 2008).

32. For writings published after 2000 that examine representations of Arabs, see John Downing and Karin Wilkins, "Mediating Terrorism: Text and Protest in Interpretations of *The Siege*,"

Critical Studies in Media Communication 19, no. 4 (December 2002): 419–437; Ervand Abrahamian, "The US Media, Huntington, and September 11," Third World Quarterly 24, no. 2 (2003): 529–44; Debra Merskin, "The Construction of Arabs as Enemies: Post–September 11 Discourse of George W. Bush," Mass Communication and Society 77, no. 2 (May 2004): 157–75; Susan Nance, How the Arabian Nights Inspired the American Dream, 1790–1935 (Chapel Hill: University of North Carolina Press, 2009); Dina Ibrahim, "Framing of Arab Countries on American News Networks Following the September 11 Attacks," Journal of Arab and Muslim Research 1, no. 3 (2009): 279–96; Karin Wilkins, Home/land/security: What We Learn about Arab Communities from Action-Adventure Films (New York: Rowman & Littlefield, 2009); Mehdi Semati, "Islamophobia, Culture and Race in the Age of Empire," Cultural Studies 24, no. 2 (2010): 256–75; Robert Morlino, "'Our Enemies among Us': The Portrayal of Arab and Muslim Americans in Post-9/11 American Media," in Civil Rights in Peril: The Targeting of Arabs and Muslims, ed. Elaine C. Hagopian (Chicago: Haymarket Books, 2004), 71–103; Evelyn Alsultany, "The Prime-Time Plight of Arab-Muslim-Americans after 9/11: Configurations of Race and Nation in TV Dramas," in Race and Arab Americans before and after 9/11: From Invisible Citizens to Visible Subjects, ed. Nadine Naber and Amaney Jamal (Syracuse: Syracuse University Press 2008), 204–28; Douglas Little, American Orientalism: The United States and the Middle East since 1945 (New York: I. B. Tauris, 2003).

33. Brian T. Edwards, Morocco Bound: Disorienting America's Maghreb, from Casablanca to the Marrakech Express (Durham, NC: Duke University Press, 2005).

34. Shaheen, Reel Bad Arabs, 28–29.

35. Ibid., 21.

36. Jarmakani, Imagining Arab Womanhood: The Cultural Mythology of Veils, Harems, and Belly Dancers in the US. (New York: Palgrave, 2008).

37. Alia Yunis and Gaelle Duthler, "Tramps vs. Sweethearts: Changing Images of Arab and American Women in Hollywood Films," Middle East Journal of Culture and Communication 4, No. 2 (2011): 225–43.

38. McAlister notes that between 1968 and 1976, Palestinians and Palestinian sympathizers led twenty-nine hijackings, forming a central part of the U.S. news cycle and becoming a popular theme in Hollywood films in the 1970s and 1980s. See Melani McAlister, Epic Encounters: Culture, Media, and U.S. Interests in the Middle East, 1945–2000 (Berkeley: University of California Press, 2001), 200.

39. For more on representations of Arabs in U.S. popular culture, see Ella Shohat, "Gender and the Culture of Empire," in Studlar and Bernstein, Visions of the East; Shohat and Stam, Unthinking Eurocentrism; Shaheen, The TV Arab and Reel Bad Arabs. Also see Little, American Orientalism; and Linda Steet, Veils and Daggers: A Century of National Geographic's Representation of the Arab World (Philadelphia: Temple University Press, 2000). Also see Edward Said, Covering Islam (New York: Vintage, 1997).

40. Arab American Institute, www.aaiusa.org/educational_packet.htm.

41. For more on racial casting during the War on Terror, see Junaid Rana, "When Pakistanis Became Middle Eastern: Visualizing Racial Targets in the Global War on Terror," in The Cultural Politics of the Middle East in the Americas, ed. Evelyn Alsultany and Ella Shohat (Ann Arbor: University of Michigan Press, forthcoming).

42. For analysis and criticism of Three Kings and The Siege, see Tim Jon Semmerling, "Evil" Arabs in American Popular Film (Austin: University of Texas Press, 2006); McAlister, Epic Encounters, 260; Shaheen, Reel Bad Arabs, 11; Wilking and Downing, "Mediating Terrorism"; Lila Kitaeff, "Three Kings: Neocolonial Arab Representation," Jump Cut: A Review of Contemporary Media 46 (2003): 1–16; and Khadija F. El Alaoui, "Mission Impossible: Wealth

at Home and Justice Abroad in Liberal Hollywood" (Paper presented at the annual meeting of the American Studies Association, Albuquerque, NM, October 16, 2008).

43. Mario L. Barnes, Erwin Chemerinsky, and Trina Jones, "A Post-Race Equal Protection?" *Georgetown Law Journal* 98 (2010), 967–1004.

44. Ibid., 973.

45. Ibid., 968.

46. Howard Winant, *The New Politics of Race: Globalism, Difference, Justice* (Minneapolis: University of Minnesota Press, 2004), xiii.

47. Ibid.

48. Ibid., xiii–xiv.

49. Jodi Melamed, "The Spirit of Neoliberalism: From Racial Liberalism to Neoliberal Multiculturalism," *Social Text* 23, no. 4, issue 89 (Winter 2006): 1–24. Also see Eduardo Bonilla-Silva, *Racism without Racists: Color-Blind Racism and the Persistence of Racial Inequality in the United States*, 2nd ed. (New York: Rowman and Littlefield, 2006). Also see Tim Wise, *Colorblind: The Rise of Post-Racial Politics and the Retreat from Racial Equity* (San Francisco: City Lights Books, 2010).

50. Melamed, "The Spirit of Neoliberalism," 18.

51. These landmark cases include *City of Richmond v. Croson*, 1989; *Adarand Constructors, Inc. v. Peña*, 1995; *Hopwood v. University of Texas Law School*, 1996; passage of Proposition 209 in California in 1997, followed by similar proposition passed in Washington (1998), Florida (2000), and Michigan (2008).

52. Barnes, Chemerinsky, and Jones, "A Post-Race Equal Protection?," 976.

53. Ella Shohat and Robert Stam, "De-Eurocentricizing Cultural Studies," in *Internationalizing Cultural Studies: An Anthology*, ed. M. Ackbar Abbas and John Nguyet Emi (Oxford: Blackwell, 2005), 484. For an overview of debates on political correctness on college campuses, see McAlister, *Epic Encounters*; and Patricia Aufderheide, ed., *Beyond PC: Toward a Politics of Understanding* (St. Paul, MN: Graywolf Press, 1992).

54. See Shohat and Stam, *Unthinking Eurocentrism*; and Herman Gray, *Watching Race: Television and the Struggle for Blackness* (Minneapolis: University of Minnesota Press, 1995).

55. Shohat and Stam, *Unthinking Eurocentrism*, 200–201.

56. Laurence Michalak, "Improvements in the Image of Arabs and Muslims in American Cinema," *Awrak Al Awsat* [Middle East Research Competition and the Center for Social and Economic Researches and Studies, Tunis], no. 2 (2009): 39–54.

57. On representations of Native Americans, see Shari Huhndorf, *Going Native: Indians in the American Cultural Imagination* (Ithaca, NY: Cornell University Press, 2001); and Philip J. Deloria, *Playing Indian* (New Haven, CT: Yale University Press, 1999). On representations of Latinos, see William Anthony Nericcio, *Tex[t]-Mex: Seductive Hallucinations of the "Mexican" in America* (Austin: University of Texas Press, 2007); Charles Ramirez Berg, *Latino Images in Film: Stereotypes, Subversion, and Resistance* (Austin: University of Texas Press, 2002); Clara E. Rodriguez, *Heroes, Lovers, and Others: The Story of Latinos in Hollywood* (Oxford: Oxford University Press, 2004); Arlene Dávila, *Latino Spin: Public Image and the Whitewashing of Race* (New York: New York University Press, 2008). On representations of Asian Americans, see David Palumbo-Liu, *Asian/American: Historical Crossings of a Racial Frontier* (Stanford: Stanford University Press, 1999); Peter X. Feng, ed., *Screening Asian Americans* (New Brunswick, NJ: Rutgers University, 2002); Kent A. Ono and Vincent N. Pham, *Asian Americans and the Media* (Cambridge: Polity Press, 2008); Gina Marchetti, *Romance and the "Yellow Peril": Race, Sex, and Discursive Strategies in Hollywood Fiction* (Berkeley: University of California

Press, 1994); Robert G. Lee, *Orientals: Asian Americans in Popular Culture* (Philadelphia: Temple University Press, 1999); and Elaine Kim, *Slaying the Dragon Reloaded: Asian Women in Hollywood and Beyond* (San Francisco: Asian Women United, 2010). For more on media representations of African Americans, see, for example, Gray, *Watching Race*; Christine Acham, *Revolution Televised: Prime Time and the Struggle for Black Power* (Minneapolis: University of Minnesota Press, 2004); and Darnell M. Hunt, *Channeling Blackness: Studies on Television and Race in America* (New York: Oxford University Press, 2004). Also see Donald Bogle, *Coons, Mulattoes, Mammies & Bucks: An Interpretive History of Blacks in American Films* (New York: Continuum International, 1994).

58. My thanks to Amy Sara Carroll for engaging with my work and coming up with this term.

59. See Mamdani, *Good Muslim, Bad Muslim*.

60. This phenomenon of using racial representations in the service of a postracial or even nonracial national imaginary can be seen in the case of Puerto Rico. Yeidy Rivero examines how *Mi Familia*, the first Puerto Rican sitcom featuring a black family after a history of representing blackness through blackface, "normalized Puerto Rico's hegemonic construction of a nonracist society" by claiming to not be about race or racism (150). She demonstrates how the sitcom, in refusing to acknowledge or deal with racism, participated in normalizing the idea of a mestizo Puerto Rico that had no racial problems. See Yeidy M. Rivero, *Tuning Out Blackness: Race and Nation in the History of Puerto Rican Television* (Durham, NC: Duke University Press, 2005).

61. Gray, *Watching Race*.

62. Herman Gray, "The Politics of Representation on Network Television," in *Media and Cultural Studies: Keyworks*, ed. Meenakshi Gigi Durham and Douglas Kellner (Oxford: Blackwell, 2001), 449.

NOTES TO CHAPTER 1

1. "Fox TV Accused of Stereotyping American Muslims," *Free Republic*, January 13, 2005, www.freerepublic.com/focus/f-news/1320357/posts (accessed May 16, 2011).

2. "24 under Fire from Muslim Groups," *BBC News*, January 19, 2007, http://news.bbc. co.uk/2/hi/entertainment/6280315.stm (accessed May 16, 2011). CAIR has also created an advertising campaign to counteract negative stereotypes. For an analysis of its ad campaign, see Evelyn Alsultany, "Selling American Diversity and Muslim American Identity through Non-Profit Advertising Post-9/11," *American Quarterly* 59, no. 3 (September 2007): 593–622 and chapter 5.

3. Critics of CAIR include www.jihadwatch.org and www.frontpagemag.com.

4. "24 Comes under Muslim Fire," *Northern Territory News* (Australia), January 29, 2007: 23.

5. I use "Arab/Muslim" not to denote that these identities are one and the same but rather to point to how Arab and Muslim identities are conflated.

6. This PSA was broadcast during one of the program's commercial breaks on Monday, February 7, 2005, FOX.

7. "Is Torture on Hot Fox TV Show 24 Encouraging US Soldiers to Abuse Detainees?," *Democracy Now*, February 22, 2007, www.democracynow.org/2007/2/22/is_torture_on_hit _fox_tv (accessed May 10, 2011).

8. Jane Meyer, "Whatever It Takes," *New Yorker*, February 19, 2007, www.newyorker.com /reporting/2007/02/19/070219fa_fact_mayer?currentPage=all (accessed May 10, 2011).

9. Ibid.

10. Martin Miller, "24 Gets a Lesson in Torture from the Experts," *Los Angeles Times*, February 13, 2007, http://articles.latimes.com/2007/feb/13/entertainment/et-torture13; David Bauder, "Group: TV Torture Influencing Real Life," *USA Today*, February 11, 2007, www.usatoday.com/life/television/2007-02-11-tv-torture_x.htm; Meyer, "Whatever It Takes."

11. 24, FOX, November 2001–9; *Threat Matrix*, ABC, September 2003–January 2004; *The Grid*, TNT, July–August 2004; *Sleeper Cell*, Showtime, December 2005–December 2006; *The Wanted*, NBC, July 2009.

12. *Threat Matrix*, ABC, September 18, 2003–January 29, 2004; 24, FOX, Season 6, January 14–May 21, 2007.

13. "Al-Fatiha," *Sleeper Cell*, Showtime, Season 1, Episode 1, December 4, 2005.

14. "Day 4: 7pm–8pm," 24, FOX, March 14, 2005.

15. Waleed Mahdi argues that Islam is portrayed as inspiring U.S. patriotism in Hollywood films after 9/11, for example, in *Traitor* (2008). Waleed Mahdi, "US vs. Arab/Muslim Trauma Unpacked: An Analysis of the Challenging Mode of Depiction in *Traitor*" (Paper presented at the annual meeting of the Middle East Studies Association, Boston, MA, 2009).

16. "Inter Arma Silent Leges," *The Practice*, ABC, Season 6, Episode 9, December 9, 2001. For an analysis of this episode and representations of Arab Americans as victims of post-9/11 hate crimes on TV dramas, see Evelyn Alsultany, "The Primetime Plight of Arab-Muslim-Americans after 9/11: Configurations of Race and Nation in TV Dramas," in *Race and Arab Americans before and after September 11th: From Invisible Citizens to Visible Subjects*, ed. Nadine Naber and Amaney Jamal (Syracuse, NY: Syracuse University Press, 2007), 204–28 and chapter 2.

17. "Suspicion," *7th Heaven*, WB, Season 6, Episode 12, January 21, 2002.

18. "Scholar," *Sleeper Cell*, Showtime, Season 1, Episode 4, December 7, 2005.

19. See Jack G. Shaheen, *Reel Bad Arabs: How Hollywood Vilifies a People* (Northampton, MA: Interlink Publishing Group, 2001).

20. Stuart Hall, "Racist Ideologies and the Media," in *Media Studies: A Reader*, 2nd ed., ed. Paul Marris and Sue Thornham (New York: New York University Press, 2000), 273.

21. My use of "cultural capital" comes from Pierre Bourdieu, *The Field of Cultural Production* (New York: Columbia University Press, 1993).

22. Mahmood Mamdani, *Good Muslim, Bad Muslim: America, the Cold War, and the Roots of Terror* (New York: Pantheon Books, 2004).

23. Even recent films with positive representations of Arab and Muslim characters, such as *The Visitor* (2007) and *Sorry, Haters* (2005), are framed in the context of 9/11. *Little Mosque on the Prairie* (2007–2012), a sitcom televised by the Canadian Broadcasting Corporation has not crossed over into the United States.

24. Andy Patrizio, "Aladdin: Special Edition," IGN Entertainment, IGN.com, September 17, 2004, http://dvd.ign.com/articles/549/549036p1.html (accessed May 14, 2011).

25. See Mamdani, *Good Muslim, Bad Muslim*.

26. For more on the significance of how the news media portrays Arab violence as terrorism through framing sympathy, violence, and context, see the documentary *Peace, Propaganda, and the Promised Land: U.S. Media and the Israeli-Palestinian Conflict* (Media Education Foundation, 2003).

27. Herman Gray, *Watching Race: Television and the Struggle for Blackness* (Minneapolis: University of Minnesota Press, 1995), 163.

28. Dorothy Rabinowitz, "Bloody Good," *Wall Street Journal*, December 2, 2005, http://online.wsj.com/article/SB113348291480011881.html?mod=2_1168_1.

29. Joy Press, "There Goes the Neighborhood: A Suburban Miniseries Drops in on the Terrorists Next Door," *Village Voice*, November 15, 2005, www.villagevoice.com /screens/0547,tv1,70218,28.html.

30. Gillian Flynn, "TV Review: Sleeper Cell," *Entertainment Weekly*, no. 852 (December 2, 2005), www.ew.com/ew/article/0,,1134552,00.html.

31. John Leonard, "There Goes the Neighborhood," *New York* 38, no. 43 (November 27, 2005), http://nymag.com/nymetro/arts/tv/reviews/15177/.

32. Joan Juliet Buck, "Sleeper Cell," *Vogue* 195, no. 12 (December 2005): 254.

33. Comment by Mike Rankin, Tampa Film Fan Blog, March 25, 2007, http://tampafilm-fan.com/blog/2007/03/23/tv-miniseries-reviewsleeper-cellamerican-terror/ (accessed January 11, 2008).

34. Comment by SGT SIEBRASSSE, August 7, 2007, http://tampafilmfan.com/ blog/2007/03/23/tv-miniseries-reviewsleeper-cellamerican-terror/ (accessed January 11, 2008). Here and in subsequent Internet posts, quotations are presented without emendation.

35. Comment by Isebella, November 4, 2007, http://tampafilmfan.com/blog/2007/03/23/ tv-miniseries-reviewsleeper-cellamerican-terror/ (accessed January 11, 2008).

36. For commentary on *The Wanted*, see David Zurawik, "The Wanted: NBC News Show an Embarrassment," *Baltimore Sun*, July 21, 2009, http://weblogs.baltimoresun.com/entertain-ment/zontv/2009/07/the_wanted_nbc_news_terrorism.html; Brian Lowry, "The Wanted," *Variety*, July 20, 2009, www.variety.com/review/VE1117940697.html?categoryid=32&cs=1; and viewer comments on the Internet Movie Database, www.imdb.com/title/tt1468817 /usercomments (accessed March 12, 2010).

37. Comment by TrentB, Metacritic, "*Sleeper Cell*: Season 1," December 13, 2006, www .metacritic.com/tv/sleeper-cell/season-1/user-reviews (accessed March 13, 2010).

38. Comment by Sue Barnham, TV Squad, "*Sleeper Cell*: Faith," December, 31, 2006, www .tvsquad.com/2006/12/13/sleeper-cell-faith/ (accessed May 14, 2011).

39. Juana Maria Rodriguez, *Queer Latinidad: Identity Practice, Discursive Spaces* (New York: New York University Press, 2003), 118.

40. Dan Iverson, "*Sleeper Cell*: American Terror Review," IGN, January 26, 2007, http:// tv.ign.com/articles/758/758753p1.html (accessed March 13, 2010).

41. Michael Medved, "Tickets to Terror," FOX, January 4, 2006.

42. Lillie Chouliaraki, *The Spectatorship of Suffering* (Thousand Oaks, CA: Sage, 2006), 30.

43. See Susan Sontag, *On Photography* (New York: Farrar, Straus and Giroux, 1977).

44. Jean Baudrillard, *Simulacra and Simulation* (Ann Arbor: University of Michigan Press, 1995).

45. Susan Willis, *The Portents of the Real: A Primer for Post-9/11 America* (New York: Verso, 2005), 4–5.

46. Rebecca Leung, "Abuse of Iraqi POWs by GIs Probed," *60 Minutes II*, April 28, 2004, www.cbsnews.com/stories/2004/04/27/60II/main614063.shtml (accessed February 18, 2011).

47. Dick Meyer, "Rush: MPs Just 'Blowing Off Steam,'" CBSNews.com, May 6, 2004, www.cbsnews.com/stories/2004/05/06/opinion/meyer/main616021.shtml (accessed February 18, 2011).

48. For more on these strategies, see Steven Peacock, ed., *Reading 24: TV against the Clock* (New York: I. B. Tauris, 2007).

49. Alfred W. McCoy, "The Myth of the Ticking Time Bomb," *Progressive*, October 2006, www.progressive.org/mag_mccoy1006 (accessed May 14, 2011).

50. Sharon Sutherland and Sarah Swan, "'Tell Me Where the Bomb Is, or I Will Kill Your Son': Situational Morality on 24," in Peacock, *Reading 24: TV against the Clock*, 119–32.

51. Miller, "24 Gets a Lesson in Torture."

52. Andrew Buncombe, "U.S. Military Tells Jack Bauer: Cut Out the Torture Scenes??? Or Else!," *Independent* (London), February 13, 2007, Transcript Policy Section, 2.

53. Greenhill, "24 on the Brain," *Los Angeles Times*, May 28, 2007: A27.

54. Dahlia Lithwick, "The Fiction behind Torture Policy: The Lawyers Designing Interrogation Techniques Cited Jack Bauer More Frequently than the Constitution," *Newsweek*, July 26, 2008, www.newsweek.com/id/149009.

55. Ibid. For examples of how the U.S. government redefined torture, see "Bad Methods; President Bush's Alternative Techniques for Questioning Terrorism Suspects Have No Basis in Science or Law," *Washington Post*, June 1, 2007: A14, www.washingtonpost.com/wp-dyn /content/article/2007/05/31/AR2007053102007.html (accessed May 14, 2011); M. Greg Bloche and Jonathan Marks, "Doing unto Others as They Did unto Us: The Path to Torture," *New York Times*, November 14, 2005, 21.

56. The Heritage Foundation is the largest right-wing think tank in Washington, D.C. Its mission is to "formulate and promote conservative public policies based on the principles of free enterprise, limited government, individual freedom, traditional American values, and a strong national defense" (www.heritage.org/about/). The foundation supports faith-based initiatives, school vouchers, banning abortion, and overturning affirmative action. The Heritage Foundation is very influential on Capitol Hill and takes credit for much of Bush's foreign and domestic policies. Remarks by Homeland Security Secretary Michael Chertoff at a Heritage Foundation Discussion, "Fact vs. Fiction in the War on Terror," Ronald Reagan Building, Washington, DC, Major Leaders Special Transcripts, Federal News Service, June 23, 2006.

57. Emilio Karim Dabul, "In Defense of '24': An Arab-American Defends the Real-Life Bauers," *Wall Street Journal*, Editorial Page, February 7, 2007, www.opinionjournal.com /la/?id=110009633 (accessed September 6, 2007).

58. Caren Kaplan, "Precision Targets: GPS and the Militarization of U.S. Consumer Identity," *American Quarterly* 58, no. 3 (September 2006): 705.

59. Miller, "24 Gets a Lesson in Torture."

60. Robert Siegel, "Torture's Wider Use Brings New Concerns," *All Things Considered*, NPR, March 13, 2007, 8:00 P.M.

61. ABC News/Washington Post Poll, May 20–23, 2004. See David Morris and Gary Langer, "Terrorist Suspect Treatment: Most Americans Oppose Torture Techniques," *ABC News*, May 27, 2004, http://abcnews.go.com/sections/us/polls/torture_poll_040527.html (accessed October 8, 2008).

62. Brigitte L. Nacos and Oscar Torres-Reyna, *Fueling Our Fears: Stereotyping, Media Coverage, and Public Opinion of Muslim Americans* (Lanham, MD: Rowman and Littlefield, 2007), 86.

63. Mark Bowden, "The Dark Art of Interrogation," *Atlantic Monthly* (October 2003): 53, www.theatlantic.com/doc/200310/bowden (accessed October 14, 2008).

64. Nacos and Torres-Reyna, *Fueling Our Fears*, 91.

65. Douglas L. Howard, "'You're Going to Tell Me Everything You Know': Torture and Morality in FOX's 24," in Peacock, *Reading 24*, 142.

66. Melani McAlister, *Epic Encounters: Culture, Media, and U.S. Interests in the Middle East, 1945–2000* (Berkeley: University of California Press, 2001), 6.

67. The term *imagined communities* originates with Benedict Anderson, *Imagined Communities: Reflections on the Origin and Spread of Nationalism* (New York: Verso, 1983).

68. My use of "interpellation" comes from Louis Althusser, "Ideology and Ideological State Apparatuses," in *Lenin and Philosophy and Other Essays* (New York: Monthly Review Press, 2001), 85–126.

NOTES TO CHAPTER 2

An earlier version of this chapter appeared in Nadine Naber and Amaney Jamal, eds., *Race and Arab Americans before and after 9/11: From Invisible Citizens to Visible Subjects* (Syracuse: Syracuse University Press, 2007).

1. Richard Cohen, "Profiles in Evasiveness," *Washington Post*, Editorial, October 11, 2001: A33.

2. Mona Charen, "Religious War?," *Jewish World Review*, September 21, 2001. Citation found in American-Arab Anti-Discrimination Committee, "Report on Hate Crimes and Discrimination against Arab Americans: The Post-September 11 Backlash," (Washington, DC: American-Arab Anti-Discrimination Committee Research Institute, 2003), www.adc .org/hatecrimes/pdf/2003_report_web.pdf (accessed January 30, 2008).

3. Rep. John Cooksey (R-LA) on Louisiana radio stations on September 17, 2001. Citation found in American-Arab Anti-Discrimination Committee, "Report on Hate Crimes."

4. Anthony D. Romero, preface to "Sanctioned Bias: Racial Profiling Since 9/11," ACLU Racial Profiling Report, February 2004, www.aclu.org (accessed September 30, 2008).

5. ACLU Fact Sheet on PATRIOT Act II, ACLU, March 28, 2003, www.aclu.org /national-security/aclu-fact-sheet-patriot-act-ii (accessed June 16, 2011).

6. Ibid.

7. "Liberal" programs are those whose plots tend to advocate for the underdog and whose messages seem concerned with lessening social hierarchies; either explicitly or implicitly, they usually support civil rights for Arab and Muslim Americans. "Conservative" programs are those whose messages tend to support institutions of power—such as the government, the police, and the military—and whose plots legitimize hierarchies of power; not surprisingly, these shows tend to be less sympathetic and express fewer qualms about—if not outright enthusiasm for—detaining Arabs. Elaine Rapping writes that what defines liberal TV dramas of the legal variety is whether the focus is on "the importance of the criminal motives and mindset" (i.e., why the suspect committed an act of terrorism) or on the "guilty act." A focus on the guilty act and an extreme form of punishment for it is characteristic of a conservative approach. See Elayne Rapping, *Law and Justice as Seen on TV* (New York: New York University Press, 2003), 34.

8. George Lipsitz, *Time Passages: Collective Memory and American Popular Culture* (Minneapolis: University of Minnesota Press, 2001), 69–70.

9. John Fiske and John Hartley, *Reading Television* (New York: Routledge, 2003), 5.

10. For more on the relationship between law and popular culture, see, for example, David A. Black, *Law in Film: Resonance and Representation* (Urbana: University of Illinois Press, 1999); John Denver, ed., *Legal Reelism: Movies as Legal Texts* (Urbana: University of Illinois Press, 1996); and Richard K. Sherwin, *When Law Goes Pop: The Vanishing Line between Law and Popular Culture* (Chicago: University of Chicago Press, 2000).

11. "Bad to Worse." *The Practice*, ABC, Season 7, Episode 8, December 1, 2002.

12. See the Council on American-Islamic Relations' 2002 Civil Rights Report at www
.cair-net.org/civilrights2002/ (accessed January 3, 2004).

13. "Inquiry into Secret Service Agent Barred from Flight," CNN.com, www.cnn
.com/2001/US/12/28/rec.agent.airline (accessed January 3, 2004).

14. Council on American-Islamic Relations' 2002 Civil Rights Report.

15. Ann Coulter, September 13, 2001, www.anncoulter.com (accessed January 3, 2004).

16. "An Appalling Magic," *Guardian Unlimited*, May 17, 2003, www.guardian.co.uk/usa
/story/0,12271,957670,00.html (accessed January 30, 2008).

17. Toby Miller, *Technologies of Truth: Cultural Citizenship and the Popular Media* (Minneapolis: University of Minnesota Press, 1997), 24.

18. Giorgio Agamben, *Homo Sacer: Sovereign Power and Bare Life* (Stanford: Stanford
University Press, 1998), 9.

19. Rachad Antonius, "Un Racisme 'Respectable,'" in *Les relations ethniques en question:
ce qui a changé depuis de 11 Septembre 2001*, ed. Jean Renaud, Linda Pietrantonio, and Guy
Bourgeault (Montreal: University of Montreal Press, 2002).

20. "Inter Arma Silent Leges," *The Practice*, ABC, Season 6, Episode 9, December 9, 2001.

21. "Ashcroft Announces 'Voluntary Interviews' with 3,000 U.S. Visitors," IslamOnline.
net, www.islamonline.net/english/news/2002-03/21/article04.shtml (accessed January 3,
2004).

22. "Hundreds of Arabs Still Detained," CBS News, March 13, 2002, www.cbsnews.com
/stories.2002.03/13/503649.shtml (accessed January 3, 2004).

23. Leti Volpp, "The Citizen and the Terrorist," in *September 11 in History: A Watershed
Moment?*, ed. Mary Dudziak (Durham, NC: Duke University Press, 2003), 148.

24. For more on "guilt by association" after 9/11, see Nadine Naber, "The Rules of Forced
Engagement: Race, Gender, and the Culture of Fear among Arab Immigrants in San Francisco Post-9/11," *Cultural Dynamics* 18, no. 3 (2006): 235–67; Louise Cainkar, *Homeland Insecurity: The Arab American and Muslim American Experience after 9/11* (New York: Russell Sage
Foundation, 2009); Anny Bakalian and Mehdi Bozorgmehr, *Backlash 9/11: Middle Eastern
and Muslim Americans Respond* (Berkeley: University of California Press, 2009); David Cole
and James X. Dempsey, *Terrorism and the Constitution: Sacrificing Civil Liberties in the Name of
National Security* (New York: New Press, 2002).

25. For more on representations of victimhood after 9/11, see Elisabeth Anker, "Villains,
Victims and Heroes: Melodrama, Media, and September 11," *Journal of Communication* 55, no.
1 (2005): 22–37.

26. "Baby Love," *NYPD Blue*, ABC, Season 9, Episode 6, December 4, 2001.

27. Educators for Social Responsibility, "List of Publicly Reported U.S. Hate Crimes
against Arabs, Muslims, and Other South Asians from September 11 through September 26,
2001," www.esrnational.org/discrimincidents200109.htm (accessed January 3, 2004).

28. "Patriot," *Law and Order*, NBC, Season 12, Episode E2226, May 22, 2002.

29. See www.in.gov/ctasc/whatsnew/freedomcorps.pdf (accessed January 3, 2004).

30. Nat Hentoff, "The Death of Operation TIPS: Volunteer Spying Corps Dismissed,"
Village Voice, December 13, 2002, www.villagevoice.com/issues/0251/hentoff.php (accessed
January 3, 2004).

31. See, for example, "Man in Terror Scare Says Woman Is Lying," CNN, www.cnn
.com/2002/US/09/13/alligator.alley/ (accessed January 3, 2004).

32. www.cair-net.org/civilrights2002.

33. Nick Lally, "Patriotism, Violence, and Hate," *Insurgent Newspaper*, October 2001, http://theinsurgent.net/index.php?volnum=13.2&article=patriotism (accessed January 4, 2006).

34. Robert E. Pierre, "Victims of Hate, Now Feeling Forgotten," *Washington Post*, September 14, 2001: A01.

35. Ella Shohat and Robert Stam, *Unthinking Eurocentrism: Multiculturalism and the Media* (New York: Routledge, 1994), 205–6.

36. On *The Education of Max Bickford*, it is through the experiences of Professor Haskell, a white woman, that the viewer comes to sympathize with the Arab/Muslim American student. On *The Guardian*, it is through Nick Fallon, the white male lawyer, that viewers come to learn about the hate crime committed against the Arab/Muslim American store owner and his daughter. On *7th Heaven*, it is through young white female Ruthie that viewers come to know and sympathize for Arab/Muslim American Yasmine.

NOTES TO CHAPTER 3

1. This apt phrase comes from Gayatri Spivak, "Can the Subaltern Speak?," in *Marxism and the Interpretation of Culture*, ed. Cary Nelson and Lawrence Grossberg (Chicago: University of Illinois Press, 1988), 271–315.

2. *7th Heaven*, for example, featured two episodes with veiled Muslim American women and girls. In one episode, Ruthie's twelve-year-old friend Yasmine, who is veiled and Muslim, is harassed on the street on her way to school. Ruthie and her family are concerned for Yasmine's well-being and try to get her accepted at Ruthie's private school. When Yasmine is rejected from the private school because of anti-Muslim sentiment, Ruthie quits her school in an act of solidarity with Muslims, stating that she does not want to be part of group hate ("Suspicion," *7th Heaven*, WB, Season 6, Episode 12, January 21, 2002). In another episode of *7th Heaven*, Yasmine and Ruthie spend time together and explore their cultural differences. Yasmine is portrayed as a good influence on Ruthie, who is starting to experiment with makeup, high heels, and boys. Yasmine believes they are too young for such pursuits and encourages Ruthie not to rush into such things ("Peer Pressure," *7th Heaven*, WB, Season 7, Episode 8, November 11, 2002). Both episodes focus on representing veiled Muslim girls and women as Americans who were subject to post-9/11 harassment. They are victims who become virtuous Americans. Their difference is portrayed as positive and nonthreatening, and their American identities are accentuated. On *The Education of Max Bickford*, an undergraduate student at the college who is Muslim and wears a veil receives a note under her dorm room door containing a death threat. The college classroom turns into a space to debate blame and civil rights after 9/11 ("Save the Country," *The Education of Max Bickford*, CBS, Season 1, Episode 11, January 13, 2002).

3. For example, see Ayaan Hirsi Ali, "Counterpoint: Setting Themselves Apart," *Newsweek International* (November 27, 2006).

4. Lorraine Ali, "Reform: Not Ignorant, Not Helpless," *Newsweek* (December 12, 2005): 33.

5. Radio Address by Mrs. George W. Bush, November 17, 2001, *The American Presidency Project*, ed. John T. Woolley and Gerhard Peters, www.presidency.ucsb.edu/ws/?pid=24992. http://www.presidency.ucsb.edu/ws/index.php?pid=24992 (accessed July 12, 2010).

6. Hillary Clinton, "New Hope for Afghanistan's Women," *Time* (November 24, 2001), www.time.com/time/nation/article/0,8599,185643,00.html (accessed June 15, 2010).

7. Richard Lacayo, "Lifting the Veil," *Time* (December 3, 2001): 34–49; "Lifting the Veil," *CNN Evening News*, November 20, 2001; "Lifting the Veil," *CNN Evening News*, September 10, 2007; "Lifting the Veil," *Anderson Cooper 360*, CNN, April 23, 2009; "Under the Veil," ABC Evening News, October 26, 2006; "Beneath the Veil," CNN Evening News, September 13, 2002; Anna Mulrine, "Unveiled Threat: The Taliban Is Relentless in Its Oppression of Afghan Women," *U.S. News & World Report* (October 15, 2001): 32–34.

8. See, for example, Richard Lacayo et al., "About Face," *Time* (December 3, 2001), www .time.com/time/magazine/article/0,9171,1001344.html (accessed June 21, 2010); and David Van Biema, Marguerite Michaels, and Nadia Mustafa, "Islam in the U.S.: Freer, But Not Friedan," *Time* (December 3, 2001), www.time.com/time/magazine/article/0,9171,1001348,00 .html#ixzz0r2vh2irx (accessed June 21, 2010).

9. Lisa Beyer, "The Women of Islam," *Time* (November 25, 2001), /www.time.com/time /world/article/0,8599,185647,00.html (accessed June 21, 2010).

10. Ibid.

11. Ibid.

12. Ibid.

13. Judith Butler, *Frames of War: When is Life Grievable?* (New York: Verso, 2010), xiii.

14. Leila Ahmed, *Women and Gender in Islam: Historical Roots of a Modern Debate* (New Haven: Yale University Press, 1992).

15. Ibid., 152.

16. Ibid., 217.

17. Minoo Moallem, *Between Warrior Brother and Veiled Sister: Islamic Fundamentalism and the Politics of Patriarchy in Iran* (Berkeley: University of California Press, 2005), 8.

18. For more on how identity can be shaped in response to external forces, see Nadine Naber, *Arab America* (New York: New York University Press, forthcoming). For more on women as signifiers of the nation, see Caren Kaplan, Norma Alarcón, and Minoo Moallem, eds., *Between Woman and Nation: Nationalisms, Transnational Feminism, and the State* (Durham, NC: Duke University Press, 1999).

19. Charles Hirschkind and Saba Mahmood, "Feminism, the Taliban, and Politics of Counter-Insurgency," *Anthropological Quarterly* 75, no 2 (Spring 2002): 341.

20. Minoo Moallem, "Transnationalism, Feminism, and Fundamentalism," in Kaplan, Alarcón, and Moallem, *Between Woman and Nation*, 320–48. See also Mahmood Mamdani, *Good Muslim, Bad Muslim: America, the Cold War, and the Roots of Terror* (New York: Pantheon Books, 2004).

21. Ibid., 61–62.

22. Hirschkind and Mahmood, "Feminism," 341.

23. For a brief history of the intellectual pioneers of political Islam, such as Jamal al-Din al-Afghani, Hassan al-Banna, Sayyid Qutb, and Abdul A'la Mawdudi, see Mamdani, *Good Muslim, Bad Muslim.* For more on women's status, role, and participation in the Middle East and Islam, see Laurie Brand, *Women, the State, and Political Liberalization: Middle Eastern and North African Experiences* (New York: Columbia University Press, 1998); Lara Deeb, *An Enchanted Modern: Gender and Public Piety in Shi'i Lebanon* (Princeton: Princeton University Press, 2006); Saba Mahmood, *The Politics of Piety: The Islamic Revival and the Feminist Subject* (Princeton: Princeton University Press, 2005); Valentin Moghadem, ed., *From Patriarchy to Empowerment: Women's Participation, Movements, and Rights in the Middle East, North Africa, and South Asia* (Syracuse: Syracuse University Press, 2007); Suad Joseph and Susan Slymovics, *Women and Power in the Middle East* (Philadelphia: University of Pennsylvania

Press, 2000); Nadje Al Ali, *Iraqi Women: Untold Stories from 1948 to the Present* (London: Zed Books, 2007); Amina Wadud, *Qur'an and Woman: Rereading the Sacred Text from a Woman's Perspective* (Oxford: Oxford University Press, 1999); Asma Barlas, "Believing Women," in *Islam: Unreading Patriarchal Interpretations of the Qur'an* (Austin: University of Texas Press, 2002); Deniz Kandiyoti, ed., *Gendering the Middle East: Emerging Perspectives* (Syracuse, NY: Syracuse University Press, 1996); Yvonne Haddad and John Esposito, eds., *Islam, Gender, and Social Change* (Oxford: Oxford University Press, 1997); Barbara Stowasser, *Women in the Qur'an, Traditions, and Interpretation* (Oxford: Oxford University Press, 1996); Fatima Mernissi, *The Veil and the Male Elite: A Feminist Interpretation of Women's Rights in Islam* (New York: Basic Books, 1992); Moallem, *Between Warrior Brother and Veiled Sister*. See also Evelyn Alsultany, Rabab Abdulhadi, and Nadine Naber, eds., *Arab and Arab American Feminisms: Gender, Violence, and Belonging* (Syracuse, NY: Syracuse University Press, 2011).

24. Moallem, *Between Warrior Brother and Veiled Sister*, 8.

25. John Esposito and Dalia Mogahed, *Who Speaks for Islam? What a Billion Muslims Really Think* (New York: Gallup Press, 2007).

26. Ibid.

27. Therese Saliba, "Military Presences and Absences: Arab Women and the Persian Gulf War," in *Seeing through the Media: The Persian Gulf War*, ed. Susan Jeffords and Lauren Rabinowitz (New Brunswick, NJ: Rutgers University Press, 1994), 126.

28. Amira Jarmakani, "Arab American Feminisms: Mobilizing the Politics of Invisibility," in Abdulhadi, Alsultany, and Naber, *Arab and Arab American Feminisms*, 227–41.

29. Susan Douglas, *Enlightened Sexism: The Seductive Message that Feminism's Work Is Done* (New York: Times Books, 2010).

30. See, for example, Sherene H. Razack, *Casting Out: The Eviction of Muslims from Western Law and Politics* (Toronto: University of Toronto Press, 2008); Lila Abu-Lughod, "Do Muslim Women Really Need Saving? Anthropological Reflections on Cultural Relativism and Its Others," *American Anthropologist* 104, no. 3 (2002): 783–90; Moallem, *Between Warrior Brother and Veiled Sister*; Amal Amireh, "Framing Nawal El Saadawi: Arab Feminism in a Transnational World," *Signs: Journal of Women in Culture and Society* 26, no. 1 (Autumn 2000): 215–49; Saliba, "Military Presences and Absences"; Ahmed, *Women and Gender*; Melani McAlister, "Suffering Sisters? American Feminists and the Problem of Female Genital Surgeries," in *Americanism: New Perspectives on the History of an Ideal*, ed. Michael Kazin and Joseph A. McCartin (Chapel Hill: University of North Carolina Press, 2006), 242–61; Laura Nader, "Orientalism, Occidentalism, and the Control of Women," *Cultural Dynamics* 11, no. 3 (1989): 323–35; Malini Johar Schueller, *U.S. Orientalisms: Race, Nation, and Gender in Literature, 1790–1890* (Ann Arbor: University of Michigan Press, 1998); Steven Salaita, *Anti-Arab Racism in the USA: Where It Comes from and What It Means for Politics Today* (London: Pluto Press, 2006); Sunaina Maira, "'Good' and 'Bad' Muslim Citizens: Feminists, Terrorists, and U.S. Orientalisms," *Feminist Studies* 35, no. 3 (Fall 2009): 631–56.

31. Krista Hunt, "'Embedded Feminism' and the War on Terror," in *(En)gendering the War on Terror: War Stories and Camouflaged Politics*, ed. Krista Hunt and Kim Rygiel, (Burlington, VT: Ashgate, 2006), 53.

32. For more on "benevolent" supremacy, see Melani McAlister, *Epic Encounters: Culture, Media, and U.S. Interests in the Middle East, 1945–2000* (Berkeley: University of California Press, 2001). For more on how foreign policies and national identity are intertwined, see Amy

Kaplan, *The Anarchy of Empire in the Making of U.S. Culture* (Cambridge, MA: Harvard University Press, 2005).

33. "Structure of feeling" is a term from Raymond Williams, *The Long Revolution* (Westport, CT: Greenwood Press, [1961] 1975), 64.

34. Sherene Razack, *Casting Out*.

35. Nonie Darwish, *Now They Call Me Infidel: Why I Renounced Jihad for America, Israel, and the War on Terror* (New York: Sentinel HC, 2006); and *Cruel and Usual Punishment: The Terrifying Global Implications of Islamic Law* (Nashville, TN: Thomas Nelson, 2008).

36. Wafa Sultan, *A God Who Hates* (New York: St. Martin's Press, 2009).

37. Robert Spencer and Phyllis Chesler, "The Violent Oppression of Women in Islam," Los Angeles: David Horowitz Freedom Center, 2007, www.scribd.com/doc/2526263/The-Violent-Oppression-of-Women-in-Islam (accessed June 21, 2010). The video is available at www.terrorismawareness.org/videos/108/the-violent-oppression-of-women-in-islam/ (accessed June 15, 2010).

38. Mohja Kahf, "The Pity Committee and the Careful Reader: How Not to Buy Stereotypes about Arab Women," in Abdulhadi, Alsultany, and Naber, *Arab and Arab American Feminisms*, 111–23. See also Amireh, "Framing Nawal El Saadawi."

39. "Crime and Punishment/Saudi Arabian Rape Case/Ali Interview," *Anderson Cooper 360*, CNN, November 29, 2007.

40. Ibid.

41. Moustafa Bayoumi, "The God That Failed: The Neo-Orientalism of Today's Muslim Commentators," in *Islamophobia/Islamophilia: Beyond the Politics of Enemy and Friend*, ed. Andrew Shryock (Bloomington: Indiana University Press, 2010), 79–93.

42. Maira, "'Good' and 'Bad' Muslim Citizens," 635.

43. Ibid., 644.

44. Jasmin Zine, "Between Orientalism and Fundamentalism: Muslim Women and Feminist Engagement," in Hunt and Rygiel, *(En)gendering the War on Terror*, 34–35.

45. See, for example, "Nigeria/Beauty Contest/Demonstrations/Allas Interview," *CNN Evening News*, November 22, 2002; "Nigeria/Miss World Contest/Riots," *NBC Evening News*, November 23, 2002; "In Depth: Miss World Beauty Pageant," *NBC Evening News*, December 7, 2002; "Divine Law," *Nightline*, ABC, July 10, 2003.

46. "FMF and NOW Protest Woman's Death Sentence at Nigerian Embassy," *Ms. Magazine*, August 29, 2002, www.msmagazine.com/news/uswirestory.asp?id=6837 (accessed June 15, 2010).

47. "Amina Lawal Wins Appeal against Stoning," September 25, 2003, http://www.msmagazine.com/news/uswirestory.asp?id=8064 (accessed June 15, 2010).

48. Jeff Koinange, "Woman Sentenced to Stoning Freed," CNN, February 23, 2004, http://edition.cnn.com/2003/WORLD/africa/09/25/nigeria.stoning/index.html (accessed March 1, 2011); and Somini Sengupta, "Facing Death for Adultery, Nigerian Woman Is Acquitted," *New York Times*, September 26, 2003, www.nytimes.com/2003/09/26/world/facing-death-for-adultery-nigerian-woman-is-acquitted.html?ref=aminalawal (accessed March 1, 2011).

49. "Can We Save Amina Lawal's Life?," *Oprah Winfrey Show*, CBS, October 4, 2002.

50. "The politics of pity," as defined by Luc Boltanski, *Distant Suffering* (Cambridge: Cambridge University Press, 1993), referred to by Lilie Chouliaraki, *The Spectatorship of Suffering* (Thousand Oaks, CA: Sage, 2006), 3.

51. Jennifer Harding and E. Deidre Pribram, "Introduction: The Case for a Cultural Emotion Studies," in *Emotions: A Cultural Studies Reader*, ed. Jennifer Harding and E. Deidre Pribram (New York: Routledge, 2009), 1, 4.

52. Chouliaraki, *The Spectatorship of Suffering*, 19.

53. Ibid., 3.

54. Wendy Brown, "Subjects of Tolerance," in *Political Theologies: Public Relations in Post-Secular World*, ed. Hent de Vries and Lawrence Eugene Sullivan (New York: Fordham University Press, 2006), 151.

55. Ibid., 166.

56. Ella Shohat and Robert Stam, *Unthinking Eurocentrism: Multiculturalism and the Media* (New York: Routledge, 1994), 170.

57. Chouliaraki, *The Spectatorship of Suffering*, 20.

58. "Can We Save Amina Lawal's Life?" *Dr. Phil* message board, Show Archive, October 2002, www.drphil.com/messageboard_archive/?IDX=messages&DiscussionID=2137&P=0 (accessed May 16, 2011).

59. Posted to the *Dr. Phil* message board by *jackattack*, at 08:16:42 on October 5, 2002, www.drphil.com/messageboard_archive/?IDX=messages&DiscussionID=2137&P=0 (accessed May 16, 2011).

60. Posted to the *Dr. Phil* message board by *nolan4444*, at 14:58:57 on November 11, 2002, www.drphil.com/messageboard_archive/?IDX=messages&DiscussionID=2137&P=0 (accessed May 16, 2011).

61. Chouliaraki, *The Spectatorship of Suffering*, 14.

62. Ibid., 11.

63. Ebony Coletu, "The New Giving Marketplace: What Does Donor's Choice Charity Commodify?" (Paper presented at the annual meeting of the American Studies Association, San Antonio, TX, November 20, 2010).

64. Laura Berlant uses the term *intimate public* in *The Female Complaint* (Durham, NC: Duke University Press, 2008), 10.

65. My use of the term *interpellation* borrows from Louis Althusser, "Ideology and Ideological State Apparatuses," in *Lenin and Philosophy and Other Essays* (New York: Monthly Review Press, 2001), 85–126.

66. Butler, *Frames of War*, 39.

NOTES TO CHAPTER 4

1. Susan J. Brison, "Gender, Terrorism, and War," *Signs: Journal of Women in Culture and Society* 28, no. 1 (2002): 437. Cited in Maureen Dowd, "Liberties: Cleopatra and Osama," *New York Times*, November 18, 2001.

2. Joel Beinin, "Is Terrorism a Useful Term in Understanding the Middle East and the Palestinian-Israeli Conflict?" *Radical History Review* 85 (Winter 2003): 13.

3. Ibid., 22.

4. Jasmin Zine, "Between Orientalism and Fundamentalism: Muslim Women and Feminist Engagement," in *(En)gendering the War on Terror: War Stories and Camouflaged Politics*, ed. Krista Hunt and Kim Rygiel (Burlington, VT: Ashgate, 2006), 44.

5. Amy Kaplan, "Violent Belongings and the Question of Empire Today—Presidential Address to the American Studies Association, October 17, 2003," *American Quarterly* 56, no. 1 (March 2004): 7.

6. For how emotions are not self-evident but socially constructed, see Jennifer Harding and E. Deidre Pribram, "Introduction: The Case for a Cultural Emotion Studies," in *Emotions: A Cultural Studies Reader*, ed. Jennifer Harding and E. Deidre Pribram (New York: Routledge, 2009).

7. Barbie Zelizer and Stuart Allen, "Introduction: When Trauma Shapes the News," in *Journalism after September 11*, ed. Barbie Zelizer and Stuart Allen (New York: Routledge, 2002), 11.

8. "Giuliani Rejects $10 Million from Saudi Prince," CNN.com, October 12, 2001, http://archives.cnn.com/2001/US/10/11/rec.giuliani.prince/index.html (accessed November 17, 2008).

9. Thomas Friedman, "Foreign Affairs; Saudi Royals and Reality," *New York Times*, October 16, 2001, www.nytimes.com/2001/10/16/opinion/foreign-affairs-saudi-royals-and-reality.html (accessed May 16, 2011).

10. Nicholas D. Kristof, "Behind the Terrorists," *New York Times*, May 7, 2002, http://query.nytimes.com/gst/fullpage.html?res=9A0CE1DA1730F934A35756C0A9649C8B63 (accessed November 10, 2008).

11. Michael Elliot, "The Shoe Bomber's World," *Time* (February 25, 2002): 50.

12. Edward Rothstein, "Connections; Exploring the Flaws in the Notion of the 'Root Causes' of Terror," *New York Times*, November 17, 2001.

13. See Neve Gordon and George Lopez, "Terrorism in the Arab-Israeli Conflict," in *Ethics in International Affairs: Theories and Cases*, ed. Andrew Valls (New York: Rowman and Littlefield, 2000), 99–113; and Mark Juergensmeyer, *Terror in the Mind of God: The Global Rise of Religious Violence*, 3rd ed. (Berkeley: University of California Press, 2005).

14. For articles on McVeigh, see David Lewis, "Background of Timothy McVeigh Slowly Being Revealed," *CNN News*, April 25, 1995; John Holliman, "Timothy McVeigh Agitated by Waco Events," *CNN News*, April 22, 1995; "McVeigh: Another Quiet Loner," *St. Petersburg Times* (FL), April 23, 1995: 1A; George Gordon, "Computer Nerd Who Turned into America's Bloodiest Killer: How the Gulf War and Waco Fueled the Paranoid of the Man behind the Oklahoma City Bomb," *Daily Mail* (London), April 24, 1995: 12; John Kifner, "Terror in Oklahoma: The Suspect; Authorities Hold a Man of 'Extreme Right-Wing Views,'" *New York Times*, April 22, 1995; Robert D. McFadden, "One Man's Complex Path to Extremism," *New York Times*, April 23, 1995.

15. Juergensmeyer, *Terror in the Mind of God*.

16. Edward Rothstein, "Connections: Cherished Ideas Refracted in History's Lens," *New York Times*, September 7, 2002, http://query.nytimes.com/gst/fullpage.html?res=9904E2D7133EF934A3575AC0A9649C8B63 (accessed November 10, 2008).

17. For more on the clash of civilizations theory, see Bernard Lewis, "The Roots of Muslim Rage," *Atlantic Monthly* 226, no. 3 (September 1990): 47–60; and Samuel P. Huntington, "The Clash of Civilizations?," *Foreign Affairs* 72, no. 3 (Summer 1993): 22–49.

18. See Saba Mahmood, "Secularism, Hermeneutics, and Empire: The Politics of Islamic Reformation," *Public Culture* 18, no. 2 (2006): 323–47.

19. Estimates vary on the number of deaths in Iraq as a result of the sanctions. Low estimates are at about 250,000. In 2005 British MP George Galloway declared on CNN that millions of Iraqi's died, many of them children, http://transcripts.cnn.com/TRANSCRIPTS/0505/17/se.01.html. Columbia University professor Richard Garfield estimates 500,000 deaths between 1990 and 2002, www.casi.org.uk/info/garfield/dr-garfield.html. However, Michael Spagat has argued that Saddam Hussein's regime likely fabricated the

numbers to encourage easing of the sanctions. Spagat points out that the high estimates are almost as mythical as Saddam Hussein's WMDs. Former U.S. Attorney General Ramsey Clark charged the United States and others for crimes against Iraqis, causing the deaths of more than 1.5 million people, including 750,000 children under five, www.twf.org/News /Y1997/Ramsey.html.

20. See Mahmood Mamdani, *Good Muslim, Bad Muslim: America, The Cold War, and the Roots of Terror* (New York: Three Leaves, 2005).

21. For more on biographic writing and interpretation, see Ebony Coletu, "Forms of Submission: Acts of Writing in Moments of Need" (PhD diss., Stanford University, 2008).

22. Several alternative news media sites, such as NPR, mention that Lindh refused to be involved in Al Qaeda's missions against the United States and Israel and did not pledge allegiance to Al Qaeda but rather to jihad. NPR also reported that he was not fighting for Al Qaeda but for the Taliban against the Northern Alliance and that Lindh is against suicide bombings since the Koran forbids suicide. See, for example, "Interview: James Brosnahan Discusses His Client, John Walker Lindh," *Morning Edition*, NPR, July 16, 2002.

23. This narrative of "going Muslim" or "going native" is explicitly referred to in an article on Lindh in *Esquire* magazine, regarding the lawyers who took up defending Lindh's case: "They did not get to know him in their time with him—but then, he was not the kind of person you got to know. He was, rather, unlike any person they'd ever met, a throwback, Fechheimer says, "to those Victorian explorers" who had to go native in order to feel authentic. He was, like Lawrence of Arabia, willing to suffer almost any kind of deprivation, if deprivation was what it took to erase the distinction between himself and his hosts." Tom Junod, "Innocent," *Esquire* (July 2006), www.esquire.com/features/ESQ0706JLINDH_106 (accessed May 16, 2011).

24. Evan Thomas, "American Taliban: A Long Strange Trip to the Taliban," *Newsweek* (December 17, 2001): 30, www.newsweek.com/2001/12/16/a-long-strange-trip-to-the-taliban .html (accessed May 16, 2011).

25. Ibid.

26. Junod, "Innocent."

27. David Eng, *Racial Castration* (Durham, NC: Duke University Press, 2005), 3.

28. Ibid, 7.

29. Ibid, 8.

30. Timothy Roche et al., "The Making of John Walker Lindh," *Time* (October, 7, 2002), www.time.com/time/magazine/article/0,9171,1003414,00.htm.

31. Julian Borger, "Bright Boy from the California Suburbs Who Turned Taliban Warrior," *Guardian*, October 5, 2002.

32. Roche et al., "The Making of John Walker Lindh."

33. For news stories that contain this narrative and visual trajectory, see "The case of the Taliban American," CNN.com, www.cnn.com/CNN/Programs/people/shows/walker/profile.html; Josh Tyrangiel, "The Taliban Next Door," *Time* (December 9, 2001), www.time .com/time/printout/0,8816,187564,00.html; "Profile: John Walker Lindh," BBC News Online: World: Americas, January 24, 2002, http://news.bbc.co.uk/2/low/americas/1779455.stm; Bill Hewitt, Maureen Harrington, and Colleen O'Connor, "The Long Road Home," *People* 58, no. 15 (October 7, 2002): 66–70; and Timothy Roche, "A Short Course in Miracles," *Time* 160, no. 5 (July 29, 2002): 34–35.

34. In January 2001 two Vermont teenagers, James Parker and Robert Tulloch, entered the home of married professors Half and Susanne Zantop and stabbed them to death. The motive

was robbery. They were charged with first degree murder. See, for example, "Youths Dreamed of Adventure, But Settled for Killing a Couple," *New York Times* (May 18, 2002), www.nytimes.com/2002/05/18/us/youths-dreamed-of-adventure-but-settled-for-killing-a-couple.html?ref=suzannezantop (accessed May 16, 2011).

35. Upon visiting the owner of the bookstore, the detectives are told that a young man, Musah Salim, was recently hired to stack books. He was fired soon after when the owner discovered that he was using his post to distribute misogynistic materials. While Salim's sexist views are linked to his belief and practice of Islam, a distinction is made between Salim's sexist Islam and the Islam practiced by the owner of the bookstore. The TV program does not seek to portray all Muslims as extremist and oppressive and thus inserts several moments of distinction in the story line. As I explore in chapter 1, this is a strategy employed by most post-9/11 TV dramas in order to circumvent reproducing stereotypes of Arabs and Muslims as terrorists. Through representing both reasonable and unreasonable Muslims, extreme and moderate forms of Islam, TV dramas can establish themselves as sensitive in representing Muslims.

36. Mucahit Bilici, "American Jihad: Representations of Islam in the United States after 9/11," *American Journal of Islamic Social Sciences* 22, no. 1 (Winter 2005): 65.

37. John Walker Lindh when asked what he was doing in Afghanistan fighting with the Taliban stated, "My heart became attached." A biography about Lindh was written with this title: Mark Kukis, *"My Heart Became Attached": The Strange Journey of John Walker Lindh* (Dulles, VA: Brassey's, 2003).

38. Junod, "Innocent."

39. Jasbir Puar, *Terrorist Assemblages: Homonationalism in Queer Times* (Durham, NC: Duke University Press, 2007), 9.

40. Ibid., 76–77.

41. David Eng, *The Feeling of Kinship: Queer Liberalism and the Racialization of Intimacy* (Durham, NC: Duke University Press, 2010), 33.

42. Ibid.

43. Arian Campo-Flores and Dirk Johnson, "From Taco Bell to Al Qaeda: How Accused 'Dirty Bomb' Plotter Jose Padilla Traveled from Gangland Chicago to Osama bin Laden's Backyard," *Newsweek* (June 24, 2002): 34.

44. Supreme Court Justice Sandra Day O'Connor defined "enemy combatant" as someone "carrying a weapon against American troops on a foreign battlefield." The U.S. Department of Defense used a broader definition: "anyone part of or supporting Taliban or Al Qaeda forces or associated forces." See Neil A. Lewis, "Indictment Portrays Padilla as Minor Figure in a Plot," *New York Times*, November 24, 2005. President Bush signed an order in 2002 to legalize the suspension of rights for persons under the category "enemy combatants." According to an MSNBC news report, "As an enemy combatant, Padilla was a candidate for a number of aggressive interrogation techniques, including manipulation of temperatures and exploitations of phobias that were for a time approved by Secretary of Defense Donald Rumsfeld. But the handling of his case—particularly of the government's refusal to allow him to have an attorney—provoked a fierce national debate over civil liberties, which eventually went to the Supreme Court in 2004." See Michael Isikoff and Mark Hosenball, "Terror Watch: The Missing Padilla Video," *Newsweek*, February 28, 2007, www.msnbc.com/id/17389175/site/newsweek (accessed November 17, 2008).

45. For more on how the category "enemy combatant" functions to dehumanize people, see Amy Kaplan, "Where Is Guantánamo?" *American Quarterly* 57, no. 3 (September 2005): 831–58.

46. See, for example, Amanda Ripley, "The Case of the Dirty Bomber," *Time* (June 16, 2002): 28–32, www.time.com/time/nation/article/0,8599,262917,00.html; and Tony Karon, "Person of the Week: Jose Padilla," *Time* (June 14, 2002), www.time.com/time/nation/article/0,8599,262269,00.html.

47. Froma Harrop, "Keep Him 'Detained'—Padilla: A Goon in Exotic Costume," *Providence Journal* (RI), May 5, 2004: B05.

48. File photo by the *Miami Herald* via AP. Laura Parker, "Padilla Charges Don't Measure Up to Accusations," *USA Today*, July 18, 2007, www.usatoday.com/news/nation/2007–07–18 –padilla-charges_n.htm (accessed November 24, 2008).

49. Ana Y. Ramos-Zayas, "Delinquent Citizenship, National Performances: Racialization, Surveillance, and the Politics of 'Worthiness' in Puerto Rican Chicago," *Latino Studies* 2 (2004): 40.

50. Ibid., 41.

51. Transcript of News Conference on Jose Padilla held by James Comey, June 1, 2004. Transcript can be found at www.cnn.com.

52. Inderpal Grewal, *Transnational America: Feminisms, Diasporas, Neoliberalisms* (Durham, NC: Duke University Press, 2005), 22.

53. See, for example, Laura Parker, "The Ordeal of Chaplain Yee," *USA Today* (May 16, 2004), www.usatoday.com/news/nation/2004–05–16–yee-cover_x.htm; Michele Norris, "Muslim Army Chaplain Recalls Guantanamo Ordeal," *All Things Considered*, NPR, October 5, 2005, www.npr.org/templates/story/story.php?storyId=4946292; Brad Wright, "Gitmo Chaplain Reprimanded for Adultery, Porn," CNN, May 6, 2004, www.cnn.com/2004 /LAW/03/22/yee/index.html; Neil Lewis and Thom Shanker, "Missteps and Confusion Seen in Muslim Chaplain's 'Spy Case,'" *New York Times*, January 3, 2004, www.nytimes .com/2004/01/04/national/04YEE.html?pagewanted=all&position=

54. James Yee, "A U.S. Army Muslim Chaplain's Struggle for Justice," *Voices*, University of California San Diego Television, April 23, 2008.

55. On the military's use of Rafael Patai's *The Arab Mind* (New York: Charles Scribner's Sons, 1973), see Brian Whitaker, "Its Best Use Is as a Doorstop," *Guardian Unlimited*, May 24, 2004, www.guardian.co.uk/world/2004/may/24/worlddispatch.usa (accessed May 16, 2011).

56. "Reid: 'I am at war with your country,'" CNN.com/Law Center, January 31, 2003, www.cnn.com/2003/LAW/01/31/reid.transcript/ (accessed December 3, 2008.)

57. Mumia Abu-Jamal, "Live from Death Row: Johnny's Real Crime," *Michigan Citizen* 24, no. 39 (August 24, 2002): A7. Another commentary sympathetic to Lindh is a Steve Earle song, "John Walker Blues," on his album *Jerusalem* (2002).

58. Alison M. Jaggar, "Love and Knowledge: Emotion in Feminist Epistemology," in *Women Knowledge, and Reality*, ed. Anny Garry and Marilyn Pearsall (New York: Routledge, 1996), 60.

59. Sunaina Maira, *Missing* (Durham, NC: Duke University Press, 2009), 214.

60. Jaggar, "Love and Knowledge," 60.

NOTES TO CHAPTER 5

An earlier version of this chapter appeared in *American Quarterly* **59, no.** 3 (2007).

1. See, for example, *New York Times*, September 21–24, 2001, specifically September 22, 2001: A26; and September 23, 2001: A47.

2. Life insurance and pharmaceutical companies had a field day advertising in the face of tragedy. LIFE (an insurance company) advertised, "Life Insurance Isn't for the People Who Die, It's for the People Who Live," capitalizing on the loss of human life and the resulting financial burden for many families. And Pfizer, a pharmaceutical company, advertised, "At Pfizer we discover and develop medicines. We wish we could make a medicine that would take away the heartache." For example, see *Newsweek* (October 8, 2001).

3. For more on post-9/11 patriotism, see Ella Shohat and Robert Stam, *Flagging Patriotism: Crises of Narcissism and Anti-Americanism* (New York: Routledge, 2007).

4. For example, see Human Rights Watch, "'We Are Not the Enemy': Hate Crimes against Arabs, Muslims, and Those Perceived to Be Arab or Muslim, after September 11," *Human Rights Watch Report* 14, no. 6 (November 2002), www.hrw.org/reports/2002/usahate/index.htm#TopOfPage (accessed March 7, 2007); the Sikh Coalition, "One Year after Brutal Attack, Sikh Hate Crime Victim Files Civil Suit against Attackers," July 12, 2005, www.sikhcoalition.org/ca_rhill.asp (accessed March 7, 2007); and Jim Forman, "Store Owner Fights Back after Attack," KING5 News, Seattle, WA, February 22, 2007, www.king5.com/topstories/stories/NW_022107WABclerkattackKC.22f8ceob.html (accessed March 7, 2007).

5. Media and Society Group, "MSRG Special Report: Restrictions on Civil Liberties, Views of Islam, and Muslim Americans," and "MSRG Special Report: U.S. War on Terror, U.S. Foreign Policy, and Anti-Americanism," Cornell University, Ithaca, NY, December 2004; www.comm.cornell.edu/msrg/report1a.pdf and www.comm.cornell.edu/msrg/report1b.pdf (accessed March 7, 2007).

6. Peter Slevin, "Arab Americans Report Abuse," *Washington Post*, July 28, 2004, www.washingtonpost.com/wp-dyn/articles/A21888-2004Jul28.html (accessed August 14, 2010).

7. Leti Volpp, "The Citizen and the Terrorist," in *September 11 in History: A Watershed Moment?*, ed. Mary L. Dudziak (Durham, NC: Duke University Press, 2003), 147–62. For a discussion of the increased racialization of Arab Americans after 9/11, see Nadine Naber and Amaney Jamal, eds., *From Invisible Citizens to Visible Subjects: Arab American Identities before and after September 11th* (Syracuse, NY: Syracuse University Press, 2007).

8. Melani McAlister, *Epic Encounters: Culture, Media, and U.S. Interests in the Middle East, 1945–2000* (Berkeley: University of California Press, 2001).

9. Stuart Hall, "The Problem of Ideology: Marxism without Guarantees," *Journal of Communication Inquiry* 10 (1986): 42.

10. The "I am an American" public service announcement can be viewed at the Ad Council's website: www.adcouncil.org/default.aspx?id=141 (accessed March 7, 2007).

11. "I am an American" (2001–present), Ad Council, http://adcouncil.org/default.aspx?id=141 (accessed May 14, 2007). Also see Sophia A. McClennen, "E Pluribus Unum, Ex Uno Plura: Legislating and Deregulating American Studies Post-9/11," *CR: The New Centennial Review* 8, no. 1 (2008), 155–85.

12. Ian F. Haney López, "White Lines," in *White by Law: The Legal Construction of Race* (New York: New York University Press, 1996).

13. Wahneema Lubiano, "Talking about the State and Imagining Alliances," in *Talking Visions: Multicultural Feminism in a Transnational Age*, ed. Ella Shohat (New York: New Museum/MIT Press, 1998), 441–50.

14. McAlister, *Epic Encounters*, 259.

15. For more on representations of the Gulf War, see Ella Shohat, "The Media's War," *Social Text* 28 (Spring 1991): 135–41.

16. Cynthia Weber, "'I Am an American': Portraits of Post-9/11 U.S. Citizens," Opendemocracy.net (September 2007).

17. Cynthia Weber, "Citizenship, Security, Humanity," *International Political Sociology* 4, no. 1 (2010): 83.

18. Council on American-Islamic Relations, www.cair.com (accessed March 7, 2007).

19. Neil MacFarquhar and David Johnston, "Scrutiny Increases for a Group Advocating for Muslims in U.S.," *New York Times*, March 14, 2007: A1.

20. CAIR planned to produce fifty-two print PSAs as part of their "Islam in America" campaign but ended up producing only six for financial reasons.

21. My use of the term *cultural citizenship* comes from Renato Rosaldo, "Cultural Citizenship, Inequality, and Multiculturalism," in *Race, Identity, and Citizenship*, ed. Rodolfo D. Torres, Louis F. Mirón, and Jonathan Xavier Inda (Oxford: Blackwell, 1999), 253–61. For more on the media's role in shaping multiculturalism, see Ella Shohat and Robert Stam, *Unthinking Eurocentrism: Multiculturalism and the Media* (New York: Routledge, 1994).

22. The ads can be viewed at www.americanmuslims.info/archive.asp (accessed March 7, 2007).

23. See the Girl Scouts web page at www.girlscouts.org/who_we_are/facts/ (accessed March 7, 2007).

24. Found at www.americanmuslims.info/archive.asp (accessed March 7, 2007).

25. See poll results at www.cnn.com/ELECTION/2004/pages/results/states/US/P/00 /epolls.0.html (accessed March 7, 2007).

26. See CAIR print ads at www.americanmuslims.info/archive.asp (accessed March 7, 2007).

27. See Mahmood Mamdani, *Good Muslim, Bad Muslim: America, the Cold War, and the Roots of Terror* (New York: Pantheon, 2004).

28. Akhil Gupta and James Ferguson, "Culture, Power, Place: Ethnography at the End of an Era," in *Culture, Power, Place: Explorations in Critical Anthropology*, ed. Akhil Gupta and James Ferguson (Durham, NC: Duke University Press, 1997), 18–19.

29. Laura Levitt, "Impossible Assimilations, American Liberalism, and Jewish Difference," *American Quarterly* 53, no. 3 (2007): 807.

30. Ibid., 827.

31. Eugene McLaughlin, "Rebranding Britain: The Life and Times of 'Cool Britannia,'" *BBC and the Open University*, www.open2.net/newbrit/pages/features/features_mclaughlin .htm (accessed March 7, 2007).

32. Ibid.

33. Ibid.

34. Mark Leonard, "Cool Britannia," *New Statesman*, http://markleonard.net/journalism/ coolbritannia/ (accessed March 7, 2007).

35. Liam Kennedy and Scott Lucas, "Enduring Freedom: Public Diplomacy and U.S. Foreign Policy," *American Quarterly* 57, no. 2 (June 2005): 309–33. For more on U.S. public diplomacy, see Penny M. Von Eschen, "Enduring Public Diplomacy," *American Quarterly* 57, no. 2 (June 2005): 335–43; and Ron Robin, "Requiem for Public Diplomacy?," *American Quarterly* 57, no. 2 (June 2005): 345–53.

36. Penny Von Eschen, *Satchmo Blows Up the World: Jazz Ambassadors Play the Cold War* (Cambridge, MA: Harvard University Press, 2004).

37. James Dao and Eric Schmitt, "A Nation Challenged: Hearts and Minds; Pentagon Readies Efforts to Sway Sentiments Abroad," *New York Times*, February 19, 2002: A1, 6. See

also "Pentagon Closes Down Controversial Office," CNN, February 26, 2002, http://archives.cnn.com/2002/US/02/26/defense.office (accessed March 7, 2007).

38. U.S. Department of State, International Information Program, April 11, 2002, http://usinfo.state.gove/regional/nea/sasia/text/0227rmfd.htm.

39. Office of the Press Secretary, "Executive Order: Establishing the Office of Global Communications," January 21, 2003, /www.whitehouse.gov/news/releases/2003/01/20030121–3.html (accessed March 7, 2007).

40. "Changing Minds, Winning Peace: A New Strategic Direction for U.S. Public Diplomacy in the Arab and Muslim World," Report of the Advisory Group on Public Diplomacy for the Arab and Muslim World. October 1, 2003.

41. Andrew Buncombe, "Bush Launches Magazine to Teach Young Arabs to Love America," *Independent News and Media* (UK), July 18, 2003, http://news.independent.co.uk/world/americas/article96619.ece (accessed March 7, 2007).

42. Louis Althusser, "Ideology and Ideological State Apparatuses," in *Lenin and Philosophy and Other Essays* (New York: Monthly Review Press, 2001).

43. "Changing Minds," 13.

44. Kennedy and Lucas, "Enduring Freedom," 325.

45. Ibid., 315.

46. See www.radiosawa.com/ (accessed March 7, 2007).

47. See www.alhurra.com/ (accessed March 7, 2007). See also William Lafi Youmans, "Humor against Hegemony: Al-Hurra, Jokes, and the Limits of American Soft Power," *Middle East Journal of Culture and Communication* 2, no. 1 (2009): 76–99.

48. Found at www.himag.com/ (website no longer available).

49. President George W. Bush, "State of the Union, 2004," January 20, 2004, www.whitehouse.gov/news/releases/2004/01/20040120–7.html (accessed March 7, 2007).

50. "U.S.-Funded Arab TV's Credibility Crisis," *60 Minutes*, CBS News, June 22, 2008.

51. William Youmans, "The War on Ideas: Alhurra and US International Broadcasting Law in the 'War on Terror,'" *Westminster Papers in Communication and Culture* 6, no. 1 (2009): 45–68; Youmans, "Humor against Hegemony."

52. Found at www.opendialogue.com (website no longer available).

53. "Changing Minds," 72.

54. Jane Perlez, "Muslim-as-Apple-Pie Videos Are Greeted with Skepticism," *New York Times*, October 30, 2002, www.nytimes.com/2002/10/30/world/muslim-as-apple-pie-videos-are-greeted-with-skepticism.html (accessed August 10, 2010).

55. See, for example, "FBI Investigating Michigan Mosque Attacks," *USA Today*, February 16, 2006, www.usatoday.com/news/nation/2006–02–16–michigan-mosque_x.htm (accessed March 7, 2007); and "Frederick Mosque Possible Target of Hate Crime: Windows Broken at Building 3 Times," NBC4.com, MD, February 28, 2007, www.nbc4.com/news/11138569/detail.html (accessed March 7, 2007).

56. The website used to be located at www.opendialogue.com but is no longer available on-line.

57. Ibid.

58. Ibid.

59. Ed Finn, "Unhip, Unhip Al Hurra: The Middle East Hates Its New TV station," Slate.com, February 20, 2004, http://slate.msn.com/id/2095806 (accessed March 7, 2007).

60. Kennedy and Lucas, "Enduring Freedom," 325.

61. "Changing Minds," 9.

62. The site www.opendialogue.com (which is no longer available) included a section for visitors to post comments.

63. Jasbir Puar, *Terrorist Assemblages: Homonationalism in Queer Times* (Durham, NC: Duke University Press, 2007), 3–4.

NOTES TO EPILOGUE

1. See, for example, Nicholas D. Kristof, "The Push to 'Otherize' Obama," Op-Ed, *New York Times*, September 21, 2008, www.nytimes.com/2008/09/21/opinion/21kristof.html; Charles A. Radin, "False Alarms," *Jewish Advocate* 199, no. 38 (September 19, 2008): 13; Fraser Sherman, "Beware! The Islamofascists Walk among Us!," *McClatchy-Tribune Business News* (May 31, 2008).

2. Debbie Schlussel, "Barack Hussein Obama: Once a Muslim, Always a Muslim" (December 18, 2006), www.debbieschlussel.com.

3. Ibid.

4. Ben Smith and Jonathan Martin, "Untraceable E-mails Spread Obama Rumor," Politico.com (October 13, 2007); Michael Barbaro, "Bloomberg, in Florida, Blasts Rumor about Obama," *New York Times*, June 21, 2008.

5. E-mail that circulated in January 2008.

6. See the film's website: http://obsessionthemovie.com. The Muslim Public Affairs Council distributed this flyer to raise awareness about *Obsession*'s hateful message: www.mpac.org /docs/Exposing-Obsession.pdf (accessed August 31, 2010).

7. Amy Chozick, "Campaign '08: Obama Walks a Fine Line with Muslims; Campaign's Efforts to Dispel Rumors Risk Offending a Base of Support," *Wall Street Journal*, June 23, 2008: A10.

8. Andrea Elliott, "Muslim Voters Detect a Snub from Obama," *New York Times*, June 24, 2008.

9. "Growing Number of Americans Say Obama Is a Muslim: Religion, Politics and the President," Pew Forum on Religion and Public Life, August 18, 2010, http://pewforum.org/ Politics-and-Elections/Growing-Number-of-Americans-Say-Obama-is-a-Muslim.aspx (accessed August 30, 2010).

10. Kurt Williamsen, "Obama Citizenship Accusations Come to a Head," *New American*, December, 2, 2008, www.thenewamerican.com/usnews/election/562 (accessed August 31, 2010).

11. "Police: Cab Driver Stabbed by Passenger Who Asked 'Are You Muslim?'" NY1 News, August 25, 2010, www.ny1.com/content/top_stories/?ArID=124338 (accessed October 14, 2010).

12. "Islamic Center Defaced with Bacon Slices," Associated Press, October 12, 2010, www .cbsnews.com/stories/2010/10/12/national/main6952008.shtml (accessed October 14, 2010).

13. Michele McPhee, "Southwest Apologizes for Removing Muslim Passenger from Flight," *AOL Travel News*, March 16, 2011, http://news.travel.aol.com/2011/03/16/southwest-apologizes-for-removing-muslim-passenger-from-flight/ (accessed March 17, 2011).

14. "Muslim Clerics Ordered off Atlantic Southeast Airlines Flight," WPIX 11, May 8, 2011, www.wpix.com/news/wpix-muslim-clerks-removed-plane-story,0,2534595.story (accessed May 20, 2011).

15. "Protest of an American Muslim Relief Group's Fundraiser Advocated Hate and Violence," Council on American Islamic-Relations, March 2, 2011, www.esquire.com/blogs /politics/orange-county-protest-5334312 (accessed March 3, 2011).

16. Ibid.

17. See, for example, Alex Seitz-Wald, "Texas Mosque and Educational Center Vandalized with Offensive Graffiti and Fire, Causing $20,000 in Damage," Think Progress, August 2, 2010, http://thinkprogress.org/2010/08/02/texas-mosque-vandalized/; Jana Shortal, "St. Cloud Graffiti May Be Investigated as Hate Crime," KARE 11 News, July 9, 2010, www.kare11.com/news/news_article.aspx?storyid=856970; "Feces Smeared on Van Parked Near Bellevue Mosque," Seattle Times, June 24, 2010, http://seattletimes.nwsource.com/html/localnews/2012202078_vansmeared25m.html (accessed August 30, 2010).

18. Lauren Russell, "Church Plans Quran-Burning Event," CNN, July 31, 2010, www.cnn.com/2010/US/07/29/florida.burn.quran.day/index.html (accessed August 30, 2010).

19. Parts of this epilogue on the "ground zero" mosque controversy were originally published as "The 'Ground Zero' Mosque Controversy and 'Post Race' Racism," States of Devotion Blog, Ann Pellegrini, Diana Taylor, and Marcial Godoy, eds., October 2010, http://hemisphericinstitute.org/devotion/2010/10/the-"ground-zero-mosque"-controversy-and-"post-race"-racism/.

20. Sheryl Gay Stolberg, "Obama Strongly Backs Islam Center Near 9/11 Site," New York Times, August 13, 2010, www.nytimes.com/2010/08/14/us/politics/14obama.html?_r=3 (accessed August 30, 2010).

21. See, for example, "Statement On Islamic Community Center Near Ground Zero," Anti-Defamation League, July 28, 2010, www.adl.org/PresRele/CvlRt_32/5820_32.htm (accessed August 30, 2010); and Evan McMorris-Santoro, "Mosque Ado about Fear-Mongering: Right Wing Takes on Muslim Worship Anywhere and Everywhere," Talking Points Memo, July 20, 2010, http://tpmmuckraker.talkingpointsmemo.com/2010/07/mosque_ado_about_fear-mongering_right_wing_takes_0_1.php (accessed August 30, 2010).

22. For a discussion on conversation enders on race, see "Introduction: Doing Race," in Doing Race: 21 Essays for the 21st Century, ed. Paula M. L. Moya and Hazel Rose Markus (New York: Norton, 2010).

23. Sheryl Gay Stolberg, "Obama Says Mosque Upholds Principle of Equal Treatment," New York Times, August 13, 2010, www.nytimes.com/2010/08/15/us/politics/15islamcenter.html (accessed October 14, 2010).

24. Patricia Hill Collins, Black Feminist Thought (New York: Routledge, 2001), 78.

25. Mark Andrejevic, "Watching Television without Pity: The Productivity of Online Fans," Television and New Media 9 (2008): 24–46.

26. Kiran Ansari, "Muslims Moving beyond Stereotypes on Screen," Chicago Tribune, www.chicagotribune.com/news/opinion/chi-movies-muslims-perspective,0,7678614.story (accessed July 25, 2008).

27. On these comedians, see, for example, Jodi Wilgoren, "Arab and Muslim Comics Turn Fear into Funny," New York Times, September 1, 2002, http://query.nytimes.com/gst/fullpage.html?res=9B05E4D8103FF932A3575AC0A9649C8B63 (accessed July 28, 2008); Jannat Jalil, "Muslim Comedians Laugh at Racism," BBC News, June 15, 2004, http://news.bbc.co.uk/2/hi/americas/3796109.stm; Roya Heydarpour, "The Comic Is Palestinian, the Jokes Bawdy," New York Times, November 21, 2006, www.nytimes.com/2006/11/21/nyregion/21ink.html?fta=y (accessed July 28, 2008); James Poniewozik, "Stand-Up Diplomacy," Time 169, no. 12 (March 19, 2007): 69; Lorraine Ali, "Mining the Middle East for Laughs," Newsweek, Web Exclusive, October 18, 2007, www.newsweek.com/id/56656 (accessed January 12, 2008); Larry Fine, "New Yorkers Laughing Again after Sept. 11 Trauma," Yahoo! News, Canada, July 19, 2002, http://ca.news.yahoo.com/020719/5/nqcj.html (accessed September 15, 2002).

28. "Pilot," Whoopi!, NBC, Season 1, Episode 1 (September 9, 2003).

29. "Pilot," *Aliens in America*, CW, Season 1, Episode 1 (October 1, 2007).

30. "Help Wanted,"*Aliens in America*, Season 1, Episode 5, CW (October 29, 2007).

31. "Camels on Hand to Celebrate Premier of 'Little Mosque on the Prairie,'" Yahoo! News, January 4, 2007, http://ca.news.yahoo.com/s/capress/070104/entertainment/tv_little_mosque (accessed January 28, 2008).

32. John Intini, "Little Mosque on the Prairie: Recreate Small-Town Canada, Then Add Muslims—For Laughs," Macleans.ca, December 11, 2006, www.macleans.ca/article.jsp?content=20061211_137752_137752 (accessed July 24, 2008).

33. Tim Surette, "Fox Importing Mosque," TV.com, June 10, 2008, www.tv.com/story/11375.html (accessed July 23, 2008).

34. Zahen Amanullah, "Comedy Has to Come from a Good Place," altmuslim.com, January 18, 2007, www.altmuslim.com/a/a/n/2439/ (accessed July 24, 2008).

35. Herman S. Gray, *Cultural Moves* (Berkeley: University of California Press, 2005), 107–8.

36. Stuart Hall, "What Is This 'Black' in Black Popular Culture?," in *Black Popular Culture*, ed. Gina Dent (Seattle: Bay Press, 1992), 21–33, 24. For an examination of minority self-representation, see, for example, Rosa Linda Fregoso, *The Bronze Screen: Chicana and Chicano Film Culture* (Minneapolis: University of Minnesota Press, 1993); Chon Noriega, *Shot in America: Television, the State, and the Rise of Chicano Cinema* (Minneapolis: University of Minnesota Press, 2000); Sarita See, *The Decolonized Eye: Filipino American Art and Performance* (Minneapolis: University of Minnesota Press, 2009); Peter X. Feng, *Identities in Motion: Asian American Film and Video* (Durham, NC: Duke University Press, 2002).

37. Stuart Hall, "New Ethnicities," in *Critical Dialogues in Cultural Studies*, ed. David Morley and Kuan-Hsing Chen (New York: Routledge, 1996), 443.

Bibliography

"24 Comes under Muslim Fire." *Northern Territory News* (Australia), January 29, 2007: 23.

"24 Under Fire from Muslim Groups." *BBC News*, January 19, 2007. http://news.bbc.co.uk/2/hi/entertainment/6280315.stm. Abu-Lughod, Lila. "Do Muslim Women Really Need Saving? Anthropological Reflections on Cultural Relativism and Its Others." *American Anthropologist* 104, no. 3 (2002): 783–90.

Abu-Jamal, Mumia. "Live from Death Row: Johnny's Real Crime." *Michigan Citizen* 24, no. 39 (August 24, 2002): A7. Ad Council. "I Am an American." 2001. http://adcouncil.org/default.aspx?id=141.

Agamben, Giorgio. *Homo Sacer: Sovereign Power and Bare Life.* Stanford, CA: Stanford University Press, 1998.

Ahmed, Leila. *Women and Gender in Islam.* New Haven, CT: Yale University Press, 1992.

"Al-Fatiha." *Sleeper Cell*, Showtime, Season 1, Episode 1 (December 4, 2005).

Ali, Lorraine. "Mining the Middle East for Laughs." *Newsweek*, October 18, 2007. www.newsweek.com/id/56656.

Alsultany, Evelyn. "The 'Ground Zero' Mosque Controversy and 'Post Race' Racism." States of Devotion Blog, Inaugural Issue, edited by Ann Pellegrini, Diana Taylor, and Marcial Godoy (October 2010). http://hemisphericinstitute.org/devotion/2010/10/the-"ground-zero-mosque"-controversy-and-"post-race"-racism/.

———. "The Primetime Plight of Arab-Muslim-Americans after 9/11: Configurations of Race and Nation in TV Dramas." In *Race and Arab Americans before and after September 11th: From Invisible Citizens to Visible Subjects*, edited by Nadine Naber and Amaney Jamal, 204–28. Syracuse: Syracuse University Press, 2007.

———. "Selling American Diversity and Muslim American Identity through Non-Profit Advertising Post-9/11." *American Quarterly* 59, no. 3 (September 2007): 593–622.

Alsultany, Evelyn, Rabab Abdulhadi, and Nadine Naber, eds. *Arab and Arab American Feminisms: Gender, Violence, and Belonging.* Syracuse: Syracuse University Press, 2011.

Althusser, Louis. "Ideology and Ideological State Apparatuses." In *Lenin and Philosophy and Other Essays*, 85–126. New York: Monthly Review Press, 2001.

Amanullah, Zahen. "Comedy Has to Come from a Good Place." altmuslim.com, January 18, 2007. www.altmuslim.com/a/a/n/2439/.

American-Arab Anti-Discrimination Committee. "Report on Hate Crimes and Discrimination against Arab Americans: The Post–September 11 Backlash." American-Arab Anti-Discrimination Committee Research Institute, Washington, DC, 2003. www.adc.org/hatecrimes/pdf/2003_report_web.pdf.

American Civil Liberties Union. "Blocking Faith, Freezing Charity." *ACLU Report*, June 16, 2009, www.aclu.org/human-rights/report-blocking-faith-freezing-charity.

"Amina Lawal Wins Appeal against Stoning." *Ms. Magazine*, September 25, 2003. www.msmagazine.com/news/uswirestory.asp?id=8064.

Amireh, Amal. "Framing Nawal El Saadawi: Arab Feminism in a Transnational World." *Signs: Journal of Women in Culture and Society* 26, no. 1 (Autumn 2000): 215–49.

"An Appalling Magic." *Guardian Unlimited*, May 17, 2003. www.guardian.co.uk/usa/story/0,12271,957670,00.html.

Anderson, Benedict. *Imagined Communities: Reflections on the Origin and Spread of Nationalism*. New York: Verso, 1991.

Andrejevic, Mark. "Watching Television without Pity: The Productivity of Online Fans." *Television and New Media* 9 (2008): 24–46.

Anker, Elisabeth. "Villains, Victims and Heroes: Melodrama, Media, and September 11." *Journal of Communication* 56, no. 1 (2006): 22–37.

Ansari, Kiran. "Muslims Moving beyond Stereotypes on Screen." *Chicago Tribune*. n.d. www.chicagotribune.com/news/opinion/chi-movies-muslims-perspective,0,7678614.story.

Anti-Defamation League. "Statement on Islamic Community Center Near Ground Zero." Anti-Defamation League Press Release. July 28, 2010. www.adl.org/PresRele/CvlRt_32/5820_32.htm.

Antonius, Rachad. "Un racisme 'respectable.'" *Les relations ethniques en question: Ce qui a changé depuis de 11 Septembre 2001*, edited by Jean Renaud, Linda Pietrantonio, and Guy Bourgeault. Montreal: University of Montreal Press, 2002.

"Ashcroft Announces 'Voluntary Interviews' with 3,000 U.S. Visitors." IslamOnline.net News. www.islamonline.net/english/news/2002–03/21/article04.shtml.

"Baby Love." *NYPD Blue*, ABC, Season 9, Episode 6 (December 4, 2001).

"Bad Methods; President Bush's Alternative Techniques for Questioning Terrorism Suspects Have No Basis in Science or Law." *Washington Post*, June 1, 2007: A14.

"Bad to Worse." *The Practice*, ABC, Season 7, Episode 8 (December 1, 2002).

Bakalian, Anny, and Mehdi Bozorgmehr. *Backlash 9/11: Middle Eastern and Muslim Americans Respond*. Berkeley: University of California Press, 2009.

Barbaro, Michael. "Bloomberg, in Florida, Blasts Rumor about Obama." *New York Times*, June 21, 2008. www.nytimes.com/2008/06/21/nyregion/21jewish.html.

Barnes, Mario L., Erwin Chemerinsky, and Trina Jones. "A Post-Race Equal Protection?" *Georgetown Law Journal* 98 (2010): 967–1004.

Bauder, David. "Group: TV Torture Influencing Real Life." *USA Today*, February 11, 2007. www.usatoday.com/life/television/2007–02–11–tv-torture_x.htm.

Baudrillard, Jean. *Simulacra and Simulation*. Ann Arbor: University of Michigan Press, 1995.

Bayoumi, Moustafa. "The God That Failed: The Neo-Orientalism of Today's Muslim Commentators." In *Islamophobia/Islamophilia: Beyond the Politics of Enemy and Friend*, edited by Andrew Shryock, 79–93. Bloomington: Indiana University Press, 2010.

Beinin, Joel. "Is Terrorism a Useful Term in Understanding the Middle East and the Palestinian-Israeli Conflict?" *Radical History Review* 85 (Winter 2003): 12–23.

"Beneath the Veil." CNN Evening News, September 13, 2002.

Berlant, Laura. *The Female Complaint*. Durham, NC: Duke University Press, 2008.

Beyer, Lisa. "The Women of Islam." *Time*, November 25, 2001. www.time.com/time/world/article/0,8599,185647,00.html.

Bilici, Mucahit. "American Jihad: Representations of Islam in the United States after 9/11." *American Journal of Islamic Social Sciences* 22, no. 1 (Winter 2005): 5–69.

Black, David A. *Law in Film: Resonance and Representation*. Urbana: University of Illinois Press, 1999.

Bloche, Greg M., and Jonathan Marks. "Doing unto Others as They Did unto Us: The Path to Torture." *The New York Times*, November 14, 2005, 21.

Boltanski, Luc. *Distant Suffering: Media, Morality, and Politics.* New York: Cambridge University Press, 1999.

Bonilla-Silva, Eduardo. *Racism without Racists: Color-Blind Racism and the Persistence of Racial Inequality in the United States.* 2nd ed. New York: Rowman and Littlefield, 2006.

Borger, Julian. "Bright Boy from the California Suburbs Who Turned Taliban Warrior." *Guardian*, October 5, 2002. www.guardian.co.uk/world/2002/oct/05/usa.afghanistan.

Bourdieu, Pierre. *The Field of Cultural Production.* New York: Columbia University Press, 1993.

Bowden, Mark. "The Dark Art of Interrogation." *Atlantic Monthly*, October 2003. www.theatlantic.com/doc/200310/bowden.

Brison, Susan J. "Gender, Terrorism, and War." *Signs: Journal of Women in Culture and Society* 28, no. 1 (2002): 435–437.

Brown, Wendy. "Subjects of Tolerance." In *Political Theologies: Public Relations in a Post-Secular World*, edited by Hent de Vries and Lawrence Eugene Sullivan, 298–317. New York: Fordham University Press, 2006.

Buck, Joan Juliet. *Vogue* 195, no. 12 (December 2005): 254.

Buncombe, Andrew. "Bush Launches Magazine to Teach Young Arabs to Love America." *Independent News and Media* (UK), July 18, 2003. http://news.independent.co.uk/world/americas/article96619.ece.

———. "U.S. Military Tells Jack Bauer: Cut Out the Torture Scenes??? Or Else!" *Independent* (London), February 13, 2007.

Bush, George W. "Address to a Joint Session of Congress and the American People." September 20, 2001, www.whitehouse.gov/news/releases/2001/09/20010920–8.html.

———. "A Nation Challenged; Excerpts from the President's Remarks on the War on Terrorism." *New York Times*, October 12, 2001.

———. "State of the Union, 2004." January 20, 2004. www.whitehouse.gov/news/releases/2004/01/20040120–7.html.

Butler, Judith. *Frames of War: When Is Life Grievable?* New York: Verso, 2010.

Cainkar, Louise. *Homeland Insecurity: The Arab American and Muslim American Experience after 9/11.* New York: Russell Sage Foundation, 2009.

"Camels on Hand to Celebrate Premier of 'Little Mosque on the Prairie.'" *Yahoo! News*, January 4, 2007. http://ca.news.yahoo.com/s/capress/070104/entertainment/tv_little_mosque.

Campo-Flores, Arian, and Dirk Johnson. "From Taco Bell to Al Qaeda: How Accused 'Dirty Bomb' Plotter Jose Padilla Traveled from Gangland Chicago to Osama bin Laden's Backyard." *Newsweek*, June 24, 2002: 34.

"Can We Save Amina Lawal's Life?" *Oprah Winfrey Show*, CBS (October 4, 2002).

"Can We Save Amina Lawal's Life?" Dr. Phil Message Board, Show Archive (October 2002). www.drphil.com/messageboard_archive/?IDX=messages&DiscussionID=2137&P=0.

Carlson, Peter. "Jack Bauer of 24, the Interrogator's Marquis de Sade?" *Washington Post*, February 20, 2007: C1.

Carter, John. "Political Correctness Kills." *Washington Times*, December 11, 2009. http://carter.house.gov/index.cfm?sectionid=104&sectiontree=6,104&itemid=1110.

"The Case of the Taliban American." CNN.com. www.cnn.com/CNN/Programs/people/shows/walker/profile.html.

Chang, Nancy. *Silencing Political Dissent: How Post-September 11 Anti-Terrorism Measures Threaten Our Civil Liberties.* New York: Seven Stories, 2002.

"Changing Minds, Winning Peace: A New Strategic Direction for U.S. Public Diplomacy in the Arab and Muslim World." *Report of the Advisory Group on Public Diplomacy for the Arab and Muslim World*. October 1, 2003.

"Chapter Seventy-Four." *Boston Public*, FOX, Episode 74 (December 19, 2003).

Chertoff, Michael. "Fact vs. Fiction in the War on Terror." Ronald Reagan Building, Washington, DC. Major Leaders Special Transcripts, Federal News Service, June 23, 2006.

Chouliaraki, Lilie. *The Spectatorship of Suffering*. Thousand Oaks, CA: Sage, 2006.

Chozick, Amy. "Campaign '08: Obama Walks a Fine Line with Muslims; Campaign's Efforts to Dispel Rumors Risk Offending a Base of Support." *Wall Street Journal*, June 23, 2008: A10.

Clinton, Hillary. "New Hope for Afghanistan's Women." *Time*, November 24, 2001. www.time.com/time/nation/article/0,8599,185643,00.html.

Cohen, Richard. "Profiles in Evasiveness." *Washington Post*, October 11, 2001, Editorial: A33.

Cole, David, and James X. Dempsey. *Terrorism and the Constitution: Sacrificing Civil Liberties in the name of National Security*. New York: New Press, 2002.

Coletu, Ebony. "Forms of Submission: Acts of Writing in Moments of Need." PhD diss., Stanford University, 2008.

———. "The New Giving Marketplace: What Does Donor's Choice Charity Commodify?" Paper presented at the annual meeting of the American Studies Association, San Antonio, TX, November 20, 2010.

Collins, Patricia Hill. *Black Feminist Thought*. New York: Routledge, 2001.

Council of American Muslims for Understanding. "Share Values Initiative." www.opendialogue.com, 2002.

Council on American-Islamic Relations. "Islam in America." Ad Campaign, 2003. www.americanmuslims.info/archive.asp.

———. "Protest of an American Muslim Relief Group's Fundraiser Advocated Hate and Violence." March 2, 2011. www.esquire.com/blogs/politics/orange-county-protest-5334312.

———. "The Status of Muslim Civil Rights in the United States 2002: Stereotypes and Civil Liberties." Civil Rights Report, 2002. www.cair.com/CivilRights/CivilRightsReports/2002Report.aspx.

"Crime and Punishment/Saudi Arabian Rape Case/Ali Interview." *Anderson Cooper 360*, CNN, November 29, 2007.

Dabul, Emilio Karim. "In Defense of 24: An Arab-American Defends the Real-Life Bauers." *Wall Street Journal*, Editorial Page, February 7, 2007. www.opinionjournal.com/la/?id=110009633.

Dao, James, and Eric Schmitt. "A Nation Challenged: Hearts and Minds; Pentagon Readies Efforts to Sway Sentiments Abroad." *New York Times*, February 19, 2002: A1.

"Day 4: 3–4pm." 24, FOX (February 14, 2005).

"Day 4: 7pm–8pm." 24, FOX (March 14, 2005).

Deeb, Lara. *An Enchanted Modern: Gender and Public Piety in Shi'I Lebanon*. Princeton: Princeton University Press, 2006.

Denver, John, ed. *Legal Reelism: Movies as Legal Texts*. Urbana: University of Illinois Press, 1996.

Douglas, Susan. *Enlightened Sexism: The Seductive Message that Feminism's Work Is Done*. New York: Times Books, 2010.

Dowd, Maureen. "Liberties: Cleopatra and Osama." *New York Times*, November 18, 2001.

Downing, John, and Karin Wilkins. "Mediating Terrorism: Text and Protest in Interpretations of *The Siege*." *Critical Studies in Media Communication* 19, no. 4 (December 2002): 419–37.

Educators for Social Responsibility. "List of Publicly Reported U.S. Hate Crimes against Arabs, Muslims, and Other South Asians from September 11 through September 26, 2001." www.esrnational.org/discrimincidents200109.htm

Edwards, Brian T. *Morocco Bound: Disorienting America's Maghreb, from Casablanca to the Marrakech Express.* Durham, NC: Duke University Press, 2005.

Elliot, Michael. "The Shoe Bomber's World." *Time*, February 25, 2002: 47–50. www.time .com/time/world/article/0,8599,203478,00.html.

Elliott, Andrea. "Muslim Voters Detect a Snub from Obama." *New York Times*, June 24, 2008.

Eng, David. *The Feeling of Kinship: Queer Liberalism and the Racialization of Intimacy.* Durham, NC: Duke University Press, 2010.

———. *Racial Castration.* Durham, NC: Duke University Press, 2005.

Esposito, John, and Dalia Mogahed. *Who Speaks for Islam? What a Billion Muslims Really Think.* New York: Gallup Press, 2007.

"FBI Investigating Michigan Mosque Attacks." *USA Today*, February 16, 2006. www .usatoday.com/news/nation/2006–02–16–michigan-mosque_x.htm.

"Feces Smeared on Van Parked Near Bellevue Mosque." *Seattle Times*, June 24, 2010. http:// seattletimes.nwsource.com/html/localnews/2012202078_vansmeared25m.html.

Fine, Larry. "New Yorkers Laughing Again after Sept. 11 Trauma." *Yahoo! News*, Canada, July 19, 2002. http://ca.news.yahoo.com/020719/5/nqcj.html.

Finn, Ed. "Unhip, Unhip Al Hurra: The Middle East Hates Its New TV Station." Slate.com, February 20, 2004. http://slate.msn.com/id/2095806.

Fiske, John, and John Hartley. *Reading Television.* New York: Routledge, 2003.

Flynn, Gillian. "TV Review: *Sleeper Cell,*" *Entertainment Weekly* 852 (December 2, 2005): 67.

"FMF and NOW Protest Woman's Death Sentence at Nigerian Embassy." *Ms. Magazine*, August 29, 2002. www.msmagazine.com/news/uswirestory.asp?id=6837.

Forman, Jim. "Store Owner Fights Back after Attack." *KING5 News*, Seattle, WA, February 22, 2007. www.king5.com/topstories/stories/NW_022107WABclerkattackKC.22f8ce0b .html.

"Fox TV Accused of Stereotyping American Muslims." *Free Republic*, January 13, 2005. www .freerepublic.com/focus/f-news/1320357/posts.

"Frederick Mosque Possible Target of Hate Crime: Windows Broken at Building 3 Times." NBC4.com, Maryland, February 28, 2007. www.nbc4.com/news/11138569/detail.html.

Friedman, Thomas. "Foreign Affairs; Saudi Royals and Reality." *New York Times*, October 16, 2001. www.nytimes.com/2001/10/16/opinion/foreign-affairs-saudi-royals-and-reality.html.

"Getting to Know You." *7th Heaven*, WB, Season 8, Episode 7 (November 3, 2003).

Girl Scouts of the United States of America. "Who We Are." www.girlscouts.org /who_we_are/facts/.

"Giuliani Rejects $10 million from Saudi Prince." CNN.com, October 12, 2001. http:// archives.cnn.com/2001/US/10/11/rec.giuliani.prince/index.html.

Gordon, George. "Computer Nerd Who Turned into America's Bloodiest Killer: How the Gulf War and Waco Fueled the Paranoia of the Man behind the Oklahoma City Bomb." *Daily Mail* (London), April 24, 1995: 12.

Gordon, Neve, and George Lopez. "Terrorism in the Arab-Israeli Conflict." In *Ethics in International Affairs: Theories and Cases*, edited by Andrew Valls, 99–113. New York: Rowman and Littlefield, 2000.

Gray, Herman S. *Cultural Moves.* Berkeley: University of California Press, 2005.

———. "The Politics of Representation on Network Television." In *Media and Cultural Studies: Keyworks*, edited by Meenakshi Gigi Durham and Douglas Kellner, 439–61. Oxford: Blackwell, 2001.

———. *Watching Race: Television and the Struggle for Blackness*. Minneapolis: University of Minnesota Press, 1995.

Greenhill, Kelly M. "24 on the Brain." *Los Angeles Times*, May 28, 2007: A27.

Grewal, Inderpal. *Transnational America: Feminisms, Diasporas, Neoliberalisms*. Durham, NC: Duke University Press, 2005.

"Growing Number of Americans Say Obama Is a Muslim: Religion, Politics and the President." Pew Forum on Religion and Public Life, August 18, 2010. http://pewforum.org/Politics-and-Elections/Growing-Number-of-Americans-Say-Obama-is-a-Muslim.aspx.

Gupta, Akhil, and James Ferguson. "Culture, Power, Place: Ethnography at the End of an Era." In *Culture, Power, Place: Explorations in Critical Anthropology*, edited by Akhil Gupta and James Ferguson, 1–32. Durham, NC: Duke University Press, 1997.

Hall, Stuart. "New Ethnicities." In *Critical Dialogues in Cultural Studies*, edited by Kuan-Hsing Chen and David Morley, 441–49. New York: Routledge, 1996.

———. "The Problem of Ideology: Marxism without Guarantees." *Journal of Communication Inquiry* 10 (1986): 28–44.

———. "Racist Ideologies and the Media." In *Media Studies: A Reader*, 2nd ed., edited by Paul Marris and Sue Thornham, 271–282. New York: New York University Press, 2000.

———. "What Is This 'Black' in Black Popular Culture?" In *Black Popular Culture*, edited by Gina Dent, 21–33. Seattle: Bay Press, 1992.

Haney López, Ian F. *White by Law: The Legal Construction of Race*. New York: New York University Press, 1996.

Harding, Jennifer, and E. Deidre Pribram. "Introduction: The Case for a Cultural Emotion Studies." In *Emotions: A Cultural Studies Reader*, edited by Jennifer Harding and E. Deidre Pribram, 1–24. New York: Routledge, 2009.

Harrop, Froma. "Keep Him 'Detained'—Padilla: A Goon in Exotic Costume." *Providence Journal* (Rhode Island), May 5, 2004: B05.

"Help Wanted."*Aliens in America*, CW, Season 1, Episode 5 (October 29, 2007).

Hentoff, Nat. "The Death of Operation TIPS: Volunteer Spying Corps Dismissed." *Village Voice*, December 13, 2002. www.villagevoice.com/issues/0251/hentoff.php.

Hewitt, Bill, Maureen Harrington, and Colleen O'Connor. "The Long Road Home." *People* 58, no. 15 (October 7, 2002): 66–70.

Heydarpour, Roya. "The Comic Is Palestinian, the Jokes Bawdy." *New York Times*, November 21, 2006. www.nytimes.com/2006/11/21/nyregion/21ink.html?fta=y.

Hirschkind, Charles, and Saba Mahmood. "Feminism, the Taliban, and Politics of Counter-Insurgency." *Anthropological Quarterly* 75, no. 2 (Spring 2002): 341.

Holliman, John. "Timothy McVeigh Agitated by Waco Events." *CNN*, April 22, 1995.

Howard, Douglas L. "'You're Going to Tell Me Everything You Know:' Torture and Morality in FOX's *24*." In *Reading 24: TV against the Clock*, edited by Steven Peacock, 120–48. New York: I. B. Tauris, 2007.

Howell, Sally, and Andrew Shyrock. "Cracking Down on Diaspora: Arab Detroit and America's 'War on Terror.'" *Anthropological Quarterly* 76, no. 3 (2003): 443–62.

Human Rights Watch. "'We Are Not the Enemy': Hate Crimes against Arabs, Muslims, and Those Perceived to Be Arab or Muslim, after September 11." *Human Rights Watch*

Report 14, no. 6 (November 2002). www.hrw.org/reports/2002/usahate/index .htm#TopOfPage.

"Hundreds of Arabs Still Detained." March 13, 2002. *CBS News.* www.cbsnews.com /stories.2002.03/13/503649.shtml.

Hunt, Krista. "'Embedded Feminism' and the War on Terror." In *(En)gendering the War on Terror: War Stories and Camouflaged Politics*, edited by Krista Hunt and Kim Rygiel, 51–96. Burlington, VT: Ashgate, 2006.

"In Depth: Miss World Beauty Pageant." *NBC Evening News*, December 7, 2002.

"Inquiry into Secret Service Agent Barred from Flight." *CNN.com*, December 28, 2001. www .cnn.com/2001/US/12/28/rec.agent.airline.

"Inter Arma Silent Leges." *The Practice*, ABC, Season 6, Episode 9 (December 9, 2001).

"Interview: James Brosnahan Discusses His Client, John Walker Lindh." *Morning Edition*, NPR, July 16, 2002.

Intini, John. "Little Mosque on the Prairie: Recreate Small-Town Canada, Then Add Muslims—For Laughs." *Macleans.ca*, December 11, 2006. www.macleans.ca/article .jsp?content=20061211_137752_137752.

Isikoff, Michael, and Mark Hosenball. "Terror Watch: The Missing Padilla Video." *Newsweek*, February 28, 2007. www.msnbc.com/id/17389175/site/newsweek.

"Islamic Center Defaced with Bacon Slices." *Associated Press*, October 12, 2010. www.cbsnews .com/stories/2010/10/12/national/main6952008.shtml.

"Is Torture on Hot Fox TV Show 24 Encouraging US Soldiers to Abuse Detainees?" *Democracy Now*, February 22, 2007. www.democracynow.org/2007/2/22 /is_torture_on_hit_fox_tv.

Iverson, Dan. "*Sleeper Cell*: American Terror Review." IGN.com, January 26, 2007. http:// tv.ign.com/articles/758/758753p1.html.

Jaggar, Alison M. "Love and Knowledge: Emotion in Feminist Epistemology." In *Women Knowledge, and Reality*, edited by Anny Garry and Marilyn Pearsall, 166–90. New York: Routledge, 1996.

Jalil, Jannat. "Muslim Comedians Laugh at Racism." *BBC News*, June 15, 2004. http://news. bbc.co.uk/2/hi/americas/3796109.stm.

Jarmakani, Amira. "Arab American Feminisms: Mobilizing the Politics of Invisibility." In *Arab and Arab American Feminisms: Gender, Violence, and Belonging*, edited by Rabab Abdulhadi, Evelyn Alsultany, and Nadine Naber, 227–41. Syracuse: Syracuse University Press, 2011.

———. *Imagining Arab Womanhood: The Cultural Mythology of Veils, Harems, and Belly Dancers in the U.S.* New York: Palgrave, 2008.

Joseph, Suad, and Susan Slymovics. *Women and Power in the Middle East.* Philadelphia: University of Pennsylvania Press, 2000.

Juergensmeyer, Mark. *Terror in the Eyes of God: The Global Rise of Religious Violence.* 3rd ed. Berkeley: University of California Press, 2000.

Junod, Tom. "Innocent." *Esquire*, July 2006. www.esquire.com/features /ESQ0706JLINDH_106.

Kahf, Mohja. "The Pity Committee and the Careful Reader: How Not to Buy Stereotypes about Arab Women." In *Arab and Arab American Feminisms: Gender, Violence, and Belonging*, edited by Rabab Abdulhadi, Evelyn Alsultany, and Nadine Naber, 111–23. Syracuse: Syracuse University Press, 2011.

Kandiyoti, Deniz, ed. *Gendering the Middle East: Emerging Perspectives*. Syracuse: Syracuse University Press, 1996.

Kaplan, Amy. *The Anarchy of Empire in the Making of U.S. Culture*. Cambridge, MA: Harvard University Press, 2005.

———. "Violent Belongings and the Question of Empire Today—Presidential Address to the American Studies Association, October 17, 2003." *American Quarterly* 56, no. 1 (March 2004): 1–18.

———. "Where Is Guantánamo?" *American Quarterly* 57, no. 3 (September 2005): 831–58.

Kaplan, Caren. "Precision Targets: GPS and the Militarization of U.S. Consumer Identity." *American Quarterly* 58, no. 3 (September 2006): 705.

Kaplan, Caren, Norma Alarcón, and Minoo Moallem, eds. *Between Woman and Nation: Nationalisms, Transnational Feminism, and the State*. Durham, NC: Duke University Press, 1999.

Kaptur, Marcy. "Kaptur Bill Safeguards Civil Liberties for All: H. Res. 234 Seeks to Protect Against Religious, Ethnic Persecution." Press release, Rep. Marcy Kaptur (D-OH), May 15, 2003. www.adc.org/index.php?id=1803.

Karon, Tony. "Person of the Week: Jose Padilla." *Time*, June 14, 2002. www.time.com/time /nation/article/0,8599,262269,00.html.

Kennedy, Liam, and Scott Lucas. "Enduring Freedom: Public Diplomacy and U.S. Foreign Policy." *American Quarterly* 57, no. 2 (June 2005): 309–33.

Kifner, John F. "Terror in Oklahoma: The Suspect; Authorities Hold a Man of 'Extreme Right-Wing Views.'" *New York Times*, April 22, 1995, National Desk, sec. 1: 9.

Koinange, Jeff. "Woman Sentenced to Stoning Freed." *CNN*, February 23, 2004. http://edition.cnn.com/2003/WORLD/africa/09/25/nigeria.stoning/index.html.

Kristof, Nicholas D. "Behind the Terrorists." *New York Times*, May 7, 2002. http://query.nytimes.com/gst/fullpage.html?res=9A0CE1DA1730F934A35756C0A9649C8B63.

———. "The Push to 'Otherize' Obama." Op-Ed, *New York Times*, September 21, 2008.

Kukis, Mark. *"My Heart Became Attached": The Strange Journey of John Walker Lindh*. Dulles, VA: Brassey's, 2003.

Lacayo, Richard. "Lifting the Veil." *Time*, December 3, 2001: 34–49.

Lacayo, Richard, Hannah Beech, Hannah Bloch, Matthew Forney, Terry McCarthy, Jeff Chu, Jeffrey Ressner, Alex Perry, Tim McGirk, and John F. Dickerson. "About Face." *Time*, December 3, 2001. www.time.com/time/magazine/article/0,9171,1001344,00.html.

Lally, Nick. "Patriotism, Violence, and Hate." *Insurgent Newspaper*, October 2001. http:// theinsurgent.net/index.php?volnum=13.2&article=patriotism.

"Laura Bush Radio Address." *American Presidency Project*, edited by John T. Woolley and Gerhard Peters. Santa Barbara, CA. November 17, 2001. www.presidency.ucsb.edu /ws/?pid=24992.http://www.presidency.ucsb.edu/ws/index.php?pid=24992.

Leonard, John. "There Goes the Neighborhood." *New York* 38, no. 43 (December 5, 2005): 90.

Leonard, Mark. "Cool Britannia." *New Statesman*. http://markleonard.net/journalism/ coolbritannia/.

Leung, Rebecca. "Abuse of Iraqi POWs by GIs Probed." *60 Minutes II*, April 28, 2004. www .cbsnews.com/stories/2004/04/27/60II/main614063.shtml.

Levitt, Laura. "Impossible Assimilations, American Liberalism, and Jewish Difference." *American Quarterly* 53, no. 3 (2007): 807–23.

Lewis, David. "Background of Timothy McVeigh Slowly Being Revealed." *CNN News*, April 25, 1995.

Lewis, Neil A. "Indictment Portrays Padilla as Minor Figure in a Plot." *New York Times,* November 24, 2005.

Lewis, Neil, and Thom Shanker. "Missteps and Confusion Seen in Muslim Chaplain's 'Spy Case.'" *New York Times,* January 3, 2004. www.nytimes.com/2004/01/04 /national/04YEE.html?pagewanted=all&position=.

"Lifting the Veil." *CNN Evening News,* CNN, November 20, 2001.

"Lifting the Veil." *CNN Evening News,* CNN, September 10, 2007.

"Lifting the Veil." *Anderson Cooper 360,* CNN, April 23, 2009.

Lipsitz, George. *Time Passages: Collective Memory and American Popular Culture.* Minneapolis: University of Minnesota Press, 2001.

Lithwick, Dahlia. "The Fiction behind Torture Policy: The Lawyers Designing Interrogation Techniques Cited Jack Bauer More Frequently than the Constitution." *Newsweek,* July 26, 2008. www.newsweek.com/id/149009.

Lowry, Brian. "The Wanted." *Variety,* July 20, 2009. www.variety.com/review/VE1117940697 .html?categoryid=32&cs=1.

Lubiano, Wahneema. "Talking about the State and Imagining Alliances." In *Talking Visions: Multicultural Feminism in a Transnational Age,* edited by Ella Shohat, 441–50. New York: New Museum/MIT Press, 1998.

MacFarquhar, Neil, and David Johnston. "Scrutiny Increases for a Group Advocating for Muslims in U.S." *New York Times,* March 14, 2007: A1.

Maher, Bill. *Real Time with Bill Maher.* HBO, March 19, 2004. www.hbo.com/billmaher /new_rules/.

Mahdi, Waleed. "US vs. Arab/Muslim Trauma Unpacked: An Analysis of the Challenging Mode of Depiction in *Traitor.*" Paper presented at the annual meeting of the Middle East Studies Association, Boston, MA, 2009.

Mahmood, Saba. "Secularism, Hermeneutics, and Empire: The Politics of Islamic Reformation." *Public Culture* 18, no. 2 (2006): 323–47.

Maira, Sunaina. "'Good' and 'Bad' Muslim Citizens: Feminists, Terrorists, and U.S. Orientalisms." *Feminist Studies* 35, no. 3 (Fall 2009): 631–56.

———. *Missing: Youth, Citizenship, and Empire after 9/11.* Durham, NC: Duke University Press, 2009.

Malkin, Michelle. "Racial Profiling: A Matter of Survival." *USA Today,* August 16, 2004. www.usatoday.com/news/opinion/editorials/2004–08–16–racial-profiling_x.htm.

Mamdani, Mahmood. *Good Muslim, Bad Muslim: America, the Cold War, and the Roots of Terror.* New York: Pantheon Books, 2004.

"Man in Terror Scare Says Woman Is Lying." CNN, September 13, 2002. www.cnn .com/2002/US/09/13/alligator.alley/.

"McVeigh: Another Quiet Loner." *St. Petersburg Times* (FL), April 23, 1995: 1A.

McAlister, Melani. *Epic Encounters: Culture, Media, and U.S. Interests in the Middle East, 1945–2000.* Berkeley: University of California Press, 2001.

———. "Suffering Sisters? American Feminists and the Problem of Female Genital Surgeries." In *Americanism: New Perspectives on the History of an Ideal,* edited by Michael Kazin and Joseph A. McCartin, 242–61. Chapel Hill: University of North Carolina Press, 2006.

McClennen, Sophia A. "E Pluribus Unum, Ex Uno Plura: Legislating and Deregulating American Studies Post-9/11." *CR: The New Centennial Review* 8, no. 1 (2008): 155–85.

McCoy, Alfred W. "The Myth of the Ticking Time Bomb." *Progressive,* October 2006.

McFadden, Robert. "One Man's Complex Path to Extremism." *New York Times*, National Desk, April 23, 1995.

McLaughlin, Eugene. "Rebranding Britain: The Life and Times of 'Cool Britannia.'" *BBC* and the Open University. n.d. www.open2.net/newbrit/pages/features/features_mclaughlin.htm.

McMorris-Santoro, Evan. "Mosque Ado about Fear-Mongering: Right Wing Takes on Muslim Worship Anywhere and Everywhere." *Talking Points Memo*, July 20, 2010. http://tpmmuckraker.talkingpointsmemo.com/2010/07/mosque_ado_about_fear-mongering_right_wing_takes_o_1.php.

McPhee, Michele. "Southwest Apologizes for Removing Muslim Passenger from Flight." *AOL Travel News*, March 16, 2011. http://news.travel.aol.com/2011/03/16/southwest-apologizes-for-removing-muslim-passenger-from-flight/.

Media and Society Group. "MSRG Special Report: Restrictions on Civil Liberties, Views of Islam, and Muslim Americans," and "MSRG Special Report: U.S. War on Terror, U.S. Foreign Policy, and Anti-Americanism." Cornell University, Ithaca, NY, December 2004. www.comm.cornell.edu/msrg/report1a.pdf; http://www.comm.cornell.edu/msrg/report1b.pdf.

Medved, Michael. "Tickets to Terror." FOX, January 4, 2006.

Melamed, Jodi. "The Spirit of Neoliberalism: From Racial Liberalism to Neoliberal Multiculturalism." *Social Text* 24, No. 4 (Winter 2006): 1–24.

Mernissi, Fatima. *The Veil and the Male Elite: A Feminist Interpretation of Women's Rights in Islam*. New York: Basic Books, 1992.

Meyer, Dick. "Rush: MPs Just 'Blowing Off Steam.'" CBSNews.com, May 6, 2004. www.cbsnews.com/stories/2004/05/06/opinion/meyer/main616021.shtml.

Meyer, Jane. "Whatever It Takes." *New Yorker*, February 19, 2007. www.newyorker.com/reporting/2007/02/19/070219fa_fact_mayer?currentPage=all.

Michalak, Laurence. "Improvements in the Image of Arabs and Muslims in American Cinema." *Awrak Al Awsat* [Middle East Research Competition and Center for Social and Economic Researches and Studies, Tunis], no. 2 (2009): 39–54.

Miller, Martin. "24 Gets a Lesson in Torture from the Experts." *Los Angeles Times*, February 13, 2007: E1.

Moallem, Minoo. *Between Warrior Brother and Veiled Sister: Islamic Fundamentalism and the Politics of Patriarchy in Iran*. Berkeley: University of California Press, 2005.

Moghadem, Valentin, ed. *From Patriarchy to Empowerment: Women's Participation, Movements, and Rights in the Middle East, North Africa, and South Asia*. Syracuse: Syracuse University Press, 2007.

Morris, David, and Gary Langer. "Terrorist Suspect Treatment: Most Americans Oppose Torture Techniques." *ABC News*, May 27, 2004. http://abcnews.go.com/sections/us/polls/torture_poll_040527.html.

Moya, Paula M. L., and Hazel Rose Markus, eds. *Doing Race: 21 Essays for the 21st Century*. New York: Norton, 2010.

Mulrine, Anne. "Unveiled Threat: The Taliban Is Relentless in Its Oppression of Afghan Women." *U.S. News & World Report*, October 15, 2001: 32–34.

Naber, Nadine. *Arab America*. New York: New York University Press, 2012.

———. "The Rules of Forced Engagement: Race, Gender, and the Culture of Fear among Arab Immigrants in San Francisco Post-9/11." *Cultural Dynamics* 18, no. 3 (2006): 235–67.

Naber, Nadine, and Amaney Jamal, eds. *Race and Arab Americans before and after 9/11: From Invisible Citizens to Visible Subjects.* Syracuse: Syracuse University Press, 2007.

Nacos, Brigitte L., and Oscar Torres-Reyna. *Fueling Our Fears: Stereotyping, Media Coverage, and Public Opinion of Muslim Americans.* Lanham, MD: Rowman and Littlefield, 2007.

Nguyen, Tram. *We Are All Suspects Now: Untold Stories from Immigrant Communities after 9/11.* Boston: Beacon Press, 2005.

"Nigeria/Beauty Contest/Demonstrations/Allas Interview." *CNN Evening News*, November 22, 2002.

"Nigeria/Miss World Contest/Riots." *NBC Evening News*, November 23, 2002.

Noriega, Chon. *Shot in America: Television, the State, and the Rise of Chicano Cinema.* Minneapolis: University of Minnesota Press, 2000.

Norris, Michele. "Muslim Army Chaplain Recalls Guantanamo Ordeal." *All Things Considered*, NPR, October 5, 2005. www.npr.org/templates/story/story .php?storyId=4946292.

Office of the Press Secretary. "Executive Order: Establishing the Office of Global Communications." January 21, 2003. www.whitehouse.gov/news/releases/2003/01/20030121–3.html.

Parker, Laura. "The Ordeal of Chaplain Yee." *USA Today.* May 16, 2004. www.cnn.com/2003 /US/09/20/chaplain.arrest.

———. "Padilla Charges Don't Measure Up to Accusations." *USA Today*, July 18, 2007. www .usatoday.com/news/nation/2007–07–18–padilla-charges_n.htm.

"Patriot." *Law and Order*, NBC, Season 12, Episode E2226 (May 22, 2002).

Patrizio, Andy. "Aladdin: Special Edition." IGN Entertainment, IGN.com, September 17, 2004. http://dvd.ign.com/articles/549/549036p1.html.

Peace, Propaganda, and the Promised Land: U.S. Media and the Israeli-Palestinian Conflict. Media Education Foundation, 2003.

Peacock, Steven, ed. *Reading 24: TV against the Clock.* New York: I. B. Tauris, 2007.

"Peer Pressure." *7th Heaven*, WB, Season 7, Episode 8 (November 11, 2002).

Perlez, Jane. "Muslim-as-Apple-Pie Videos Are Greeted with Skepticism." *New York Times*, October 30, 2002. www.nytimes.com/2002/10/30/world/muslim-as-apple-pie-videos-are -greeted-with-skepticism.html.

"Pentagon Closes Down Controversial Office." CNN, February 26, 2002. http://archives.cnn. com/2002/US/02/26/defense.office.

Pierre, Robert E. "Victims of Hate, Now Feeling Forgotten." *Washington Post*, September 14, 2001: A1.

"Pilot." *Whoopi*, NBC, Season 1, Episode 1 (September 9, 2003).

"Pilot." *Aliens in America*, CW, Season 1, Episode 1 (October 1, 2007).

"Police: Cab Driver Stabbed by Passenger Who Asked 'Are You Muslim?'" *NY1 News*, August 25, 2010. www.ny1.com/content/top_stories/?ArID=124338.

Poniewozik, James. "Stand-Up Diplomacy." *Time*, March 19, 2007.

Press, Joy. "There Goes the Neighborhood: A Suburban Miniseries Drops in on the Terrorists Next Door." *Village Voice*, November 21, 2005. www.villagevoice.com /screens/0547,tv1,70218,28.html.

"Profile: John Walker Lindh." *BBC News Online.* World: Americas, January 24, 2002. http:// news.bbc.co.uk/2/hi/americas/1779455.stm.

Puar, Jasbir. *Terrorist Assemblages: Homonationalism in Queer Times.* Durham, NC: Duke University Press, 2007.

Rabinowitz, Dorothy. "Bloody Good." *Wall Street Journal.* December 2, 2005: W8.

Radin, Charles, "False Alarms." *Jewish Advocate* 199, no. 38 (September 19, 2008): 13.

Ramos-Zayas, Ana Y. "Delinquent Citizenship, National Performances: Racialization, Surveillance, and the Politics of 'Worthiness' in Puerto Rican Chicago." *Latino Studies* 2 (2004): 26–44.

Rana, Junaid. *Terrifying Muslims: Race and Labor in the South Asian Diaspora.* Durham, NC: Duke University Press, 2011.

———. "Tracing the Muslim Body: Race, US Deportation, and Pakistani Return Migration." In *The Sun Never Sets: South Asian Migrants in the Circuits of US Power,* edited by Vivek Bald, Miabi Chatterji, Sujani Reddy, and Manu Vimalassary. New York: New York University Press, forthcoming.

Rapping, Elayne. *Law and Justice as Seen on TV.* New York: New York University Press, 2003.

Razack, Sherene H. *Casting Out: The Eviction of Muslims from Western Law and Politics.* Toronto: University of Toronto Press, 2008.

"Reid: 'I Am at War with Your Country.'" CNN.com/Law Center, January 31, 2003. www .cnn.com/2003/LAW/01/31/reid.transcript/.

Reuters Wire Staff. "Muslim Clerics Ordered Off Atlantic Southeast Airlines Flight." WPIX 11, May 8, 2011. www.wpix.com/news/wpix-muslim-clerics-removed-plane-story,0,2534595 .story.

Ripley, Amanda. "The Case of the Dirty Bomber." *Time,* June 24, 2002: 28–32. www.time .com/time/nation/article/0,8599,262917,00.html.

Robin, Ron. "Requiem for Public Diplomacy?" *American Quarterly* 57 no. 2 (June 2005): 345–53.

Roche, Timothy. "A Short Course in Miracles." *Time* 160, no. 5 (July 29, 2002): 34–35.

Roche, Timothy, Brian Bennett, Anne Berryman, Hilary Hylton, Siobhan Morrissey, and Amanda Radwan. "The Making of John Walker Lindh." *Time,* October 7, 2002. www .time.com/time/magazine/article/0,9171,1003414,00.htm.

Rodriguez, Juana Maria. *Queer Latinidad: Identity Practice, Discursive Spaces.* New York: New York University Press, 2003.

Romero, Anthony D. "Sanctioned Bias: Racial Profiling Since 9/11." ACLU Racial Profiling Report, February 2004. www.aclu.org.

Rosaldo, Renato. "Cultural Citizenship, Inequality, and Multiculturalism." In *Race, Identity, and Citizenship,* edited by Rodolfo D. Torres, Louis F. Mirón, and Jonathan Xavier Inda, 253–61. Oxford: Blackwell, 1999.

Rothstein, Edward. "Connections; Cherished Ideas Refracted in History's Lens." *New York Times,* September 7, 2002. http://query.nytimes.com/gst/fullpage.html?res=9904E2D7133 EF934A3575AC0A9649C8B63.

———. "Connections; Exploring the Flaws in the Notion of the 'Root Causes' of Terror." *New York Times,* November 17, 2001.

Russell, Lauren. "Church Plans Quran-Burning Event." CNN, July 31, 2010. www.cnn .com/2010/US/07/29/florida.burn.quran.day/index.html.

Said, Edward W. *Covering Islam: How the Media and Experts Determine How We See the Rest of the World.* New York: Vintage, 1997.

———. *Orientalism.* New York: Vintage, 1979.

Salaita, Steven. *Anti-Arab Racism in the U.S.A: Where It Comes From and What It Means for Politics Today.* London: Pluto Press, 2006.

Saliba, Therese. "Military Presences and Absences: Arab Women and the Persian Gulf War." In *Food for Our Grandmothers: Writings by Arab-American and Arab-Canadian Feminists*, edited by Joanna Kadi, 125–132. Boston: South End Press, 1999.

"Save the Country." *The Education of Max Bickford*, CBS, Season 1, Episode 11 (Jan. 13, 2002).

"Scholar." *Sleeper Cell*, Showtime, Season 1, Episode 4 (December 7, 2005).

Schlussel, Debbie. "Barack Hussein Obama: Once a Muslim, Always a Muslim," December 18, 2006. www.debbieschlussel.com.

Schueller, Malini Johar. *U.S. Orientalisms: Race, Nation, and Gender in Literature, 1790–1890*. Ann Arbor: University of Michigan Press, 1998.

See, Sarita. *The Decolonized Eye: Filipino American Art and Performance*. Minneapolis: University of Minnesota Press, 2009.

Seitz-Wald, Alex. "Texas Mosque and Educational Center Vandalized with Offensive Graffiti and Fire, Causing $20,000 in Damage." Think Progress, August 2, 2010. http://thinkprogress.org/2010/08/02/texas-mosque-vandalized/.

Semmerling, Tim Jon. *"Evil" Arabs in American Popular Film*. Austin: University of Texas Press, 2006.

Sengupta, Somini. "Facing Death for Adultery, Nigerian Woman Is Acquitted." *New York Times*, September 26, 2003. www.nytimes.com/2003/09/26/world/facing-death-for-adultery-nigerian-woman-is-acquitted.html?ref=aminalawal.

Shaheen, Jack G. *Guilty: Hollywood's Verdict after 9/11*. Northampton, MA: Olive Branch Press, 2008.

———. *Reel Bad Arabs: How Hollywood Vilifies a People*. Northampton, MA: Interlink Publishing Group, 2001.

———. *The TV Arab*. Bowling Green, OH: Bowling Green State University Popular Press, 1984.

Sherman, Fraser. "Beware! The Islamofascists Walk Among Us!" *McClatchy-Tribune Business News*, May 31, 2008.

Sherwin, Richard K. *When Law Goes Pop: The Vanishing Line between Law and Popular Culture*. Chicago: University of Chicago Press, 2000.

Shohat, Ella. "The Media's War." *Social Text* 28 (Spring 1991): 135–41.

Shohat, Ella, and Robert Stam. "De-Eurocentricizing Cultural Studies." In *Internationalizing Cultural Studies: An Anthology*, edited by M. Ackbar Abbas and John Nguyet Emi, 481–98. Oxford: Blackwell, 2005.

———. *Flagging Patriotism: Crises of Narcissism and Anti-Americanism*. New York: Routledge, 2007.

———. *Unthinking Eurocentrism: Multiculturalism and the Media*. New York: Routledge, 1994.

Shortal, Jana. "St. Cloud Graffiti May Be Investigated as Hate Crime." *KARE 11 News*, July 9, 2010. www.kare11.com/news/news_article.aspx?storyid=856970.

Siegel, Robert. "Torture's Wider Use Brings New Concerns." *All Things Considered*, NPR, March 13, 2007.

Sikh Coalition. "One Year after Brutal Attack, Sikh Hate Crime Victim Files Civil Suit against Attackers." July 12, 2005. www.sikhcoalition.org/ca_rhill.asp.

Slevin, Peter. "Arab Americans Report Abuse." *Washington Post*, July 28, 2004. www.washingtonpost.com/wp-dyn/articles/A21888-2004Jul28.html.

Smith, Ben, and Jonathan Martin. "Untraceable E-Mails Spread Obama Rumor." Politico.com, October 13, 2007.

Sontag, Susan. *On Photography*. New York: Farrar, Straus and Giroux, 1977.

Spencer, Robert, and Phyllis Chesler. "The Violent Oppression of Women in Islam." David Horowitz Freedom Center, 2007. www.scribd.com/doc/2526263/The -Violent-Oppression-of-Women-in-Islam; www.terrorismawareness.org/videos/108 /the-violent-oppression-of-women-in-islam/.

Spivak, Gayatri. "Can the Subaltern Speak?" In *Marxism and the Interpretation of Culture*, edited by Cary Nelson and Lawrence Grossberg, 271–315. Chicago: University of Illinois Press, 1988.

Stolberg, Sheryl Gay. "Obama Says Mosque Upholds Principle of Equal Treatment." *New York Times*, August 13, 2010. www.nytimes.com/2010/08/14/us/politics/14obama .html?_r=3.

Surette, Tim. "Fox Importing Mosque." TV.com, June 10, 2008.

"Suspicion." *7th Heaven*, WB, Season 6, Episode 12 (January 21, 2002).

Sutherland, Sharon, and Sarah Swan. "'Tell Me Where the Bomb Is, Or I Will Kill Your Son': Situational Morality on 24." In *Reading 24: TV against the Clock*, edited by Steven Peacock, 119–32. New York: I. B. Tauris, 2007.

Thomas, Evan. "American Taliban: A Long Strange Trip to the Taliban." *Newsweek*, December 17, 2001: 30. www.newsweek.com/2001/12/16/a-long-strange-trip-to-the -taliban.html.

Tyrangiel, Josh. "The Taliban Next Door." *Time*, December 9, 2001. www.time.com/time /printout/0,8816,187564,00.html.

"Under the Veil." ABC, *Nightline* (October 26, 2006).

U.S. Department of State. International Information Program, April 11, 2002. http://usinfo. state.gove/regional/nea/sasia/text/0227rmfd.htm.

"U.S.-Funded Arab TV's Credibility Crisis." *60 Minutes*, CBS News, June 22, 2008.

"U.S. President National Exit Poll" CNN, 2005. www.cnn.com/ELECTION/2004/pages /results/states/US/P/00/epolls.0.htm.

Van Biema, David, Marguerite Michaels, and Nadia Mustafa. "Islam: In the U.S.: Freer, But Not Friedan." *Time*, December 3, 2001. www.time.com/time/magazine /article/0,9171,1001348,00.html#ixzz0r2vh2irx.

Volpp, Leti. "The Citizen and the Terrorist." In *September 11 in History: A Watershed Moment?*, edited by Mary L. Dudziak, 147–62. Durham, NC: Duke University Press, 2003.

Von Eschen, Penny M. "Enduring Public Diplomacy." *American Quarterly* 57 no. 2 (June 2005): 335–43.

———. *Satchmo Blows Up the World: Jazz Ambassadors Play the Cold War*. Cambridge, MA: Harvard University Press, 2004.

Wadud, Amina. *Qur'an and Woman: Rereading the Sacred Text from a Woman's Perspective*. Oxford: Oxford University Press, 1999.

Weber, Cynthia. "Citizenship, Security, Humanity." *International Political Sociology* 4, no. 1 (2010): 83.

———. *"I am an American": Filming the Fear of Difference*. Chicago: University of Chicago Press, 2011.

———. "'I Am an American': Portraits of Post-9/11 US Citizens." *Opendemocracy.net* (September 2007).

Whitaker, Brian. "Its Best Use Is as a Doorstop." *Guardian Unlimited*, May 24, 2004. www .guardian.co.uk/world/2004/may/24/worlddispatch.usa.

Wilgoren, Jodi. "Arab and Muslim Comics Turn Fear into Funny." *New York Times*, September 1, 2002. http://query.nytimes.com/gst/fullpage.html?res=9B05E4D8103FF932A3575A CoA9649C8B63.

Williamsen, Kurt. "Obama Citizenship Accusations Come to a Head." *New American*, December 2, 2008. www.thenewamerican.com/usnews/election/562.

Willis, Susan. *The Portents of the Real: A Primer for Post-9/11 America*. New York: Verso, 2005.

Winant, Howard. *The New Politics of Race: Globalism, Difference, Justice*. Minneapolis: University of Minnesota Press, 2004.

Wise, Tim. *Colorblind: The Rise of Post-Racial Politics and the Retreat from Racial Equity*. San Francisco: City Lights Books, 2010.

Wright, Brad. "Gitmo Chaplain Reprimanded for Adultery, Porn." CNN, May 6, 2004. http://www.cnn.com/2004/LAW/03/22/yee/index.html.

Yee, James. "A U.S. Army Muslim Chaplain's Struggle for Justice." *Voices*, UCSB, UCVT (April 23, 2008).

Youmans, William Lafi. "Humor against Hegemony: Al-Hurra, Jokes, and the Limits of American Soft Power." *Middle East Journal of Culture and Communication* 2 (2009): 76–99.

———. "The War on Ideas: Alhurra and US International Broadcasting Law in the 'War on Terror.'" *Westminster Papers in Communication and Culture* 6, no. 1 (2009): 45–68.

"Youths Dreamed of Adventure. But Settled for Killing a Couple." *New York Times*, May 18, 2002. www.nytimes.com/2002/05/18/us/youths-dreamed-of-adventure-but-settled-for -killing-a-couple.html?ref=suzannezantop.

Yunis, Alia, and Gaelle Duthler. "Tramps vs. Sweethearts: Changing Images of Arab and American Women in Hollywood Films." *Middle East Journal of Culture and Communication* 4, no. 2 (2011): 225–43.

Zelizer, Barbie, and Stuart Allen. "Introduction: When Trauma Shapes the News." In *Journalism after September 11*, edited by Barbie Zelizer and Stuart Allen, 1–32. New York: Routledge, 2002.

Zine, Jasmine. "Between Orientalism and Fundamentalism: Muslim Women and Feminist Engagement," In *(En)gendering the War on Terror: War Stories and Camouflaged Politics*, edited by Krista Hunt and Kim Rygiel, 27–50. Burlington, VT: Ashgate, 2006.

Zurawik, David. "*The Wanted*: NBC News Show an Embarrassment." *Baltimore Sun blog*, July 21, 2009. http://weblogs.baltimoresun.com/entertainment/zontv/2009/07/the_wanted_ nbc_news_terrorism.html.

Index

7th Heaven, 1, 3, 22, 71, 179n7, 179n10, 190n36, 190n2

24, 2–3, 18–19, 30, 33–36, 140, 170; Criticism of, 18–19; Examples of simplified complex representations and, 20–26; Racial casting in, 9–10; Technology in, 42–43; Torture in, 40–46; Women in, 71

Abu Ghraib, 40–44, 58, 119, 127, 170
Abu-Jamal, Mumia, 130
Ad Council, 132, 134–39, 148, 160; And other ad campaigns, 140–43
Advisory Group on Public Diplomacy for the Arab and Muslim World, 132, 150, 159
Affect, 16, 71, 74, 128, 169; Excess of, 72, 75, 90, 94, 103; Politics of affective worthiness, 126; Regulation of, 72. *See also* Benevolent emotions; Compassion; Dissenting feelings; Emotional hegemony; Emotive public; Empathy; Mourning; Outlaw emotion; Outrage; Pity; Remorse; Structure of feeling; and Sympathy
Afghan War, 6, 29, 39, 53, 58; Justifications for, 73, 76, 80, 82–83
Agamben, Giorgio, 53, 56
Ahmed, Leila, 79
Alhurra Television, 151–52, 159
Aliens in America, 172–73, 176
Allen, Stuart, 103
Ambiguous assimilative diversity, 134–37, 141, 161
Ambivalence, 53; In *The Practice*, 52–58
American-Arab Anti-Discrimination Committee, 4, 170
American Civil Liberties Union, 47–48
American Taliban. *See* Lindh, John Walker
Amnesty International, 4, 91–92
Anti-Semitism, 9, 86, 115–20, 127
Antonius, Rachad, 53

Arab American Institute, 170
Arabs and Muslims: Artists, 170–71; "Bad," 8, 11, 15, 28, 31–32, 72, 147; Challenging conflation of, 23, 32–33; As citizen-patriots, 142–44; Conflation of, 9–10, 29, 73, 103, 142; Diverse identities of, 23, 34, 36, 146, 176–77; "Good," 8, 10–11, 15, 18, 28, 31–32, 72, 85–86, 141–43, 147–48, 155, 157, 160–61; Organizations, 170; As patriotic, 13–14, 21–22, 31, 60–63, 69, 102, 138, 141, 146, 148, 154, 161, 169, 177; Plight after 9/11, 16, 22–23, 48–50, 57–58, 62–72, 86, 99, 171; As traitors, 109, 127, 130; Viewers' ideas concerning, 31–37; World population of, 9. *See also* Terrorism; Victims
Assimilation, 14, 154, 161. *See also* Ambiguous assimilative diversity

Baudrillard, Jean, 39
Bayoumi, Moustafa, 85
"Behind the veil," 75–76
Benevolent emotions, 49, 57, 68–74; Post-race racism and, 50–51; Regret, 49, 65–66
Bilici, Mucahit, 119
Bin Laden, Osama, 73, 101, 104, 128, 129, 163, 165
Boltanski, Luc, 87, 91–92
Bonilla-Silva, Eduardo, 12
Borders, 54–55, 57, 91
Boston Public, 3, 179n10
Brown, Wendy, 90
Bush, George W., 1–2, 40, 56, 100, 132; Policies of, 5, 6, 66, 123, 150–51, 197n44
Butler, Judith, 71, 79, 99

Chouliaraki, Lillie, 97–98
Civil liberties, 6, 19, 139, 197n44; Suspension of, 57, 61–63, 133
Civil rights movement, 11–12, 28, 70, 137, 146; Co-optation of, 12–13

Clarion Fund, 163
Clash of civilizations, 107–8, 140–41, 195n17
Collins, Patricia Hill, 169
Colonialism, 8, 79, 105–6
Community, 172–76
Compassion, 88–92, 96, 98, 102
Cordoba Initiative, 167–68
Council on American-Islamic Relations,
    4, 18, 51, 132; Advertising campaign, 134,
    140–48, 170; Mission, 139–40
Cultural citizenship, 142, 148, 200n21
Cultural studies, 13–14
Culture talk, 29–30

Darwish, Nonie. See Native informants
Deportation, 5, 15, 53, 57–59, 137, 172, 180n14
Detention, 5, 28, 47–48, 69–70, 127, 152;
    Representations of, 22, 58–62, 65; Support
    for, 133, 188n7; "Voluntary," 60–62
Dirty bomber. See Padilla, Jose
Dissenting feelings, 131
Diversity, 13, 31, 77, 86, 133–34, 169, 176–77;
    American identity and, 53–54, 154–57
Diversity patriotism, 17; Ambiguous
    assimilative diversity and, 135–37, 139;
    Approximating sameness through the
    "good Muslim" and, 141–48; Definition,
    134; And diminishing difference, 148;
    Gone global, 134, 152–53, 157; Limits of,
    159–61; And narratives of exclusion, 148
Douglas, Susan, 83
Dr. Phil Show, 92

The Education of Max Bickford, 3, 71, 190n36,
    190n2
Embedded feminism, 83
Emotional hegemony, 130–31
Emotive public, 86, 98
Empathy, 72, 130
Empire, 103–4, 128, 130–31, 169. See also
    Imperialism
Enemy combatant, 5, 125, 129, 180n16;
    Definitions, 123, 197n44
Eng, David, 111–12
Enlightened sexism, 83
Exceptionalism, 38, 54, 58; Logic of exception,
    16, 44, 50, 52–54, 56–58, 63, 65–69, 123

Exclusionary logics, 16, 71

Failed heterosexuality. See Terrorism, failed
    heterosexuality and
Feminism: Arab and Muslim, 79, 81–83;
    Colonial, 79; Co-optation of, 17, 79–83,
    86, 91, 98
Feminist Majority Foundation, 83, 87
Ferguson, James, 148
Field of meaning, 7, 14, 44
Fiske, John, 48–49
Friedman, Thomas, 56, 104
Fundamentalism, fundamentalist, 29, 79;
    Association with Islam, 79–80, 117–18; As
    the cause of terrorism, 106–8; Colonialism
    and, 79–80; John Walker Lindh and, 109–12,
    120; As modern formation, 79–80; U.S.
    Cold War policies and, 79–80, 83, 98–99

Giuliani, Rudolph, 42, 104, 132
Going Muslim, 110–11, 113–14, 119–22, 125–28,
    196n23
Going Native. See Going Muslim
Gray, Herman, vii, 13, 15, 31, 171
Grewal, Inderpal, 126
The Grid, 2, 20
"Ground zero mosque," 167–69
Guantanamo Bay prison, 12, 58, 127, 130, 138,
    170
Gulf War, 13, 29, 42, 137
Gupta, Akhil, 148

Hall, Stuart, 27, 176–77
Hartley, John, 48–49
Hate crimes, 2, 4, 31, 49, 71–72, 102, 166–67;
    Representations of, 14–26, 31, 49, 63–66,
    68, 169; Responses to, 133, 135, 157
The Heritage Foundation, 42, 187n56
Hi Magazine, 151, 159
Hirschkind, Charles, 80
Hirsi Ali, Ayaan. See Native informants
Homonationalism, 121–22
Human Rights First, 19, 41, 43–44
Hunt, Krista, 83

Ideological field. See Field of meaning
Imagined community, 46, 133, 137, 161

Immigration, 55, 57, 70, 142, 152–53, 156–57;
    Policies, 6, 59
Imperialism, 54, 58, 75, 91, 101, 121;
    Advertising and, 149–50; Freedom and,
    159; "Oppressed Muslim women" and,
    83–85
Internment of the psyche, 5
Iraq War, 3, 6, 13, 29, 82, 130, 138
Islam: Challenging misperceptions of,
    139–41, 146–48, 160; As incompatible with
    democracy, 108; As compatible with the
    United States, 22, 134, 143–44, 152–53,
    156–59; Disclaimers about, 74, 77–78, 89;
    Diversity of, 23, 32, 82, 141–42; Misogyny
    and representations of, 75–76, 81–82, 119–20;
    Monolithic images of, 49, 73–74, 76, 80–81,
    83–84, 93–94, 168–69; Native informants
    and, 84–86; And non-Arabs, 29, 103, 105,
    110; As pathological, 123, 127; As vehicle of
    dissent, 79
Islamic Circle of North America Relief
    Organization, 166–67
Israel, Israeli, 8, 30, 101, 105–6, 108, 127–28;
    Criticism of, 84–85, 140, 159

Jaggar, Alison, 131
Jarmakani, Amira, 82

Kahf, Mohja, 84, 171
Kaplan, Amy, 102
Kaplan, Caren, 42–43
Kennedy, Liam, 151, 159

Law and Order, 3, 29, 50, 63; John Walker
    Lindh and, 113–20, 123; Patriotism and
    racism in, 66–68
Lawal, Amina, 87–92, 98–99; Viewer
    responses to, 92–96
The Left/liberal, 32–33, 48, 56–57, 69–70, 87,
    148; Dramatic use of, 52, 57; Education,
    120–22; Indictment of, 106–7, 112
Leonard, Mark, 149
Levitt, Laura, 148
Liberal pluralism, 176
Lindh, John Walker, 103, 108–11, 119–20, 126,
    130, 196n22–23; Non-normative sexuality
    of, 111–13, 120–22; Queering of, 112

Lipsitz, George, 48
Little Mosque on the Prairie, 172, 174–76
Lubiano, Wahneema, 137
Lucas, Scott, 151, 159

Maher, Bill, 100, 102, 121
Mahmood, Saba, 80
Maira, Sunaina, 85–86, 131
Mamdani, Mahmood, 14–15, 29–30, 80
McAlister, Melani, 8–9, 13, 46, 137
McVeigh, Timothy, 36, 105, 106
Melamed, Jodi, 12
Miller, Toby, 52
Moallem, Minoo, 79–81
Mourning, 49; Benevolence and, 49, 58,
    62–63; Centrality to post-9/11 racial logic,
    65, 68, 70
Multicultural movement, 11–12, 21, 168;
    Co-optation of, 13
Multicultural sensitivity, 4, 38, 69, 169
Multiculturalism, 12–13, 15–17, 91, 176;
    Commodification of, 28; Liberal, 148;
    Neoliberal, 12; Projecting, 13, 26, 133; In
    television dramas, 45, 82
Muslim Public Affairs Council, 170

Naber, Nadine, 5
National Organization for Women, 87
National security, 11, 45, 48, 68, 144, 146–47,
    168; In television dramas, 56–57, 61–62;
    Threats to, 4–6, 20, 29, 32–34, 38, 42, 68
National Security Entry-Exit Registration
    System, 5
Native informant, 84–86, 90, 99
NYPD Blue, 3, 49–50, 63–66; Preferred
    meaning in, 65

Obama, Barack, 11, 160; Post-race racism and,
    163–66
Office of Global Communications, 150–51
Office of Strategic Influence, 149–50
Oklahoma City bombing, 36–37
Oppressed Muslim woman, 71, 74; In
    advertising, 146; Arab/Muslim conflation
    and, 73; Excess of affect and, 16, 72, 90–91,
    94, 98–99, 103; Iterations of simplified
    complex representations and, 75, 84, 86;

And the "liberated American woman,"
83; Used to gain support for military
intervention, 83; U.S. imperialism and,
79–80, 84. *See also* Lawal, Amina
Oprah Winfrey Show, 74–75, 87–88; And
compassion, 88–90; Moral and political
actors, 91–92; And online message boards,
92–98; And tolerance, 90–91
Orientalism, 7, 9, 85–86, 128, 181n31
Outlaw emotion, 131
Outrage, 17, 31, 72–78, 81–83, 86–91; Of
viewers, 92, 94–99

Padilla, Jose, 103, 108, 122–27, 197n44
Parents Television Council, 19, 41, 43
Patriotism, 63–66, 68, 148–49; Arab/Muslim
representations and, 13, 21–22, 28, 59–61,
102, 177; National service and, 142–44, 146
Pedagogy, 36
Pity, 72–74, 76–77, 84, 90, 118; Politics of,
87–88, 92, 98–99; Regimes of, 97
Politically correct/political correctness, 6, 12,
32, 38, 107, 168; In *The Practice*, 52–57
Politics of invisibility, 82
Politics of worthiness, 125
Postfeminism, 82–83, 91, 99, 117
Post-race, 21, 29, 31, 106, 117, 134; Barack
Obama and, 163–166; And co-optation,
11–15, 82–83, 98; Emotions, 50, 72, 75, 102
The Practice, 3, 22, 49–50, 51–52, 58–62;
Ambivalence in, 51, 53–56, 58; Detention
in, 59; Left/right binary in, 52, 54, 57;
Logic of exceptional racism in, 52–58;
Preferred meaning in, 56, 58, 61–62
Preferred meaning, 49–50
Puar, Jasbir, 121–22, 161
Public diplomacy, 132, 149–52, 159
Public service announcements, 18, 133–38,
140–48, 160; Critiques of, 138–39;
Corporate, 152; And heterosexual family
values, 134, 144; Nation building and, 148–
49; As performative speech act, 143–44

Racial casting, 10, 182n41
Racial profiling, 6, 9–11, 47–48, 152, 172,
175–76; In air travel, 15, 57; In television
dramas, 3, 51–55

Racialization, 53–55, 57–60, 111, 122, 126, 137;
Of Arabs, 14; Of Muslims and Islam, 103,
167–68
Racism, 2–5, 31, 86, 149, 176–77; As
aberration, 50–51; As ambivalent, 53;
Circumventing accusations of 26, 38;
Color-blind, 12, 149, 165; Conflation with
patriotism, 63–66; Denial of, 11, 69, 168–
69; As exceptional, 51–57, 69; Inferential,
27; Institutionalized, 6, 11–12, 15, 29, 62;
Legitimizing, 6, 16, 45, 49–50; Post-race,
7, 13, 50–51, 98, 163–66; Respectable,
53–54, 56
Radio Sawa, 151
Ramos-Zayas, Ana Y., 124–25
Razack, Sherene, 83–84
"The real," 39
Reid, Richard, 129–30
Remorse, 49, 56–57, 68–70, 72
Respectable racism. *See* Racism, respectable
The Right/conservative, 6, 12, 31–33, 37–38,
102, 112; Anti-Muslim activism, 140, 163,
166–67; And causes of terrorism, 106–8;
Dramatic use of, 52, 57; Native informants
and, 84–86; Television programs, 48,
188n7; Torture and, 40
Rodriguez, Juana Maria, 37
Rumsfeld, Donald, 150, 197n41

Saliba, Therese, 82
Sanctions, 30–31, 108, 128, 130, 195n19
Saudi Arabia, 104–5, 108, 152, 175; Women in,
73, 76–78, 85
Saving Muslim women, 73, 83, 98–99
September 11, 2001, 1–5, 9, 17, 47, 50, 54;
Causes of, 80, 82, 104, 106, 119; Coverage
of, 103
Shaheen, Jack G., 8
Shared Values Initiative, 134, 152, 156–60
Shoe bomber. *See* Reid, Richard
Shohat, Ella, 13–14, 69
Simplified complex representations: Absence
and, 31; Challenges to, 170–76; Challenging
the Arab/Muslim conflation with diverse
Muslim identities, 23, 40; Concessions of,
30–31; Critics' responses to, 31–34; Definition
of, 14–15, 21; Disclaimers, 86; Excess of

sympathy and, 75; Explanations for terrorism, 29, 128–31; Fictionalizing the Middle Eastern or Muslim country, 26; Flipping the enemy, 23–24; Good/bad coupling, 31; Humanizing the enemy, 24–26; Inserting patriotic Arab or Muslim Americans, 21–22; Islam and, 74–75, 78; Limited impact of, 32; Obscuring the "why," 103; Projecting a multicultural U.S. society, 26; Regulating sympathy and, 103; Strategies of, 21–26, 44–45, 84; Sympathizing with the plight of Arab and Muslim Americans after 9/11, 22–23; Viewers' responses to, 34–38. *See also* Diversity patriotism; Going Muslim; Oppressed Muslim woman; Sympathy, excess of

Sleeper Cell (TV show), 2, 9, 20–23, 25–26, 29–30, 45–46; Torture in, 41; Viewer responses to, 31–37

Sleeper cell (term), 10, 23, 25, 68, 163

Stam, Robert, 13–14, 69

Stereotype/stereotyping, 2–3, 11, 13–14, 20–21, 27, 74, 146; African American, 169; Arab/Muslim terrorist, 14, 16, 18–19, 38, 78; Challenging, 26, 28–31, 44, 69, 94, 170–75; Conversion to Islam and, 110; Perpetuation of, 27–28; Rehabilitation of, 14

Structure of feeling, 83, 193n33

Sultan, Wafa: *See* Native informant

Symbolic castration, 118, 120, 125

Sympathetic representations, 2, 4; Logic of exception and, 16, 50, 69–70, 169; Proliferation of, 7, 10–11, 15–16

Sympathy, 4, 16, 23, 30, 56–57, 68; Absence of, 103–4; Bridges to, 69; Evoking, 49; Excess of, 72, 75, 86; As key emotion, 72; Public, 17; Race and, 126, 130; Regulation of, 83, 97, 103, 110, 117–20, 128; Terrorism and, 31, 78, 102, 128; Uses of, 106

Terrorism: As catchall for all political violence, 101–2; Civilizational argument for, 106–7, 111–12; Context and, 18, 27, 45, 78, 101–3, 128; Failed heterosexuality and, 109–12, 119, 121, 126; As incomprehensible,

32, 75; Psychological explanations for, 110, 119–20, 123; Root causes, 56, 101–3, 105–8, 118–20, 125, 128

They hate us for our freedom, 6–7, 38, 56, 73

Threat Matrix, 2, 20, 21

Ticking time bomb scenario, 36, 40, 45

Tolerance, 90, 138, 142–46, 148

Torture, 39, 58, 104, 127; 24 and, 19–21, 40–45; Debates about, 16, 40; Ineffectiveness of, 41; As necessary evil, 40; Patriotism and, 42; Public opinion of, 42–44, 170; Television news and, 44

USA PATRIOT Act, 5–6, 12, 47–48, 58, 65, 102

Victims, 49, 62; Of terrorism, 30, 138, 168; Of torture, 40. *See also* Hate crimes; Oppressed Muslim woman; Lawal, Amina

Vigilantism, 66–67

Volpp, Leti, 59, 133

Von Eschen, Penny, 149

The Wanted, 20, 35–36

War on Terror, 1–4, 7, 18–19; And Arab/Muslim conflation, 9; As common interest, 38; Conflation with television dramas, 35–37; Diversity and 134, 160, 169; Field of explanation of, 29, 103; Ideological hegemony and, 150, 160; Mediation of, 38–42; Oppressed Muslim woman and, 73–74, 79, 83–84, 86; Sexuality and, 121; Sites of, 29; State of exception and, 53, 67–69

Weber, Cynthia, 138–39

West Point Military Academy, 19, 41, 44

Whoopi!, 172–73, 176

Willis, Susan, 39

Winant, Howard, 12

Yee, James, 127, 138

Youmans, William, 152

Zelizer, Barbie, 103

Zine, Jasmin, 86, 101

About the Author

Evelyn Alsultany is Associate Professor in the Program in American Culture at the University of Michigan. She is coeditor of *Arab and Arab American Feminisms* and guest curator of *Reclaiming Identity: Dismantling Arab Stereotypes* (www.arabstereotypes.org). Her coedited volume *Between the Middle East and the Americas* is forthcoming.